HERE IS QUEER

Nationalisms, Sexualities, and the Literatures of Canada

What is the connection between Oscar Wilde and the literary history of Canada? Where do we locate gender and sexuality in the performance of Canadian ethnicities? How might the sexual sloganeering of Queer Nation illuminate the cultural angst of Northrop Frye? Peter Dickinson explores these and other questions in this book, the first full-length study to consider how the interconnected concepts of nationalism and sexuality have helped shape the production and reception of Canadian, Québécois, and First Nations literatures.

The main focus of Dickinson's study is contemporary – the fiction, drama, and poetry of Timothy Findley, Michel Tremblay, Tomson Highway, Nicole Brossard, Daphne Marlatt, and others. Juxtaposing an alternative sexual politics against the predominantly nationalist literary framework of literary criticism in Canada, he argues that the historical construction of Canada's literatures around the apparent absence of a coherent national identity presupposes the presence of a subversive, destabilizing sexual identity. To Frye's 'Where is here?' Dickinson answers emphatically, 'Here is queer.'

Drawing on a wide and eclectic body of postcolonial, gay and lesbian, and Canadian literary scholarship, *Here Is Queer* extends in new and exciting ways our thinking about Canada's 'famous problem of identity.' Dickinson brings to his work a familiarity and ease with contemporary queer theory and Canadian cultural criticism that will appeal to readers interested in issues of nationality, sexuality, politics, identity, and literature.

PETER DICKINSON holds a PhD from the University of British Columbia. He lives in Vancouver.

HERE IS QUEER

Nationalisms, Sexualities, and the Literatures of Canada

Peter Dickinson

UNIVERSITY OF TORONTO PRESS
Toronto Buffalo London

Toronto Buffalo London
Printed in Canada

ISBN 0-8020-4403-4 (cloth)
ISBN 0-8020-8210-6 (paper)

Printed on acid-free paper

Canadian Cataloguing in Publication Data

Dickinson, Peter, 1968–
Here is queer : nationalisms, sexualities, and the literatures of Canada

Includes bibliographical references and index.
ISBN 0-8020-4403-4 (bound) ISBN 0-8020-8210-6 (pbk.)

1. Homosexuality in literature. 2. Canadian literature – 20th century – History and criticism. I. Title.

PS8101.H6D52 1998 C810.9'353 C98-931663-7
PR9185.5.H6D52 1998

This book has been published with the help of a grant from the Humanities and Social Sciences Federation of Canada, using funds provided by the Social Sciences and Humanities Research Council of Canada.

University of Toronto Press acknowledges the financial assistance to its publishing program of the Canada Council for the Arts and the Ontario Arts Council.

for Richard

Contents

Acknowledgments

As I explain at greater length in the Coda to this book, its broad parameters were conceived during the autumn of 1993, when Little Sister's Book and Art Emporium, in Vancouver, was still in the initial stage of its court battle with Canada Customs. That battle is far from over, and a portion of the proceeds from the sale of this book will go to support the Little Sister's Legal Defense Fund.

Margery Fee not only encouraged me to pursue the project, she also agreed to supervise it during its earlier incarnation as a Ph.D. thesis in the Department of English at the University of British Columbia. I am profoundly grateful to her for the enthusiasm, guidance, and critical stimulation she provided throughout the long haul of its completion and revision. I also benefited immensely from the careful and considered readings offered by the other members of my thesis committee, Alec Globe and Sherrill Grace.

Countless others have contributed, in ways many of them could not imagine, to the creation of this book. Among those I wish to thank are: Dennis Denisoff, M. Morgan Holmes, Gabriele Helms, Patrick Patterson and the entire staff at UBC's Interlibrary Loan Office, Julie Beddoes, Lorraine York, Terry Goldie, Patricia Merivale, Ralph Sarkonak, Barbara Gabriel, George Piggford, W.H. New, Patrick Campbell, Patricia Whitney, Claire Wilkshire, Louise Ladouceur, and Janine Fuller. I am especially indebted to the scholarly example of Robert K. Martin, who has been a perceptive reader and generous supporter of my writing (even when I stubbornly refuse to follow his advice), and whose pioneering work in gay criticism and theory remains a constant source of inspiration.

At University of Toronto Press, Linda Hutcheon provided much-needed encouragement at the outset, as did Gerald Hallowell. Emily Andrew has been a superb editor and insightful interlocutor from the moment she received the rough-hewn, dot matrix–printed pages of my original manuscript, responding to my increasingly anxious electronic queries about the review process with clarity, humour, and grace. Her engaged colloquy and suggestions for revision, along with those of the anonymous readers of my manuscript, have without a doubt made this a better book. Thanks, as well, to Ken Lewis for his expert and intuitive copy-editing.

Generous financial assistance was provided by the Social Sciences and Humanities Research Council of Canada.

Finally, this book could not have been written without the intellectual and emotional support of Richard Cavell: it is dedicated to him in admiration and love.

HERE IS QUEER

Nationalisms, Sexualities, and the Literatures of Canada

Introduction: Here Is Queer

Consider, to begin, the following rather imperfect syllogism:

a) 'Where is here?'
b) 'We're here, we're queer, get used to it!'
c) 'Here is queer.'

Whatever you may think of my powers of deductive reasoning, the *cogito* which results from my deliberately ahistorical pairing of the social rhetorics of Northrop Frye and the gay and lesbian activist organization Queer Nation encapsulates what it is that I am trying to do in this book: that is, to fuse two different imaginative models of identity – one national, the other sexual – within an examination of the cultural production and textual dissemination of contemporary Canadian, Québécois, and First Nations literatures. More specifically, I am seeking to uncover, or 'bring out,' what I see as Canadian literary nationalism's simultaneously othered and coupled discourse, to juxtapose against the predominantly nationalist framework of literary criticism in this country an alternative politics, one propelled by questions of sexuality and, more often than not, homosexuality.

Building broadly on the insights of George Mosse, Benedict Anderson, Michel Foucault, and their subsequent interlocutors in the fields of postcolonial and queer theory, this book interrogates the (hetero)normative assumption that 'nation' and 'sexuality' are somehow discrete, autonomous, historically transcendent, and socially uninflected categories of identity. To this end, if Frye's circa-centennial speculations on national ennui ('Where is here?') amount to a failure of imagination, a refusal to conceive of 'Canada,' for example, in anything other than geopolitical terms, then Queer Nation's 'Bush-Thatcher-Mulroney era' (Warner, 'Something Queer,' 361) declaration of sexual anomie ('We're here, we're queer, get used to it!') reveals a surfeit of imagination, an extension of the notions of citizenship and community beyond the borderlines of current legal and juridical discourse. Whereas the former speech act excludes by positing a structural absence, the latter includes by announcing an embodied presence. This question of absence and presence extends to my understanding of the affiliative spaces of Canadian, Québécois, and First Nations literatures as well: not simply that there are 'other solitudes,' including queer ones, but that what gets *counted* as literature in this country is contingent upon certain supplementary socio-political discourses, such as nationalism and sexuality.

In the emerging narrative surrounding the canonization of Canadian literature – I am thinking, in particular, of the exchanges between Robert Lecker and Frank Davey, first in the pages of *Critical Inquiry* (1990), and, more recently, in Davey's *Canadian Literary Power* (1994) and Lecker's *Making It Real* (1995) – the discourse of (homo)sexuality, and its role (or non-role) in the formation and organization of a literary tradition in this country, is virtually non-existent. Instead, this narrative, especially as constructed by Lecker, has tended to focus on questions of 'nationalism,' 'mimeticism,' and some vaguely defined notion of 'institutionality.' It is only very recently that Davey has included 'gay and lesbian writing' among those 'Canadian literatures which evaded Lecker's [and, I would add, initially his own] notice' (*Canadian Literary Power*, 76).

And yet, as Eve Kosofsky Sedgwick reminds us in the sixth axiom of the introduction to *Epistemology of the Closet*, the 'master-canons' of national literatures, and the dominant curricula of Western academic institutions, are filled with their own closets. When it comes to the 'ambiguous' sexuality of 'great' thinkers and writers (Socrates, Shakespeare, Proust, to cite Sedgwick's examples), literary criticism tends to operate under the aegis of a 'Don't ask, don't tell' cultural imperative. I myself have never been good at keeping secrets. So allow me to let the cat out of the bag right away by reconfiguring slightly the aforementioned dialectic of absence and presence. In this book I contend that the identificatory *lack* upon which Canadian literary nationalism has historically been constructed – the 'where' of Frye's 'here,' for example – is in large part facilitated by, if not wholly dependent upon, a critical refusal to come to grips with the textual *superabundance* of a destabilizing and counter-normative sexuality.

This counter-normative sexuality I am labelling 'queer,' a term that applies equally in this book to the erotic triangles found in John Richardson's New World and those that resurface in Leonard Cohen's New Jerusalem; to the hyper-masculinity of Martin Allerdale Grainger's *Woodsmen of the West* and the feminist revisionism of Daphne Marlatt's *Ana Historic*; to the apparent sterility of Mrs Bentley's prairie Horizon and the unexpected verdancy of Maude Laures's desert horizon; to the sexual dissimulation inherent in Pierre X. Magnant's admission of 'une phobie d'impuissance' in *Trou de mémoire* and the sexual exhibitionism accompanying Claude's mantra of 'Chus t'un homme' at the end of *Hosanna*; to Duncan Campbell Scott's miscegenated Madonna and Tomson Highway's hybrid Trickster. This is not to say that 'here' is only or ever 'queer,' nor that resistance to a heteronormative nationalism is always or exclusively homosexual; what the range of texts discussed in this book does suggest, however, is that 'queer,' as a literary-critical category of an almost inevitable definitional elasticity, one whose inventory of sexual meanings has yet to be exhausted, challenges and upsets certain received national orthodoxies of writing in Canada.

An important corollary to this claim of national and sexual cross-identification is that if the discourse of nationalism has historically been gendered as patriarchal (a point I explore at greater length in chapter 5), then it has also frequently been eroticized as homosocial. This is the 'congruent' contradiction I attempt to elucidate in chapter 1, adapting the central thesis of Sedgwick's *Between Men* to an analysis of the triangulation of male desire in several of this country's foundational literary texts. Samuel Hearne and Chief Matonabbee; Jackie Denham and Tay John; George Stewart and Jerome Martell; Hazard Lepage and Demeter Proudfoot: Canadian literature, or at the very least *English*-Canadian literature, is riddled with male couples who displace their love for each other – and frequently their nation – across the 'body' of a woman, whom they symbolically share, or else onto a mythically feminized region or landscape, which they symbolically exploit.[1] My own national narrative of Canadian homosociality I have divided into three sections, each corresponding with a specific literary-historical period (colonial, modern, postmodern), each announced by appropriate intertitles. I have deliberately sacrificed comprehensiveness in favour of focused attention on specific key texts. These texts (including John Richardson's *Wacousta*, Sinclair Ross's *As for Me and My House*, Leonard Cohen's *Beautiful Losers*, and Hubert Aquin's *Trou de mémoire*) have been chosen as much for my own (and others') critical attachment to them as for their exemplary canonicity – and homosociality. The final section of chapter 1, 'From There to Queer,' moves outward from this concentrated reading of a contained literary system to a broader discussion of the theoretical and conceptual frameworks animating my use of the discourses of nationalism and sexuality throughout the book as a whole. Consequently, the arrangement of chapter 1 more or less enacts, at a metonymical level, the rather idiosyncratic sequencing of my subsequent chapters. In them I travel inside-out (and back again) along a Möbius strip – to borrow a metaphor from Diana Fuss (see her introduction to the important lesbian and gay studies essay collection, *Inside/Out*) – of textual analysis, critical and theoretical commentary, and historical contextualization. In so doing, I am less concerned with retracing *linearly* the familiar Canadian cultural emplotments of chronology and geography than with examining *interdiscursively* the temporal gaps and spatial fissures that make up the discontinuous national and sexual storylines of this plot, a strategy of literary recuperation that will hopefully be made clearer by the summary that follows, as well as by the chapters themselves.

Although they are related terms, 'homosocial' and 'homosexual' should not be conflated. As Robert K. Martin has put it, in his introduction to a recent *Lesbian and Gay Studies* special issue of *English Studies in Canada*, 'there are no gay men (let alone lesbians) in *Between Men*' (126). One could potentially say the same thing about the first chapter of this book; as such, the ensuing chapters constitute an attempt on my part to come to grips with this paradox. In them I seek to transform what I have been more or less calling the *absent* presence of queerness in Canadian literature into a more *manifest* or *embodied* presence. As a signifying system, the Canadian literary canon seems to have no trouble incorporating homosexuality into its rarefied textual precincts, so long, that is, as it functions primarily as a means of re-eroticizing readers' fundamentally heterosexual love for their country. But what happens when (homo)sexual *dissidence* is used to signal a somewhat more *ambivalent* attachment to the idea of nationhood? This is the question taken up in chapter 2, which deals with three important fictions by Timothy Findley: *The Wars, Famous Last Words,* and *Not Wanted on the Voyage.* Having said this, however, I must point out that chapter 2 actually opens with a brief digression on Oscar Wilde. As Sedgwick notes in 'Nationalisms and Sexualities in the Age of Wilde,' the nineteenth-century writer's 'hyper-indicativeness as a figure of his age' made him uncannily susceptible (and responsive) to 'mutual representations of emerging national and sexual claims' (243): an Irishman whose literary apotheosis in the (m)other country coincided with a public trial for 'gross indecency,' which resulted in his imprisonment and eventual exile to France. Extending Sedgwick's arguments spatially and intertextually, along a 'geography' of 'male homosocial desire,' I highlight Wilde's unique connection with the literary history of Canada, and, in particular, the ambivalent/dissident fictions of Findley. In employing the terms 'ambivalence' and 'dissidence' in this chapter, I am alluding, most directly, to the work of Homi Bhabha and Jonathan Dollimore. Building on their respective theories of the 'iterative temporality' of the nation-space and the 'transgressive agency' of sexual perversion, I want to suggest that the interplay between national ambivalence and sexual dissidence within Findley's novels displaces ideas of fixed meaning – especially regarding the commodification/conflation of identities – and frequently produces wild(e)ly divergent readings of his work.

As a writer of a certain gender, race, class, and age, Findley enjoys a rather privileged position in Canadian letters, a position that, until relatively recently, he has been loath to complicate with any overt political statements regarding his sexuality. To the extent that chapter 2 charts my own personal response to this tension in Findley's life and work, as well as my evolution as a gay reader and critic, I have chosen to place it ahead of my next chapter, which actually documents an earlier period in Canadian literary history, and which even, to a certain extent, contextualizes Findley's sexual/textual anxieties. Beginning with an analysis of the publication, in 1943, of A.J.M. Smith's *The Book of Canadian Poetry*, and culminating with a re-examination of 1967's centennial celebrations, chapter 3 analyses two writers – Patrick Anderson and Scott Symons – caught up in the intensely nationalist fervour accompanying these two decades of Canadian canon-formation. Both writers were the victims of blatantly homophobic criticism, which resulted not only in the pillorying of their work in print, but also, more dramatically, in their eventual self-imposed exiles from Canada. By focusing on Anderson and Symons, I demonstrate that at the same time as the modern (and postmodern) Canadian literary canon was being put together, the discourses of nationalism and sexuality were repeatedly yoked together by critics in order to exclude certain writers from this aggressively masculinist and heterosexual 'tradition.' Moreover, I argue that a thorough reassessment of their texts, especially in light of current postcolonial and gender theories of travel writing, implicitly critiques this very process, deconstructing the inside(r)/outside(r) binary of national, sexual, and therefore cultural authenticity.

Chapter 4 shifts the focus from English Canada to French Canada, in particular the Montreal theatre scene of the past two decades. After setting the stage with Michel Tremblay's *Hosanna,* I move on to a discussion of René-Daniel Dubois's *Being at home with Claude,* and Michel Marc Bouchard's *Les Feluettes,* assessing the extent to which homosexuality, as represented in these plays, has been tied, allegorically or otherwise, to questions of Quebec nationalism (whether it be the Duplessism of the 1940s and 1950s or the separatist struggles of the '60s and '70s). If there is indeed a link to be made, it is a profoundly paradoxical one: on the one hand, oppression of homosexuals can be seen to be emblematic of the (intra)national oppression of Quebec society by Anglo-Canada; on the other hand, there are further processes of colonization at work in the 'homosexual panic' which frequently accompanies Quebec's anti-colonial/nationalist rhetoric (as is so often the case in the work of Aquin, for example). Rather than restrict my analysis to a close reading of the written texts, I will be concentrating, as much as possible, on specific productions, as well as their critical reception, particularly in English Canada, where 'the vicissitudes of reviewing theatre for the daily press' and the 'differences between Québécois and English-Canadian theatrical practice' often seem 'to mitigate [*sic*] against ... the development of a positive tradition of inter-cultural production' (Wallace, *Producing Marginality,* 230).

Of course, this implicitly raises the whole issue of translation within and between the Canadian literatures, which, as Richard Cavell has recently demonstrated, in turn raises issues 'of originality and of nationhood' and 'the movement of empire' ('"Comparative Canadian Literature,"' 10). In chapter 5 I examine certain 'translation effects' produced by/within lesbian-feminist fiction/theory, a 'virtual' space of writing in Canada and Quebec that exceeds the distinction signalled in its 'barrier/slash' (Mezei, quoted in Godard, 'Fiction/Theory,' 4), a (re)reading and (re)writing in/of the feminine that positions language and representation, genre and gender, not in absolute opposition, but in 'differential relation' (see Tostevin, 'Contamination'). The essentially collaborative nature of fiction/theory – fostered within collectively edited journals by a community of feminist writers and academics who translate, interpret, and 'co-create' each other's work – impacts significantly on the concept of a 'singular' (i.e., 'the people-as-one') Canadian nation; it also thoroughly destabilizes the patriarchal-homosocial underpinnings of the Canadian literary system as it is discussed in chapter 1 of this book. The translation of lesbian desire 'through the body,' along a direct axis or passageway between women, renders obsolete the need for triangular mediation. As Terry Castle has recently argued in another context, 'to theorize about female-female desire ... is precisely to envision the taking apart of this supposedly intractable patriarchal structure' (72); at the very least, it is to envision the *translation* of this male structure into an explicitly *female* homosocial configuration. I focus primarily on the work of Nicole Brossard and Daphne Marlatt in this chapter, basing this somewhat arbitrary decision on their respective affiliations with *La (Nouvelle) Barre du jour* and *Tessera*, on their poetic collaborations/translations (most notably in *Mauve* and *character / jeu de lettres*), and on the fact that they have both written texts (*Le Désert mauve* and *Ana Historic*) which explore the 'effects of translation': 'from one novel to another, from one "language" to another, and of course from one woman to another' (Gould, 98).

Just as gender disrupts the all-too-frequent binary opposition between nationalism and sexuality in Canadian literature, so do race and ethnicity contribute to a net accretion in criss-crossed equations of identity. The poetry of Dionne Brand, for example, is more often classified by critics as 'West Indian' than 'Canadian,' despite the fact that she 'has lived here all [her] adult life' (Brand, *Chronicles*, 70). Moreover, these same critics frequently erase Brand's lesbianism, at the same time as they ignore her substantial contributions as a short story writer, novelist, documentary film-maker, scholar, archivist, and cultural activist. In chapter 6 I apply recent feminist and postcolonial accounts of the 'politics of location' (by, among others, Adrienne Rich, Chandra Talpade Mohanty, Caren Kaplan, and Michele Wallace) to the multiple and diasporic dis-locations inscribed within Brand's texts, showing how 'her cross-cultural position as poet [*and* film-maker *and* activist], as well as the boundary-crossing subjects she chooses to address, question the systemic pressures that shape and mis-shape our subjectivities as people defined through categories such as gender, ethnicity, class, or nation' (Brydon, 'Reading,' 86). I conclude this chapter by adapting the speech act theory which implicitly informs Bhabha's 'DissemiNation' and Judith Butler's *Gender Trouble* to an analysis of Brand's *No Language Is Neutral*, focusing on the degree to which this text 'locates' minority utterance in (performative) opposition to hegemonic nationalist and patriarchal discourses.

The challenge to Canadian literary nationalism is perhaps nowhere more evident than in the work of contemporary First Nations writers. The term 'First Nations' itself – in daring to posit prior origins, nationalities, *and* pluralisms – thoroughly destabilizes the bicultural model of Canadian literature at the same time that it raises problematic questions of cultural authenticity: where, for example, do we situate two-spirited writers like Tomson Highway within such a catch-all locution? Adapting the First World/Third World opposition inherent in postcolonial theories of 'hybridity,' and the First World–Second World specificity of queer theories of 'homosociality,' to the so-called Fourth World, in chapter 7 I examine how Highway's plays re-imagine conventional notions of Indigenous community. Close attention is paid to the performative function of the Nanabush/Trickster figure in the writing of Highway. As a trope employed counter-discursively in order to capture limited/liminal space within white textual production, Nanabush/Trickster, in his/her various incarnations and transmutations, paradoxically makes provisional the embodiment or ownership of an 'essential' ab-originality (and, by extension, all other 'nationalities'). This is accomplished in large part, as we shall see, through Nanabush/Trickster's resistance to fixed gender and sexual roles, something which Highway exploits to great effect in his plays.

Issues of performativity – the repetition and reception of various acts of identity – surface throughout this book, but most especially in my analyses of the work of Brand and Highway. It is only fitting, therefore, that I should follow chapters 6 and 7 with a concluding Coda, in which I attempt to relate the term more materially to some of the provocative (rhetorical) poses made fashionable by contemporary queer theory and, indeed, refashioned throughout this book. In the process, I draw connections between the performative and several other important *p*-words: the political, the pedagogical, and, certainly not least, the personal. A warning, in this regard: there is a lot of *me* scattered throughout the ensuing pages. This is much as I intend it. I came late to the study of Canadian literature. Even later to postcolonial and queer theory. What follows is in part my attempt to make up for lost time.

In the spirit of haste, then, let us first proceed with an object-lesson in geometry ...

1

Of Triangles and Textuality

A Syndrome without the Symptoms

Between Sir Everard Valletort and Charles de Haldimar, who, it has already been remarked, were lieutenants in Captain Blessington's company, a sentiment of friendship had been suffered to spring up almost from the moment of Sir Everard's joining.

John Richardson, *Wacousta*, 79

In *Between Men: English Literature and Male Homosocial Desire,* Eve Sedgwick writes that 'to draw the "homosocial" back into the orbit of desire, of the potentially erotic ... is to hypothesize the potential unbrokenness of a continuum between homosocial and homosexual ... "Male homosocial desire" is the name this book will give to the entire continuum' (1–2). Sedgwick goes on to situate this continuum 'within the structural context of triangular, heterosexual desire' (16). Drawing upon René Girard's schematization of erotic triangles in the male-centred novelistic tradition of Europe, Freud's psychoanalytical formulation of the Oedipal triangle, and Gayle Rubin's feminist critique of Claude Lévi-Strauss, she outlines a basic paradigm of 'male traffic in women,' whereby *active* male homosocial desire is refracted/triangulated 'asymmetrically' through the *passive* positioning of women as displaced objects of nominal/patrimonial heterosexual desire (see ch. 1, 21–7).

It is worth emphasizing here that what many have come to regard as *the* foundational text of contemporary *gay studies* was written primarily from a *feminist theoretical* position, one that sought to situate homosociality and the 'exchange of women' within the larger context of patriarchy. For Sedgwick, the erotic bonds established between men are not automatically subversive or counter-hegemonic; more often than not they signal a certain 'structural congruence.' As she puts it, 'in any male-dominated society, there is a special relationship between male homosocial (*including* homosexual) desire and the structures for maintaining and transmitting patriarchal power' (*Between*, 25). And yet, despite this caveat, Sedgwick has recently come under attack by lesbian-feminist critics like Teresa de Lauretis (in 'Film and the Visible') and Terry Castle (in *The Apparitional Lesbian*) for the narrowness of her focus on *male* homosocial desire. For her part, while she acknowledges the existence of a continuum of '"women loving women" and "women promoting the interests of women"' (3) – a continuum first theorized by Carroll Smith-Rosenberg in 'The Female World of Love and Ritual' (1975), later popularized by Adrienne Rich in 'Compulsory Heterosexuality and Lesbian Existence' (1980), and further extended by Lillian Faderman in *Surpassing the Love of Men* (1981) – Sedgwick nevertheless prefers to focus on the more dichotomous opposition between the 'homosocial' and the 'homosexual' in male-male bonds, arguing that it provides a better opportunity 'to explore the ways in which the shapes of sexuality, and what *counts* as sexuality, both depend on and affect historical power relationships' (2). And, I would add (as per the dictates of patriarchal culture), so too with nationality. Moreover, just as there are important gender differences in the continuum/continua of homosocial desire, so are those continua subject to the national and political contingencies of race and class. While my own focus in these early pages remains, for the most part, strategically oriented towards the *occlusions* of homosocial desire within canonical texts by white men in this country, I am nevertheless sensitive to the *exclusions* of gender, race, and class which these texts also perform, exclusions which subsequent chapters attempt to address, if not remedy.

For the moment, however, it would seem inevitable that my Sedgwickian analysis of Canadian literature should begin with Major John Richardson's *Wacousta* (1832), a 'foundational' text in its own right, one filled with all manner of erotic triangles, male-male attachments, and transgressive crossings ('female' to 'male,' 'white' to 'native,' 'human' to 'animal'). In *The Wacousta Syndrome*, Gaile McGregor locates Richardson's text at the origins of a trend in Canadian literary history which posits a negative response to 'nature' and the binary opposition between 'wilderness' and 'civilization' as the defining characteristics of 'the Canadian sense of self' and 'the conceptual underpinnings of the Canadian imagination' as a whole (412). However, I would like to suggest an alternative reading of *Wacousta*, one which thoroughly disrupts and destabilizes the nationalist paradigm invoked by McGregor, one which interprets the pervasive undercurrent of male homosocial desire in the text as 'symptomatic' of a completely different 'syndrome' in Canadian literature, where readerly/writerly panic is induced as much by a terror of the unknown nature of same-sex and mixed-race attachments as it is by the unknowable in nature itself.

Central to McGregor's argument is the cross-border connection between Richardson and his American literary counterpart, James Fenimore Cooper, both of whom styled their North American 'wilderness romances' on the European conventions of the genre established by Sir Walter Scott. I certainly do not discount the influence of Cooper's novels on *Wacousta*;[1] in my mind, however, it is Scott to whom Richardson owes his greatest authorial debt. Indeed, Richardson's recourse to a Jacobite Scotland reminiscent of Scott's Waverley novels as the originary setting for his own tale of competing nationalisms (British, French, and Indigenous) not only provides him with the appropriate background of political confrontation against which to construct his account of the Pontiac uprising, but also with a textbook example of Sedgwick's (homo)erotic triangle. And yet, while the romantic rivalry between Colonel de Haldimar, Clara Beverley, and Reginald Morton/Wacousta, initiated in the Old World, fuels the text's revenge plot, it is the triangulation of desire between Sir Everard Valletort, Clara de Haldimar, and Charles de Haldimar, all unfortunate victims of this revenge plot in the New World, which is more clearly homosocial.

That Richardson takes the time to establish the deep friendship between Valletort, 'a young lieutenant of the — regiment, recently arrived from England' (20), and Charles de Haldimar, 'the youngest son of the governor' (21), amidst the chaos of the first chapter is, I think, significant. The two men are presented as character types 'straight' out of a novel of sensibility: they are men of feeling and sentiment. They are also rather effete. In chapter 1, for example, we are told that Valletort possesses a 'dandyism and effeminacy of manner' and that Charles speaks 'in accents of almost feminine sweetness' (21). A little later on, in comparing him with his brother, Frederick, the narrator notes that Charles was particularly esteemed 'for those retiring, mild, winning manners, and gentle affections, added to extreme and almost feminine beauty of countenance for which he was remarkable' (44). As for Valletort's fighting prowess, the narrator discloses that while 'he concealed a brave, generous, warm and manly heart,' he was also somewhat of a '"feather-bed soldier"' (79, 80).

The exact extent and nature of the bond between the two men is revealed in chapter 6. Here we learn that Valletort counts among his 'secret' pleasures not only 'his growing friendship for the amiable and gentle Charles de Haldimar,' but also a 'scarcely to himself acknowledged' interest in Charles's sister, Clara, 'whom he only knew from the glowing descriptions of his friend, and the strong resemblance she was said to bear to him by the other officers' (80). The fact that Valletort falls in love with Clara while listening to Charles's 'eloquent praises' of her, and that brother and sister are virtual 'counterpart[s]' 'in personal attraction as in singleness of nature' (81), has striking resonances with Sedgwick's thesis of the triangulation of male homosocial desire. Consider, in this regard, the following passage:

> Never had Charles de Haldimar appeared so eminently handsome; and yet his beauty resembled that of a frail and delicate woman rather than that of one called to the manly and arduous profession of a soldier. The large, blue, long dark-lashed eye, in which a shade of languor harmonized with the soft but animated expression of the whole countenance – the dimpled mouth – the small, clear, and even teeth – all these now characterized Charles de Haldimar; and if to these we add a rich voice, full and melodious, and a smile sweet and fascinating, we shall be at no loss to account for the readiness with which Sir Everard suffered his imagination to draw on the brother for those attributes he ascribed to the sister. (87)

For her part, Clara has not even appeared in the text yet. And when she does (in chapter 19), she concedes, in response to her cousin Madeline's teasing questions, that '"I have never seen this friend of my brother ... I am disposed to like him, certainly, for the mere reason that Charles does, but this is all"' (245–6). Ironically, no sooner are Clara and Valletort united on board the schooner bound for Fort Detroit then they are promptly whisked away by the vengeance-seeking Wacousta, precipitating the litter of corpses at the end of the novel. It is important to note that Charles, Clara, and Valletort all eventually join this litter. The triangulation of desire, interrupted in the Old World, cannot be allowed to flourish again in the New World, especially if the nature of that desire is sexually suspect. The sentimental romance of Scott's novels becomes 'inverted' gothicism in Richardson's *Wacousta*, or, as the highly omniscient narrator announces in chapter 28, 'sad real[ism]':[2]

> To such of our readers as, deceived by the romantic nature of the attach-

> ment stated to have been originally entertained by Sir Everard Valletort for the unseen sister of his friend, have been led to expect a tale abounding in manifestations of its progress when the parties had actually met, we at once announce disappointment. Neither the lover of amorous adventures nor the admirer of witty dialogue, should dive into these passages ... [O]ur heroes and heroines figure under circumstances that would render wit a satire upon the understanding, and love a reflection upon the heart. (362)

The 'bounds of probability' (362) to which Richardson has confined his text ensure that 'virtue' will not be allowed to triumph amid a chaotic wilderness setting where national, social, and sexual conventions have not yet been stabilized. In this sense, the re-establishment of domestic harmony supposedly enacted in the closing tableau of 'Captain [Frederick] and Miss [Madeline] De Haldimar, Francois the Canadian, and the devoted Oucanasta' (431) is undermined by the novel's final line: 'As for poor Ellen Halloway, search has been made for her, but she never was heard of afterwards' (434). Ellen, in her transgression of both gender and racial boundaries (she masquerades as a drummerboy in order to witness the mistaken execution of her 'first' husband, Frank Halloway, and later 'goes native' for her 'second' husband, Wacousta), in 'her movement "beyond the pale" of the European fortress into the space of "savagery,"' remains an 'unassimilatable' figure of otherness within the 'garrison mentality' of a fledgling New World nation (Jones, 'Beyond,' 51, 49). As such, her ghost haunts not just Richardson's text, but arguably all of English-Canadian literature. As a symbol of 'exchange' in both patriarchal and colonial economies of power, Ellen may be located at the nexus of homosociality and 'indigenization,'[3] two overlapping discourses which together set in motion a double literary paradigm of sexual displacement and national authentification, and which achieve something of a contemporary apotheosis in Leonard Cohen's *Beautiful Losers*, where, as we shall see, Ellen resurfaces as Edith.

I would like to conclude this section by briefly contrasting Richardson's paradigmatic text of Canadian homosociality, written in the nineteenth century, with an early twentieth-century example of the genre, namely Martin Allerdale Grainger's *Woodsmen of the West* (1908). Like *Wacousta*, Grainger's text shares a fascination with the challenges of a national 'frontier' landscape, and delights in recounting the particular rituals of an all-male environment, in this case a British Columbian logging camp rather than a military base. Unlike *Wacousta*, however, *Woodsmen* is less a 'novel' per se than a sequence of dramatized personal observations (the text was apparently reconstructed from letters Grainger wrote to his future wife). To this end, the 'story' is told in the first person, with the 'narrator' even retaining the author's name and, presumably, identity. Casting aside the romantic conventions of Richardson's *Wacousta*, Grainger created in *Woodsmen* one of the first and best examples of early-Canadian literary realism.

Moreover, Grainger seems to have taken Sedgwick's concept of the triangulation of male homosocial desire – as classically demonstrated in *Wacousta* – and provided it with a further twist: the homoerotic triangle in *Woodsmen* is all male in gender.[4] While the narrator, Mart, is at once fascinated and repelled by Carter's ruthless and single-minded exploitation of both the land and his men, Bill Allen's 'admiration for his great partner glows visibly within him. He would have played Boswell to Carter's Johnson. He yields to hero-worship' (83). If there is one member of this triangle who is 'feminized' in any way, it is Allen, who, we are told, has a 'pretty' face, 'framed in fair curly hair,' suggesting, especially when clean, a vaguely 'girlish' air (120). (To be sure, Mart's English education, his 'queer way of expressing [him]self,' and his 'damaged foot' [24, 38] also set him apart from the masculine ideal embodied by Carter.)

Read intertextually via Joseph Conrad's *Heart of Darkness*, however, Allen becomes the harlequin figure to Mart and Carter's Marlow-Kurtz relationship. Indeed, by the end of *Woodsmen* Carter has succeeded in taking Mart 'to oblivion' (211 and *passim*), just as Kurtz takes Marlow to the edge of an inner abyss. In addition, the text's concluding poem/song, with its refrain of 'Farewell to loggers and my youth! / Farewell to it all: marriage is better' (217), is vaguely reminiscent of Marlow's meeting with Kurtz's 'Intended' at the end of *Heart of Darkness*. The question is, do we read it as a lament for homosociality or as a paean to heteronormativity? Certainly the photograph that serves as the first edition's frontispiece – showing a solitary male figure standing triumphantly atop the massive stump of a felled tree, and identified with the cut-line 'The Conqueror' – would seem to celebrate the 'woodsman' as quintessential exemplar of hyper-masculinity.[5] Any retreat from this all-male world, as Mart well knows, is necessarily a diminution, a feminization. As Misao Dean has recently put it, *Woodsmen* maps the 'distance between Mart's masculine ideal and his ability to achieve it ... The book's ending, with the narrator returning to a feminised "civilization" further expresses the critical moment of self-awareness and an ironic perspective on the masculine culture of agency it purports to define' (85).

This gendered moment of self-awareness ('And now I must go and scrub the kitchen floor of / The cottage next to Mrs Potts', / in [what will be] Lyall Avenue, / [outside the city limits of] / Victoria, / B.C.' read the text's final lines [217]) contains within it a kind of national epiphany as well, the domestication of the land (through clear-cut logging) constituting a form of ethnic legitimation. For, as Mart tells us much earlier in the book, 'in British Columbia ... a man could go anywhere on unoccupied Crown lands, put in a corner post, compose a rough description of one square mile of forest measured from that post, and thus secure from the Government exclusive right to the timber on that square mile ... ("No Chinese or Japanese to be employed in working the timber")' (44). As a document of Western expansion, then, Grainger's text, along with Ralph Connor's contemporaneous *The Foreigner: A Tale of Saskatchewan* (1909), and the later work of Frederick Philip Grove (*Over Prairie Trails* [1922], *Settlers of the Marsh* [1925], *A Search for America* [1927], etc.) and John Marlyn (*Under the Ribs of Death* [1957]), can be said to participate in – at the same time as it reacts against – what Daniel Coleman has recently identified as the Canadian national 'allegory of manly maturation.' That is, the immigrant other must not only be assimilated into the ideology of what it means to be 'Canadian' but also of what it means to be a 'man.'

Sinclair Ross's 'Queers'

Well ... the prairie has some queer ones.

W.O. Mitchell, *Who Has Seen the Wind*, 140

Writing in 1947, when 'queer' was used simultaneously to *denote* general non-conformity (as in strange or eccentric behaviour) and to *connote* outright deviancy (as in homosexuality), Mitchell could hardly have predicted the political and lexical distance the word would travel in the close to fifty-year history of pre- and post-Stonewall gay liberation. And while, as Terry Goldie has recently suggested, it is possible to divine something more than mere Wordsworthian 'intimations of immortality' in Brian O'Connoll's attraction to the Young Ben ('W.O. Mitchell'),[6] it is probably 'safer' to read this classic example of the Canadian 'rural *Bildungsroman*' as a simple 'coming-of-age' story rather than as a sublimated 'coming out' story. It is 'safer' because overly ardent 'queer' readings of canonical Canadian texts from the 1940s leave the contemporary critic (like Goldie and myself) open to charges of ahistoricism. (Only relatively recently, for example, has 'queer' been redeployed as a positive marker of gay subcultural affinity in slogans like 'We're here, we're queer, get used to it!')

Well aware, then, that every invocation of the term 'queer' is fraught with certain critical and political perils, I nevertheless propose to focus my homosocial gaze in this section on another Canadian Prairie classic from the 1940s, a text with its own preponderance of 'queers,' a text, moreover, which has been nationally canonized (at the 1978 Calgary Conference on the Canadian Novel, and in repeated readings thereafter) as the *locus classicus* of the Canadian *Künstlerroman*, in this case a 'failed-artist' narrative.[7] I am speaking, of course, of Sinclair Ross's celebrated novel, *As for Me and My House* (1941).

The posthumous 'outing' of Ross, and the concomitant 'uncloseting' of his first and most famous novel, has recently been undertaken with eximious exactitude by Keath Fraser in *As for Me and My Body*, where biographical criticism is taken to new lengths – quite literally in the case of Fraser's obsession with the size of Ross's penis. However, rather than 'chewing over the "intentional fallacy"' (Fraser, 16), and questions pertaining to Ross's own sexuality, I prefer to approach the text, at least initially, with a discussion of narrative point of view. In a compelling investigation into how so many eighteenth-century English novels structured as women's autobiographies (in particular, Defoe's *Roxana* and Richardson's *Clarissa*) came to be written by men, Madeleine Kahn 'offer[s] a theory of the novel as a form which allowed its authors to exploit the instability of gender categories and which is thus inseparable from its own continual reexamination and redefinition of those categories' (6). Conjoining the discourses of literary criticism and psychoanalysis to formulate her theory of 'narrative transvestism,' Kahn argues that the term 'is not a diagnosis but a metaphor: it furnishes helpful analogies to the structures that govern an essentially literary masquerade, and it directs our attention to the dialectic of display and concealment exhibited by these eighteenth-century texts – to the complex negotiations between self and other that structure both the novelist's art and the reader's response' (11). Taking my cue from Kahn, I want to suggest that the first-person narration of *As for Me and My House*, the locutionary positioning of Mrs Bentley as enigmatic diarist, constitutes a twentieth-century Canadian example of 'narrative transvestism,' and that 'the dialectic of display and concealment' exhibited by the text opens up a cross-gender space of liminal minority gay identification.

In a recent article on the 'conflicting signs' of *As for Me and My House*, Frank Davey notes that the text is read canonically as either straightforward realism, with Philip Bentley as the 'main character,' or else as an example of psychological realism, with Mrs Bentley's 'unreliability' as narrator becoming the focus of critical scrutiny. According to Davey, the emphasis on realism in both sets of readings obscures 'the novel's existence as a complex of textual signs that participate in the readerly construction of meaning' (*Canadian Literary Power*, 128). Davey himself locates within the text 'the presence of at least a triple construction – a signator, Sinclair Ross, who has constructed a text which in turn constructs its narrator by constructing the narrator's construction of events' (128). Yet, while Davey includes among the text's 'conflicting signs' issues of sexuality and cross-gender affiliations, he 'leave[s] implicit but unstated how the text reflects in turn on its male signator and on the gender questions the presence of this signator raises' (129).

Indeed, in disclaiming the label of 'realism' for *As for Me and My House*, Davey fails to endorse any alternative narrative categorizations. Most of my critical sensibilities support Davey in his refusal to fix absolute meaning either inside or outside of Ross's text. On the subject of projective readerly relations, however, my post-structuralist resolve tends to become a little limp-wristed. For, as I see it, *at least one* possible way to reconcile the male signator with *at least one* community of readers is to interpret the text, not as realism, but as homosexual fantasy.

In her very first diary entry, Mrs Bentley clearly establishes Philip's artistic sensibility, 'what he is and what he nearly was – the failure, the compromise, the going-on – it's all there – the discrepancy between the man and the little niche that holds him' (7). She also discloses that 'he likes boys – often, I think, plans the bringing-up and education of *his* boy' (9). It is only very gradually (and with great subtlety) that Mrs Bentley reveals what *she* is and what *she* nearly was: a 'barren' woman, a 'failed' artist in her own right, Philip's '[partner] in conspiracy' (20).

Into this 'house of silence and repression and restraint' (77) comes Steve, a young orphaned boy, who awakens in Philip a 'dark, strange and morbid passion,' a passion which 'account[ed] for ... the tangle of his early years, dark, strange, and morbid most of them too' (177). Suddenly Mrs Bentley, who can 'give [Steve] only a twisted, hybrid love' (146), is required to put up another 'false front,' 'enlarged this time for three': 'Philip, Steve and I. It's such a trim, efficient little sign; it's such a tough, deep-rooted tangle that it hides' (81).

'*As for Me and My House – The House of Bentley*' (81): the singularity of the pronoun and possessive in Ross's title is itself significant and points to the fact that any complete reading of the text must consider Philip and Mrs Bentley together, not as separately defined characters. Moreover, such a reading must also take into account the text's self-reflexive commentary on its own 'written' composition. At one point we are told expressly that Philip 'tried to write': 'It was a failure, of course, and it exhausted him' (45). It is thus left to Mrs Bentley, through her diary, to elaborate an 'illusion' of Horizon, and concomitantly, of herself: 'Over the tea and sponge cake I had a few gaunt moments, looking down a corridor of years and Horizons, at the end of which was a mirror and my own reflection' (109). Of course, if occasionally Mrs Bentley does not like what she sees, neither does Horizon: 'Right to my face Horizon tells me I'm a queer one' (203).

The image of the mirror, or looking-glass, also figures implicitly in the riddle which Paul Kirby poses to Mrs Bentley at the end of the novel:

> 'Why is a raven like a writing-desk?'
>
> 'A nonsense riddle in *Alice in Wonderland*,' I replied. 'There isn't an answer, and those are crows, not ravens.'
>
> 'Once the raven, too, had a croak in his name,' he said cryptically, 'and there was a time when all pens scratched.' (208)

This riddle, with its phallic *double entendre* (pen/penis), points in turn to one of the text's central ambiguities: Mrs Bentley's name; or, rather, her lack of a *Christian* name. According to Robert Kroetsch, in his afterword to the New Canadian Library edition of *As for Me and My House*, Ross's refusal 'to "name" Mrs. Bentley' is part of the text's 'splendid dance of ... evasions' (221). But surely it is also a clue. Philip Bentley, Mrs Philip Bentley: might not the two characters be one and the same person? The homo-narcissistic implications of this hypothesis become provocatively apparent when, at the end of the novel, Mrs 'Philip' Bentley decides to name Judith West's child, now 'her' son, 'Philip,' after his father, 'Philip,' a man who, 's/he' tells us in her initial diary entry, 'has a way of building in his own image, too' (9).

In 'The Fear of Women in Prairie Fiction,' another important essay on *As for Me and My House*, Kroetsch discusses the 'evasion' of sex in Ross's novel. However, in repeatedly posing the rhetorical question 'How do you make love in a new country?' Kroetsch fails to consider the fact that Ross's refusal to answer that question in his text might in fact betray a dis-ease with heterosexuality as a compulsory institution rather than with female sexuality and eroticism per se. Kroetsch's disingenuousness is all the more ironic in this regard given the links he makes in this essay between *As for Me and My House* and Willa Cather's *My Antonia*. After all, Cather was a lesbian who repeatedly wrote 'across gender and sexuality,' peopling her fiction with a wide spectrum of gay men.[8]

In this sense, the narrative confusion created by Ross's text is at least doubly transvestic, signalling what Marjorie Garber, in *Vested Interests*, refers to as a 'category crisis.' Both the male 'signator' and the male 'protagonist' create in Mrs Bentley a writerly 'persona' through which to reflect/refract their sexual/textual desires. And I would like to suggest that the 'object' of these desires is not the pale-faced soprano, Judith West, but Philip's 'parody-double' (Kroetsch, 'The Fear of Women,' 77), Paul Kirby, whose Carrollian etymologies, puns, and riddles remind us that the gaps, silences, indirections, and prevarications surrounding words are part of the projective fantasy of any narrative: 'I think of Paul, and wonder might it have been different if we had known each other earlier. Then the currents might have taken and fulfilled me. I might not still be nailed by them against a heedless wall' (209). Extending Mrs Bentley's writerly fantasy (and my readerly one) even further, beyond the bounds of her text, if Ross locates in *As for Me and My House* a tale of 'closeted' homosocial/sexual martyrdom, then surely *Sawbones Memorial* (1974) represents a textual 'coming out' of sorts, an attempt to integrate more fully a self-identified gay character (in this case, Benny Fox) into his writing.

One final question that I wish to pose at the end of this section is the extent to which the modern homosocial tradition in Canadian literature can be said to have emerged as a variant of the whole *Künstlerroman* genre in this country. Consider, in this regard, another 'failed-artist narrative' from the pre-1960 period, Ernest Buckler's *The Mountain and the Valley*. Transposing Ross's Prairie setting to the Annapolis Valley of Nova Scotia, Buckler relates in a high, metaphysical style the story of David Canaan. Ironically, David, the supposedly 'gifted' child, the perpetual 'outsider,' is the only member of his family who does not make it off the farm in rural Entremont. After glimpsing a vision of the unity he has failed to achieve in his writing, David dies on the mountain that has symbolized his unattainable goal: the triumph of passion over intellect.[9] More than once in the narrative, Buckler suggests that a possible source of David's emotional disequilibrium is a conflict with his own sexuality. For example, after a scene in which David and Toby (once David's pen-pal, now married to David's twin sister, Anna – more homosocial triangulation) kill birds together, Buckler has David ruminate on the 'man-fibre' and 'man-togetherness' he shares 'with the other who was like him':

> Having spoken of and felt the same way about the thing that *made* them men, the way a man feels about a woman, there was less loneliness in him than at any other time he had walked here before. There was less loneliness, in a

> way, than if he were walking here with a woman; for though a woman you might love, your love was only possible because she was different. The only people who can take loneliness away are the people who are the same. (256)

In highly Whitmanesque prose ('man-fibre,' 'man-togetherness'), Buckler reveals in this passage (as elsewhere in his novel) a certain authorial sensitivity to, not to mention textual felicity with, the emotional investments and social emplotments of male-male desire. In so doing, he opens up another discursive space of identification and critical interrogation for those readers who prefer to interpret his text from outside the strict bounds of regional or generic classification. Here, to be sure, is a quintessential example of Maritime- or Atlantic-Canadian writing. Here too is psychological realism at its finest. But equally, to allude once again to Whitman, 'Here is adhesiveness' ('Song of the Open Road,' *Leaves of Grass*, 230) – which is to say, of course, here is queer.

Homo Pomo

> George is reading, being handsome, in a crushed red velvet shirt. He is entertaining, being a performer, which I don't get, I don't get him at all, really, why he does all this, the video-camera, the attention of the audience, seem suddenly so dreary, commonplace, a false rigour of importance hangs around the occasion with it, for what, Canadian Literature, I suppose, all that, Canadian Literature has always seemed over there, in boring-land to me, I will never write Canadian Literature.
>
> Scott Watson, 'Voice without Words,' 10

The 'George' alluded to here in Watson's 'story-*à-clef*' is George Bowering, exemplary practitioner – as some would have it – of postmodernist writing in this country, the kind of 'Canadian Literature' Watson 'will never write.'[10] In *Burning Water* (1980), the first instalment of his 'British Columbia trilogy,' Bowering cuts a wide swath across Canadian history with his parodic pen, deliberately deconstructing several time-honoured and revered national myths. Moreover, as my choice of metaphor is meant to demonstrate, he also constructs a few new sexual myths, such as the homosexual relationship he imputes between rival British and Spanish Captains George Vancouver and Francisco Quadra.

I am willing to accept the argument that Bowering's parodic break with realist modes of storytelling in *Burning Water* constitutes a politically motivated attempt to subvert dominant historical and colonial methods of representation, particularly with respect to the fostering of regional and national identity. I remain unconvinced, however, by Bowering's own assertion, in the prologue to his novel, that the (his)story he is at once deconstructing and reconstructing is one we all share: 'We all live in the same world's sea.' According to the textual 'George,' 'We cannot tell a story that leaves us outside, and when I say we, I include you' (n. pag.). As Marcia Crosby comments, 'One can only parody something that is shared, otherwise it's an "in" joke. The work is only postmodern if the reader is engaged, since it is a receiver system: the code must be learned, otherwise the work or intention of the theory is invisible' (271). Crosby, a Haida woman, points out that *Burning Water*, with its stereotypical depiction of sardonic, inscrutable, rather child-like Native men, and 'savage,' sexually willing Native women, is itself not outside the colonizing loop of representation and, in fact, even interiorizes (and thus perpetuates) its manifold national and sexual myths.

Likewise, I have serious qualms about Bowering's representation of homosexuality in his novel, which appears to have little to do with a political commitment to interrogating normative assumptions about masculinity and much to do with the standard conventions of postmodernist metafiction. That is, if part of the project of Canadian literary postmodernism is to render forever ambivalent the received narratives of nationhood, then why not extend this project to narratives of sexuality as well? Consider, in this regard, Leonard Cohen's *Beautiful Losers* (1966), hailed by critics such as Linda Hutcheon and Sylvia Söderlind as '*the* quintessential Canadian postmodern novel' (Söderlind, *Margin/Alias*, 41). Both Hutcheon and Söderlind offer brilliant readings of the 'central bizarre triangle of symbolically orphaned characters [the Anglo-Canadian I, the French-Canadian F, and the Native-Canadian Edith]' as an allegory of 'the history and political destiny of the Canadian nation' (Hutcheon, *The Canadian Postmodern*, 28). Moreover, both critics apply Mikhail Bakhtin's concepts of 'ambivalence' and 'carnivalesque' to the sex in the novel, with Hutcheon arguing that 'all the sex is deliberately non-productive biologically (i.e., mechanical, oral, anal)' (33) and Söderlind, that 'the pornography paradigm also emphasizes Cohen's (quasi-Foucauldian) preoccupation with the inscription of power relationships on the body' (43–4). What does not get discussed by either critic, however, at least not at any length, is how same-sex desire, as presented in *Beautiful Losers*, both accedes to and resists this inscription, how, in other words, homosexuality is in/an excess of (not to mention, inaccessible to) the national narrative of self-identification. This is, to be sure, somewhat understandable, given

Cohen's own authorial disavowal of the sexual activity between I and F as homo-inflected. '"[Y]ou musn't feel guilty about any of this,"' F instructs I at one point in the text, adding that what they do ('sucking each other, watching the movies, Vaseline,' etc.) '"isn't homosexuality at all."' To which I promptly responds: '"Oh, F., come off it. Homosexuality is a name"' (18).

While I applaud Cohen's (quasi-Foucauldian) narrative insights into the discursive construction of (homo)sexuality, I cannot help but read this abrogation of sexual/textual 'response-ability' as yet another colonizing *gaze*, whereby the 'homosexual panic' of supposedly 'straight' characters is assuaged at the expense of the lived experience of self-identified *gays*: the 'queer horrible acts' that I and F – as 'victim[s] of the system' – are forced to commit by the 'Roman Catholic Church of Québec' must not be equated, the text makes abundantly clear, with what the 'raging fairies' who hang out in the lobby of the System Theatre do (50, 65). 'Homosexuality is celebrated in Cohen,' according to Robert K. Martin, 'but only as a way of reinforcing heterosexuality ... As Quebec helps Canada to be more Canadian, so homosexuality helps men to be more manly' ('Two Days in Sodom,' 29). Or, as F puts it at one point in his long letter to I, 'Our queer love keeps the lines of our manhood hard and clean, so that we bring nobody but our own self to our separate marriage beds, and our women finally know us' (164–5).

Except that once again the 'indigenized'/Indigenous woman performs double duty in the overlapping triangulated narratives of national and sexual identity. The twice 'widowed' Ellen Halloway, having disappeared into the wilderness at the end of Richardson's *Wacousta*, re-emerges from 'the old Canadian trees' in Cohen's *Beautiful Losers* as Edith (60), running first into the arms of I, and then into F's warm embrace (or vice-versa, depending on whose version of events we accept). Edith, true to her vanishing tribe, the 'A—,' is both earthy and ethereal, passed back and forth between I and F 'like a package of mud,' hovering over them like a 'holy star' (231, 164). But once again like Ellen, and – even closer to home – Catherine Tekakwitha, Edith remains the 'unassimilatable' other in the cinematic melt-down that takes place in the final section of Cohen's novel, the lonely question mark at the end of all the 'what IFs?' surrounding the future of Canada and Quebec.

Among critics of Canadian postmodernism, *Beautiful Losers* is most often juxtaposed against the work of Hubert Aquin, whose best-known texts – *Prochain Épisode* (1965) and *Trou de mémoire* (1968) – bracket the publication of Cohen's novel. These two important Québécois examples of the *nouveau roman* demonstrate, according to Hutcheon, that Aquin 'appears willing to accept the fact that the act of writing itself is a truly revolutionary one. For the author, this insight involves no crude *engagement* on the level of political content; it is, in fact, through metafictional *form* that Aquin hopes to liberate his country and his literature' (*Narcissistic Narrative*, 156). The reader, too, is involved in this liberation, since 'to read is to act; to act is both to interpret and to create anew – to be revolutionary, perhaps in political as well as literary terms' (ibid., 161). While I am in complete agreement with Hutcheon's suggestion that writing, reading, and interpreting are political acts, and while I am intrigued by Söderlind's own sado-masochistic (i.e., master/slave) take on the reader's 'willing submission to the writer' (not to mention, the latter's submission to 'the cruelty of the critic' [236]), I remain concerned about a frequent tendency within literary criticism to view postmodernism and postcolonialism as little more than new formalisms. In terms of *Trou de mémoire*, my anxieties in this regard coalesce around what Söderlind calls 'the formal expressions of the colonization paradigm' (70) in that novel, particularly as they are enacted in the 'symbolic rape' of Rachel Ruskin (RR) by Pierre X. Magnant, revolutionary pharmacist and murderer of RR's sister, Joan. Just as rape is not consensual sex, so is its metaphorical deployment in a text not an authorial move to which every reader is willing to submit. Nor are critics' often 'cruel' explications of it by any means uniform, as we shall see at greater length in chapter 2 in connection with the rape in Findley's *The Wars*.

Aquin's preoccupation with African anti-colonialist struggles in general, and with the writings of Albert Memmi and Frantz Fanon in particular, is well documented by scholars. What these same scholars fail to consider, however, is that the connection Aquin felt with Fanon, for example, may not have centred solely on questions of revolutionary nationalism; it may also have had something to do with a few unresolved issues of sexuality. Contemporary postcolonial theorists owe much to the rethinking of racial alterity and national difference elaborated by Fanon in *Black Skin, White Masks* and *The Wretched of the Earth*, among other texts. In terms of critical revisioning, the Martinican/Algerian psychiatrist and philosopher becomes for Edward Said 'an advocate of post-postmodern counternarratives of liberation'; for Abdul JanMohamed, 'a Manichean theorist of colonialism as absolute negation'; for Homi Bhabha, 'another Third World post-structuralist'; and for Benita Parry, a supporter of 'her own rather optimistic vision of literature and social action' (Gates, 465). Fanon's work has, even more recently, been the focus of attention for many contemporary queer theorists, several of whom have turned to his psychoanalytical writings in order to interrogate some of 'Fanon's disquieting discussions of not only femininity but homosexuality' (Fuss, 'Interior Colonies,' 30).

For example, in his discussion of 'Negrophobia' in chapter 6 of *Black Skin, White Masks,* Fanon takes as his central example the psycho-pathological fantasy 'A Negro is raping me.' Situating his theory of sexual perversions within the broader framework of cultural constructions of racism, Fanon claims that the white woman who fears the black man really desires him. So apparently does the white man: 'the Negrophobic woman is in fact nothing but a putative sexual partner – just as the Negrophobic man is a repressed homosexual' (156). Fanon's equation of homosexuality with racism in this scenario (where we would more likely expect to find homophobia positioned), and his subsequent discussion of homosexuality as the well-spring of virtually all internalized 'hate-complexes' ('Fault, guilt, refusal of guilt, paranoia – one is back in homosexual territory' [*Black Skin,* 183]), is, to say the least, troubling. As Jonathan Dollimore remarks, according to this logic, 'the homosexual is implicated all ways round ... *repressed* homosexuality is construed as a *cause* of a violent and neurotic racism, [while] elsewhere Fanon regards *manifest* homosexuality as an *effect* of the same neurotic racism' (*Sexual Dissidence,* 345). Fuss poses the question this way: 'If racism is articulated with homosexuality instead of homophobia, where are antiracist lesbians and gay men, of all colors, to position themselves in relation to same-sex desire? Fanon's theory of sexuality offers little to anyone committed to both an anti-imperialist and an antihomophobic politics' ('Interior Colonies,' 32).

However, far from condemning Fanon altogether, queer theorists would do well to examine more closely how the homophobia in *Black Skin, White Masks* unconsciously enacts the 'fear and revulsion' principles (154) analysed by Fanon throughout the text with respect to racist stereotyping, and how this in turn points to some of the psychic limitations involved in any project of decolonization. Framed in this way, the queer theorist (who is also antiracist/-colonialist, as Fuss suggests) must turn the question around: that is, if for Fanon (same-)sexuality operates as a delimiting rather than a catalytic factor in antiracist struggles, does race function in a similar way in anti-homophobic political movements? After all, male homosocial desire – as theorized by Sedgwick in *Between Men,* and as applied by myself in this chapter – does not seem to cross colour lines that easily, frequently resulting, when it does, in cataclysm or death, as with the double suicides of Magnant and Olympe at the end of Aquin's text.

Within the context of *Trou de mémoire*, then, Fanon's comments on 'Negrophobia' complicate – to say the least – the dominant reading of the rape in that novel 'as a central metaphor, connected with a loss of memory, symbolic of the colonizer's appropriation of the colony's history' (Söderlind, 71). Rather than interpreting it 'formally' as 'nothing but a repetition of Joan's murder,' a way of 'implicat[ing] Magnant in Olympe's story' (Söderlind, 77), might it not be possible to see the rape of Rachel (still highly problematical in its own right) as a displacement of Magnant's desire for her lover Olympe, his African double, the dark other in (him)self? And what of Olympe's insistence that Rachel repeatedly recount for him 'comment s'est passé le viol' (170; 'how the rape came about' [*Blackout*, 139])? Rachel is unable to provide him with all the details, but he nonetheless writes down what little he knows in his diary. In so doing, he becomes, according to Patricia Merivale, a 'complicit perpetrator,' a 'rapist in desire and fantasy as well as in his brutal violation of RR's mental privacy' ('Hubert Aquin,' 9).[11] And yet the text is deliberately vague as to whether Olympe in his diary is identifying with Magnant as the person doing the raping or with Rachel as the person being raped: 'Chaque fois que RR recommence son récit, je me retrouve encore à Lausanne, quasiment sous la peau de RR qui se tient sous la marquise; et j'attends que Pierre X. Magnant m'aborde' (189; 'Each time RR begins her story I'm back again in Lausanne, almost in the very shoes of RR standing in the shelter of an awning, waiting for Pierre X. Maganant to accost me' [*Blackout*, 155]).

The 'agonistic relation' in which Magnant and Olympe find themselves, both psychically and genitally, can thus be seen as part of what Lee Edelman calls 'the constitutive incoherence that marks heterosexual masculinity itself' (66). In his application of Fanon to the work of James Baldwin, Edelman notes that 'white men and black men ... in ways that are crucial for relations between the "races," anxiously identify "maleness" as an attribute associated, though associated differently for each, with the condition of the other' (66–7). In the case of Aquin, this necessarily means that the pathologization of *homo*sexuality per se gets displaced across gender lines, so that Rachel's supposed lesbian seduction of her sister, Joan, becomes the most shocking 'perversity' in the novel: 'Passe encore l'homosexualité entre deux hommes; les gens la tolèrant, quand ils ne cherchent pas carrément à lui reconnaître un brin de normalité. Mais moi, femme amoureuse d'une femme, je suis une sale dégénérée, une perverse!' (125; 'Homosexuality between men? People tolerate it or even try to find something normal about it. But I, a woman in love with a woman, am a filthy degenerate, a pervert!' [*Blackout*, 99]). Certainly the overtly masculinist premises of 'Negrophobia' described by Fanon are reflected, to a partial degree, in Magnant's 'phobie d'impuissance': 'Mon comportement sexuel est à l'image d'un comportement national frappé d'impuissance: plus ça va, plus je sens bien que je veux violer ... Ce désenchantement ressemble trop à une phobie d'impuissance. Fatigué, je rêve à la plénitude du viol' (112; 'My sexual behaviour is the reflection of a national behaviour whose hallmark is impotence; the easier the going the more I want to rape ... My disenchantment is too close to being a phobia of impotence. Weary, I dream of the plenitude of rape' [*Blackout*, 90]). Whereas, in *Trou de mémoire*, Magnant tells himself that his 'puissance véritable ... échappe à ce genre de vérification génitale' (115; 'true potency ... is not subject to genital proof' [*Blackout*, 91]), for the 'Negro' in Fanon's text, 'everything takes place on the genital level' (*Black Skin*, 157). Either way, phallic deficiency and phallic plenitude in both Aquin and Fanon consolidate themselves within 'a sort of tableau of narcissism' (Gates, 465), an anamorphic hall of mirrors in which homophobia and misogyny become the manifest (although no less reprehensible to this reader) external responses to other forms of internalized self-loathing induced by colonialism.

Such a (re)doubled reading of national and sexual alterity likewise finds expression in Aquin's *Prochain Épisode*. Just as the hero of Aquin's narrative of national liberation fails to kill his enemy, H. de Heutz, in whom he recognizes an 'inverted' image of himself (as well as a 'father figure'), so is he susceptible to the sexual double-cross, the beautiful and mysterious K (*Kébec*?) being responsible – or so the text implies – for his ultimate betrayal to the authorities. Patricia Smart has indicated how this particular triangular structure – which will resurface again in chapter 4 – of Oedipal desire and rivalry is in some senses unique to Quebec. For his part, Robert Schwartzwald has noted that 'the obsession for (hetero)sexual conquest that is so prominent in Aquin's novels, complete with its litanies of masculine connoisseurship, functions as a doomed compensatory mechanism. Its invariably unsuccessful resolution barely masks the homosexual panic that really fuels Aquin's writing' ('Fear of Federasty,' 187). Moreover, commenting on Aquin's influence on Scott Symons (a connection I shall explore at greater length in chapter 3), Robert K. Martin points out that in Quebec nationalist writing, 'the desire *to rape* is accompanied by a desire *to be raped*, not on the part of women but on the part of men, in the context of national guilt. If the "missionary position" is always on top, then the antimissionary must always be buggered' ('Cheap Tricks,' 200). So too with the anti-revolutionary, it would seem. Indeed, if there is an insurrectionary bond established between writer and reader in Aquin's texts, it is one that, much like the connection forged between writer and reader in Richardson's *Wacousta* or Ross's *As for Me and My House*, is 'homoerotically charged' (Schwartzwald, 'Fear of Federasty,' 190).

From There to Queer

It has not been my intent, in constructing a national 'minority narrative' of Canadian literature in the preceding pages, 'to delineate a separate male-homosocial literary canon' (Sedgwick, *Between Men*, 17). While I firmly believe that 'que(e)rying' the canon requires making space for 'new' textual voices, I also believe that such a process requires the simultaneous rereading of 'old' voices in 'new' ways. In this sense, as Sedgwick notes, virtually every national literary 'canon as it exists is already such a [homosocial] canon, and most so when it is most heterosexual' (*Between Men*, 17) – which is also to say when a canon is *most patriarchal*. This is certainly the case with Canadian literature, whose patterns of sexual dissimulation, as we shall discover at greater length in chapter 4, were distressingly apparent to someone as virulently misogynist and homophobic as Aquin. And, moreover, as the example of Aquin further illustrates, both inside and outside the system of containment known as Canadian canon-formation, the histories of nationalism and sexuality are neither discrete nor autonomous (as the broad parameters encompassed by the Lecker-Davey debate would have us believe), but rather inextricably 'enmeshed' (Mosse, 10).

My use of the term 'enmeshed' is deliberate here; it is meant to indicate that the political and theoretical impulses motivating this book owe something to the pioneering work of historian George Mosse. In *Nationalism and Sexuality*, Mosse sketches a double history of modern European nationalism and bourgeois – or 'respectable' – sexuality as they emerged together at the end of the eighteenth century and coalesced in the early twentieth century, in part helping to facilitate the rise of German National Socialism. In so doing, Mosse points out that the normative assumptions behind our understanding of nationalism and sexuality today, assumptions which we frequently take for granted or regard as conceptually immutable, were in fact thoroughly innovative in European middle-class society two hundred years ago: 'manners and morals, as well as sexual norms, are part of the historical process ... We must appreciate the relativity of such values in order to understand how they came to be allied with nationalism. What one regards as normal or abnormal behavior, sexual or otherwise, is a product of historical development, not universal law' (3).

In this passage, Mosse clearly aligns himself with the 'social constructionist' sympathies of Benedict Anderson and Michel Foucault, who in their respective analyses of 'the origins of nationalism' and the 'history of sexuality' argue that national and sexual 'communities' are 'imagined,' or discursively produced. In what is arguably the most influential academic study of nationalism in the past decade, Anderson, for example, links the development of what he calls 'imagined nation-ness' with the 'convergence of capitalism and print technology' on language in the late fifteenth and early sixteenth centuries (46). The institutionalization of this originary, 'vernacular' nationalism, according to Anderson, was 'born' in the Americas and 'modularly' adopted/adapted, that is, refashioned and retooled, first by the colonial powers of Western Europe, and then by the anti-colonial independence movements in Asia and Africa.[12]

As Partha Chatterjee has pointed out, however, Anderson's 'constructionist' account of the origin and spread of nationalism looks suspiciously like the framework for a universal history, one that 'seals up [Anderson's] theme with a sociological determinism,' and that consequently fails to account adequately for nationalism's 'twists and turns, the suppressed possibilities, the contradictions still unresolved' (*Nationalist Thought and the Colonial World,* 21, 22). Chatterjee's 'central objection' to Anderson's argument stems from the latter's inherent conflation of nationalisms. 'The most powerful as well as the most creative results of the nationalist imagination in Asia and Africa,' he asserts in *The Nation and Its Fragments,* 'are posited not on an identity but rather on a *difference* with the "modular" forms of the national society propagated by the modern West' (5). Anti-colonial nationalisms in Asia and Africa, Chatterjee goes on to argue, have imagined an '"inner" domain' of sovereignty 'within' colonial society that at the same time manages to be 'without' it, in that the imperialist powers are excluded from it. This inner, or 'spiritual,' domain of sovereignty, which Chatterjee distinguishes from the 'material' domain and which he discusses most fully in connection with Bengal, would seem to be roughly analogous to Fanon's formulation, in *The Wretched of the Earth,* of 'national consciousness' a term which Fanon in turn distinguishes from 'nationalism' and which he claims 'takes on in Africa a special dimension': 'the awareness of a simple rule which wills that every independent nation in an Africa where colonialism is still entrenched is an encircled nation, a nation which is fragile and in permanent danger' (198–9). The difference, of course, is that Fanon, unlike Chatterjee, is writing from a psychoanalytical perspective; what Chatterjee labels the 'spiritual' springs for Fanon from 'unconscious' desires. Anderson's narrative of undifferentiated national claims tends to elide these kinds of surplus terms/discourses, at the same time as the anti-/postcolonial theorizing of Fanon and Chatterjee poses new conceptual challenges to the forms of national expression and the limits of historical imagination. 'If the nation is an imagined community,' Chatterjee ambiguously concludes, then it must in part be through the powers of imagination, the intellectual and psychological processes of invention and creation – what Fanon would no doubt call the 'Negro' or 'Native's' fantasies of racial and sexual displacement – that such a community comes into being: 'In this, *its true and essential domain*, the nation is already sovereign, even when the state is in the hands of the colonial power. The dynamics of this historical project is [*sic*] completely missed in conventional histories in which the story of nationalism begins with the contest for political power' (*The Nation*, 6; my emphasis).

There is no 'true and essential domain' of sexuality according to Foucault; but its history is very much that of a contest for power.[13] As he puts it in the first volume of *The History of Sexuality*, 'discourses on sex did not multiply apart from or against power, but in the very space and as the means of its exercise' (32). Moreover, his famous re-evaluation of the 'repressive hypothesis' locates the shift from loosely defined interdictions against certain kinds of 'sodomitical' behaviour or activity to the naming of 'homosexuality' as a category – and the 'homosexual' as a 'specific' type of (deviant) individual – firmly within the convergence of medico-juridical discourses in the late nineteenth century (see *The History of Sexuality, Vol. 1: An Introduction*, especially 17–49). Foucault is actually even more precise, pinpointing 1870 as the 'date of birth' of 'the psychological, psychiatric, medical category of homosexuality':

> As defined by the ancient civil or canonical codes, sodomy was a category of forbidden acts; their perpetrator was nothing more than the juridical subject of them. The nineteenth-century homosexual became a personage, a past, a case history, and a childhood, in addition to being a type of life, a life form, a morphology, with an indiscreet anatomy and possibly a mysterious physiology ... The sodomite had been a temporary aberration; the homosexual was now a species. (43)

More recent scholarship, however, suggests that the 'Great Paradigm Shift' in 'the modern homo/heterosexual definition' (Sedgwick, *Epistemology*, 44, 45) recorded by Foucault in the first volume of *The History of Sexuality* may in fact have been initiated earlier, and sustained over a much longer historical period and in a much more complex way. Foucault was constantly modifying and revising his own argument in the subsequent volumes of *The History of Sexuality*, returning to the examples of ancient Greece and Rome in order to outline an 'ethic of care of the self' based on the 'uses of pleasure' (to modify slightly the titles of volumes 3 and 2, respectively). Across all three volumes – indeed, one might even say throughout his entire oeuvre – Foucault is most concerned with documenting the specific techniques and practices of the body (what he calls 'technologies of the self'), a project which he describes as a 'history of [sexual] "ethics," understood as the elaboration of a form of relation to self that enables an individual to fashion himself [*sic*] into a subject of ethical conduct' (*The Use of Pleasure*, 251).

Ed Cohen, whose own project of constructing a 'genealogy of a discourse on male sexualities' in *Talk on the Wilde Side* owes much to the work of Foucault, acknowledges that the increasingly polemical divide among historians and theorists of sexuality and sexual communities 'is itself constructed upon political questions represented through concrete historical and semantic issues. For what appears to be at stake in the historiographic debates about dating "homosexuality" is how we ought to evaluate the ways this concept still organizes our own engagements with and transformations of the current historical moment' (211); or, perhaps more pertinently, the ways in which these largely academic debates *fail to organize* urban gay communities whose collective engagements with history (on the day-to-day level of protest and activism) remain for the most part framed within a paradigm of identity politics. As Steven Epstein suggests, 'constructionism poses a real and direct threat to the ethnic legitimation [of the "gay masses"]: people who base their claims to social rights on the basis of a group identity will not appreciate being told that that identity is just a social construct' (22).

Rejecting both 'strict constructionism' and 'strict essentialism' as theoretically inadequate and politically ineffective positions from which to analyse homosexual identity, Epstein nevertheless strategically modifies some key essentialist tenets in developing his concept of 'gay ethnicity' as a 'politically defensible starting point from which the gay movement can evolve in a progressive direction' (27–8). Such a 'modified constructionism,' according to Epstein, 'implies a more comprehensive understanding of power, and of the dialectical relationship between identities as self-expressions and identities as ascriptive impositions' (44). Similarly, in her reading of the Subaltern Studies collective's attempts to 'situate' subaltern consciousness (and, concomitantly, postcolonial agency) within the narrative 'metalepsis' of elite historiography, Gayatri Spivak endorses what she sees 'as a *strategic* use of positivist essentialism in a scrupulously visible political interest' ('Subaltern Studies,' 205). To be sure, Epstein's 'modified constructionism' and Spivak's 'strategic essentialism' are not political panaceas; they are merely elegant rhetorical circumventions of an ongoing theoretical impasse. In practice, there will always remain a danger that what begins as provisional and interventionary will eventually solidify into a permanent re-entrenchment of absolutist positions. 'This is not an argument *against* using identity categories,' to quote from Judith Butler in *Bodies That Matter*, 'but it is a reminder of the risk that attends every such use' (228). In keeping with the situationally dependent nature of strategy, however, I would add that in certain circumstances it may just be that the 'risk' is well worth taking.[14]

In the politically volatile and emotionally charged debates around postcolonial and queer studies, unanimity of opinion is rarely in evidence. Nor should it be. Still, as Fuss has persuasively argued, 'the bar between essentialism and constructionism is by no means as solid and unassailable as advocates of both sides assume it to be' (*Essentially Speaking*, xii). Indeed, more and more critics are beginning to speak in terms of 'co-implications' (Mohanty, 'On Race and Voice') and 'cross-identifications' (Butler and Martin), to theorize difference as historically contextual and relationally contingent. That is, within the overlapping ideologies of race, gender, and sexuality, both whites and blacks, men and women, straights and gays 'share certain histories as well as certain responsibilities' (Mohanty, 'On Race and Voice,' 195).

As I see it, one of my primary responsibilities in this book is to rethink the hotly contested issue of identity, both nationally and sexually. This necessarily means beginning with where I am: a white Anglo-Scots gay male literary critic living in Vancouver, British Columbia, Canada (from here – where? – the positionalities, as Stephen Dedalus discovered, proliferate outward exponentially). However, moving forward from this locational context – be it corporeal, institutional, geographical, or whatever – requires something more, a sort of referential leap of faith, an absenting of identity before the presence of alterity. What I mean by this apparent tautology is that the process of *self*-identification will always in some senses be partial and incomplete because the social parameters governing a given identity are constituted in relation to and circumscribed in terms of that which is *other*. To resituate this statement within the discursive formations of nationalism and sexuality, at least as they are operating in this book, any evaluative methodology I come up with to account for their respective 'engagements with and transformations of' contemporary Canadian literature must first of all see – as George Mosse so clearly points out – nationalism as sexuality's other, and vice-versa. In this sense, I am attempting to heed the call announced by Schwartzwald at the end of his essay on the 'problematics of identity in Québec,' an essay to which I will have occasion to refer again in chapter 4. He concludes his analysis of the conscription and naturalization of sexual difference within Québécois social theorists' narratives of national identity by suggesting to both 'theorists of the subject-nation' *and* 'sex-gender theorists' a mutual interrogation of and 'constructive engagement' with each other's 'variegated claims' on the 'unavoidably common terrain of identity' (290, 291).

Of course, as Henry Abelove and others have so astutely intuited, one such 'constructive engagement' – or 'enmeshment,' to return to Mosse's phrase – of the national and the sexual is encapsulated in the tactics and strategies deployed by, not to mention the very name of, 'Queer Nation' (see Abelove, 'From Thoreau to Queer Politics'). In an article that is equal parts theoretical rumination, documentary history, and radical manifesto, Lauren Berlant and Elizabeth Freeman maintain that 'Queer Nation's outspoken promotion of a national sexuality not only discloses that mainstream national identity touts a subliminal sexuality more official than a state flower or national bird, but also makes explicit how thoroughly the local experience of the body is framed by laws, policies, and social customs regulating sexuality' (195). Trading upon (or, more properly, 'camping') the structures of identification and the economies of exchange central to the promotion and maintenance of a nationalist-capitalist ideology, the organization's intertwining of the national with the sexual, its commingling of multiple and manifold publics, polities, communities, and symbolic cultures, according to Berlant and Freeman, is both a reclamation of nationality (specifically for 'pleasure') and a subversion of it. Queer Nation's insurrectionary rhetoric claims all social spaces 'as "national" sites ripe both for transgression and legitimate visibility. Its tactics are to cross borders, to occupy spaces, and to mime the privileges of normality' (Berlant and Freeman, 196).

On the subject of borders, and the crossing of borders, perhaps no one has written more eloquently or more powerfully than Gloria Anzaldúa. In *Borderlands / La Frontera: The New Mestiza*, she describes, in poetry and prose, her experience as a 'border woman,' growing up Chicana and lesbian along the U.S./Mexican border in southwestern Texas, caught between two different cultures, two different languages, two different models of sexual behaviour. Commenting on this liminal space, and her contradictory and shifting occupation of it, Anzaldúa writes: 'A borderland is a vague and undetermined place created by the emotional residue of an unnatural boundary. It is in a constant state of transition. The prohibited and forbidden are its inhabitants. *Los atravesados* live here: the squint-eyed, the perverse, the queer, the troublesome, the mongrel, the mulatto, the half-breed' (3). This territory, as Anzaldúa acknowledges, is by no means an easy or comfortable area to inhabit. And yet, the experience of 'constantly "crossing over,"' of repeatedly transgressing the boundaries/limits/margins of nationalism and sexuality, of undergoing 'this racial, ideological, cultural and biological cross-pollination,' does contribute to the formation of what Anzaldúa calls 'an "alien" consciousness,' 'a new *mestiza* consciousness,' 'a consciousness of the Borderlands' (78).[15]

To be sure, minorities (national, sexual, racial, gender, class) have always been more attuned to the permeability of borders than have dominant groups. In this post-NAFTA era, however, Anzaldúa's remarks take on added significance, if only because free trade seems to have resulted in a tightening rather than a relaxing of borders: financial capital and raw materials may pass back and forth relatively unrestricted, but not people, especially if those people are dark-skinned and speak Spanish. Although expressed differently than in Mexico, 'border consciousness,' and particularly consciousness of the U.S. border, 'has a long history in Canada' as well (Brown, 14). Distinguishing between 'borderlines' and 'borderlands,' Russell Brown argues that whereas the former 'defines Canada in terms of difference, in terms of what lies on its other side, or of what it does not, or will not, admit,' the latter is 'a place that draws all things into it, a place identified with the middle ground, with the union of opposites, and with mediation' (44). It is worth emphasizing here that Brown is speaking primarily about English Canadians' experiences of borders, especially *inter*nationally *vis-à-vis* the U.S. behemoth, where narratives of national identity have traditionally been melted down rather than multiplied out. Brown devotes little attention to the *intra*-national play of borders within the 'imagined community' known as Canada, both in terms of the 'borderlines' and 'borderlands' between English Canada and Quebec, for example, or between English Canada / Quebec and the First Nations.

Avoiding such potentially problematic binarisms, Marshall McLuhan argued, a decade or more before Brown (published in 1977, McLuhan's essay was originally broadcast on the CBC in 1967), that Canada constitutes a 'borderline case,' plain and simple. Well, perhaps not so simple. For, according to McLuhan, 'Canada is a land of *multiple* borderlines, psychic, social, and geographic' (244; my emphasis); each borderline, moreover, 'is an area of spiraling repetition and replay, of both inputs and feedback, of both interlace and interface, an area of "double ends joined," of rebirth and metamorphosis' (247). This condition of multiple borderlines contributes to what McLuhan calls 'Canada's low-profile [national] identity' (246), which, far from being a hindrance in the 'global village,' 'nourishes flexibility' and 'approaches the ideal pattern of electronic living' (247, 248). As McLuhan argued elsewhere, in *Culture Is Our Business*, 'homogeneity, the old ideal of *nation*, is useless in the global theatre of gaps and interfaces' (170).

In this regard, McLuhan – whose *The Gutenberg Galaxy* anticipated Benedict Anderson's central thesis by some twenty years – provides me with my strongest conceptual link back to a more specifically Canadian *literary* context. For it is McLuhan to whom Northrop Frye appeals near the end of his 'Conclusion' to the first edition of the *Literary History of Canada* (1965) in arguing that contemporary Canadian literature is, in effect, post-national: 'The writers of the last decade, at least, have begun to write in a world which is post-Canadian, as it is post-American, post-British, and post everything except the world itself' (*The Bush Garden*, 249). Frye put it even more explicitly two years later – this time without recourse to McLuhan – in *The Modern Century*: 'What is important about the last century, in [Canada], is not that we have been a nation for a hundred years, but that we have had a hundred years in which to make the transition from a pre-national to a post-national consciousness' (17). Picking up, in many respects, where McLuhan and Frye leave off, Frank Davey has recently invoked the term 'post-national' in his survey of 'the politics of the Anglophone-Canadian novel since 1967.' 'What this array of post-centennial Canadian fiction appears most strongly to announce,' according to Davey, 'is the arrival of the post-national state – a state invisible to its own citizens, indistinguishable from its own fellows, maintained by invisible political forces' (*Post-National*, 266).

Post-national, of course, is not the same as post-national*ist*. In the present 'global village' of crumbling economic borders (NAFTA, the European Union, Microsoft) and resurrected ethnic and political ones (the 'Balkanization' of the former Soviet Union and Yugoslavia, for example), various 'franchise' and 'tribal' nationalisms are flourishing, a situation from which Canada, Quebec, and even the newly corporatized university are also not exempt. While my own use of 'post-national' is necessarily imbricated with the successive meanings that critics like McLuhan, Frye, and Davey have attached to the term, I want also to stress that my application of it to various texts throughout this book is roughly analogous to my use of the literary-critical terms 'postcolonial' and 'postmodernist.' That is, what I take to be post-national, postcolonial, and postmodernist Canadian fictions are those texts which seem to situate themselves *in between* (1) a not-so-distant imperial past and an increasingly corporate future (hence 'post,' a prefix I understand to mean here both 'posterior' to, that is, coming after or later in a temporal or serial sense – as in post-classical or post-Impressionist – *and* 'anterior' to, that is, coming before or prior to in a more spatial sense – as in post-frontal lobotomy);[16] and (2) theories of identity, citizenship, power, and art that project evaluative criteria based on notions of belonging, truth, authority, convention, and fact (hence 'national,' 'colonial,' and 'modernist').

Ironically, the 'social imagination' which Frye outlines at the beginning of his 'Conclusion,' an imagination that 'explores and settles and develops' according to 'its own rhythms of growth' and 'modes of expression,' is anything but post-national (*The Bush Garden*, 215); it is, in fact, grounded in the myth of two founding nations. In declaring that 'Canada has two languages and literatures,' Frye also rather blithely claims that 'Canada began as an obstacle, blocking the way to the treasures of the east' (216, 217). This simultaneous absorption and elision of Indigenous and ethnic peoples and writing into the cultural history and literature of Canada posits Frye's 'social imagination' as arbiter of discursive absence, its apparent autonomous presence (within – and without – his text) determining what *does not exist*, what *is not there*.

Consequently, Canadian literature, at least as it is constructed by Frye in his 'Conclusion,' not only functions as 'an indispensable aid to the knowledge of Canada' (215), but also – to borrow a locution from Diana Fuss – 'as an indispensable interior exclusion' ('Inside/Out,' 3). Indeed, Fuss's description of homosexuality's necessarily oppositional status in relation to the 'compulsory' regime of heterosexuality would seem to apply equally well to the structures of exclusion and interiorization at work in the Canadian 'garrison mentality': 'an outside which is inside interiority making the articulation of the latter possible, a transgression of the border which is necessary to constitute the border as such' ('Inside/Out,' 3; see my discussion of borders, above). But, as Himani

Bannerji has recently stated, in her introduction to *Returning the Gaze*, 'an absence ... as much as a presence, is a good point for a beginning' (xii). So too, I would add, with an inside or an outside. Indeed, in positing 'Canadian' national identity as an absence, Frye's choice of interrogative adverb actually incorporates into the enunciative present both the notions of positionality ('here') and community, or collectivity ('we're'). 'Queer,' as an inclusive term, an expansive signifier, a transitive word with linguistic roots, as I have come to discover, in reaching 'across' boundaries, in standing 'athwart' various social communities,[17] would seem especially suited to negotiating the distance between 'here' and 'we're.' Thus, my initial response to the 'absent presences' and 'interior exclusions' operating within what Frye sees as Canada's 'famous problem of identity' is not simply to replace his rhetorical question '"Where is here?"' (*The Bush Garden*, 220) with another equally rhetorical one of my own, but rather, to provide one possible (polemical?) answer to it: 'Here is queer.'

2

'Running Wilde': National Ambivalence and Sexual Dissidence in Timothy Findley's Fictions

Wilde proceeded to the Queen's Hotel for dinner, escorted by Boyle and several other gentlemen. Little ragamuffins chased his carriage down Yonge Street shouting, 'Oscar, Oscar is running Wilde.' Wilde loved it. In Toronto he had the busiest itinerary in Canada, and he fulfilled his social obligations with vigour and unswerving graciousness. No one could accuse him of laziness.

Kevin O'Brien, *Oscar Wilde in Canada*, 97

I think, too, constantly of Oscar Wilde, who came here [to Dieppe] after being released from gaol – and the Mayor refused to let him stay because – *you will drive away all the English tourists, Mister Wilde!* Well, he didn't drive *us* away – dear Oscar. And here we are enjoying splendid food and the rest we have needed now, for a year.

Timothy Findley, *Inside Memory*, 207

In 1882, having published only a few socialist fairy tales and a slim volume of poetry (*Poems* [1881]), and with his first play (*Vera* [1880]) having closed before it opened,[1] Oscar Wilde, at the age of twenty-seven, embarked on a lecture tour of North America. Although not having yet secured the pre-eminent position he felt he deserved, Wilde was by no means an obscure figure in English literary society at the time. As one of the more flamboyant standard-bearers of a new artistic movement in Britain known as Aestheticism, he had achieved, at the very least, a measure of notoriety. Satirized routinely in George du Maurier's *Punch* cartoons, Wilde, through the dissemination of these images, actually came to instantiate corporeally the dandy and aesthete (his penchant for 'cello coats,' 'Super Fancy Angola suits,' 'plum-colored breeches and silk stockings,' all manner of capes and cloaks, and, of course, those green carnations, already legendary [see Ellmann, 87]). Indeed, it was Wilde – and not the more prominent philosophers/practitioners of the movement, such as William Morris, John Ruskin, Walter Pater, Dante Gabriel Rossetti, Algernon Charles Swinburne, and James Whistler – who was singled out for ridicule by Gilbert and Sullivan in their operetta *Patience* (1881), whose 'rival aesthetes,' Reginald Bunthorpe and Archibald Grosvenor, are both loosely based on Wilde (see Ellmann, 134–6).

Ironically, it was the producer of *Patience*, Richard D'Oyly Carte, who initially approached Wilde about lecturing in the United States and Canada. D'Oyly Carte had brought a production of *Patience* to New York in September 1881 and was anxious to promote a series of speaking engagements by one of the leading exponents of Aestheticism as a tie-in for his audiences, 'obviously want[ing] Wilde to be the living embodiment of what his opera was satirizing, in case Americans and Canadians did not get the joke' (O'Brien, 24). Being in rather desperate (creative as well as financial) straits, Wilde agreed at once to the tour, and set sail for New York on 24 December 1881.

After a somewhat rocky start on the east coast of the United States, Wilde abandoned his rather ponderous and overly academic lecture entitled 'The English Renaissance' – in which he offered a broad history of the Aesthetic Movement and attempted to reconcile its divergent strains (i.e., the Pater-Swinburne-Whistler school of private creative art versus the Ruskin-Morris-Rossetti school of public decorative art) through dictums similar to the Decadent mantra of 'art for art's sake' taken up in the 1890s – in favour of more audience-friendly talks entitled 'The Decorative Arts' and 'The House Beautiful,' and the lecture tour gathered momentum, garnering critical praise, winning over cynics and would-be detractors, and attracting larger and larger audiences. The Canadian leg of Wilde's North American itinerary – which took the writer to Ontario, Quebec, and the Maritimes – has been meticulously documented by Kevin O'Brien in his book *Oscar Wilde in Canada*. It has also recently served as the backdrop to Jim Bartley's critically acclaimed play *Stephen and Mr. Wilde*, which examines the societal gulf between Wilde and Stephen Davenport, an American ex-slave and valet who accompanied Wilde on tour.[2] Wilde's Toronto engagement, in particular, demonstrates how his reception in Canada as 'an apostle for the arts' – to quote the subtitle of O'Brien's study – was further complicated by an accretion of discourses of (homo)sexuality and nationalism onto the simultaneously foregrounded and de-familiarized, at once specularized and de-localized, citings/sitings/sightings of Wilde's own body.

Of course, the fact that Wilde's body was used 'so insistently as an index to such erotic and political meanings' (Sedgwick, 'Nationalisms,' 242) attests to the intense media scrutiny he was under even at this early stage in his career. And even in such a far-flung outpost of Empire as Toronto, Canada! According to O'Brien, most of the newspaper reports on the two lectures Wilde delivered in Toronto were highly favourable. The one negative example that O'Brien cites, from the *Evening Telegram*, takes an interesting approach in its disparagement of the famous aesthete, noting that 'Miss Oscar Wilde seems to be a charming young lady, although her costume is rather unfeminine,' and that 'there is a great deal of good sense in what she says about hanging pictures, putting down carpets, papering the walls, and painting the legs of the piano' (quoted in O'Brien, 107). In the following day's issue, the *Evening Telegram* goes even further, constructing a mock dialogue between the paper's editor and the simpering Wilde:

> 'Dear, innocent Oscar, I forgot you were a passionate loving woman, rich in girlish innocence. Oh, Oscar! will you crown the spring-time of my life by taking a seat on the top of that register?' The fair creature sighed again. A plaintive, gentle, kind, Sunday-school sort of sigh, and she seated herself on the register, her feet about a foot from the floor, and the extremities of her pants about a foot from her feet ... In a devotional, revival meeting kind of voice, she at length said, 'I am a man ... A yearner, it is true, after the lovable and the emotional, the beautiful and the soulful, but still a man. A base thing made of clay and with a knowledge of the taste of beer. Yes, I am a man. It is a painful thing for me to say. It is the skeleton in our own family, the blot on my life, the clog which drags me down and embitters my existence. Oh! if I only had been a woman!' And saying this, Mr. Wilde joined the editor and they both wept. It was a touching sight. The one seated in the waste paper basket, the other on top of the register, and both their souls going out to each other in tears. (Quoted in O'Brien, 108)

I have quoted this extraordinary passage at such length in order to demonstrate how what was ostensibly written as derisive satire is in fact thoroughly imbricated in the emerging discourse of nineteenth-century sexology, a discourse with which Wilde – as transitional figure, as embodied type – is also inextricably intertwined. In the concluding chapter of *Male Subjectivity at the Margins*, Kaja Silverman notes that between 1862 and 1895 (the date of Wilde's trials), male same-sex desire was frequently explained (and often defended) by sexologists like Havelock Ellis and Karl Heinrich Ulrichs as '"*anima muliebris in corpore virili inclusa*" – a female soul enclosed in a man's body' (340). This is in keeping with Foucault's argument in the first volume of *The History of Sexuality* – outlined above, in chapter 1 – that 'homosexuality appeared as one of the forms of sexuality when it was transposed from the practice of sodomy onto a kind of interior androgyny, *a hermaphrodism of the soul*' (43; my emphasis). In this sense, the *Evening Telegram*'s tongue-in-cheek epistemological inquiry into Wilde's closet (to skew Sedgwick's phrase) succeeds in 'outing' him thirteen years before the Marquis of Queensberry, whose libellous slander against Wilde was, after all, still framed within a discourse of sodomy, albeit one subject to its own shifting parameters.[3]

While the *Evening Telegram* foregrounded questions of sexual difference in its effete, feminized portrait of Wilde, another Toronto newspaper demonstrated that Wilde's body was also subject to certain destabilizing and counter-normative nationalist inscriptions. As the son of Lady 'Speranza' Wilde, a celebrated Fenian poet, and as a somewhat reluctant spokesperson for Irish republicanism in his own right, Wilde's outsider status in relation to the domestic spaces of the English metropole meant that, in addition to his sexuality, 'the consciousness of foundational and/or incipient national *difference* already internal to national *definition* must have been part of what Wilde literally embodied' (Sedgwick, 'Nationalisms,' 242). This is certainly what he embodied to Patrick Boyle, editor of the *Irish Canadian*, who greeted Wilde at the train station in Toronto '"on behalf of our Irish citizens,"' and whose paper, in announcing Wilde's lecture, wished its '"distinguished young fellow-countryman"' a capacity audience 'for the sake of "his patriotic and talented mother, the gifted Speranza"' (O'Brien, 97). In hindsight, of course, what these two excerpts from the local Toronto press demonstrate most forcibly is how Wilde's 'othered' national identity (i.e., not British) would eventually become the very precondition of his subsequent sexual transgressions, at least in terms of the (de)regulation of sameness and difference. That is, if the (always already) degenerate Irish Wilde can 'masquerade' as English (in his comedies satirizing social manners no less than in his own 'ventriloquized' speech and deportment), then what is to prevent him from 'posing' as a sodomite or, worse yet, a woman? To put this another way, a certain 'tendency' towards 'deviancy' is already inherent in Wilde's blood.

Terry Eagleton frames the confluence of regulatory discourses within

Wilde more positively in the foreword to his play *Saint Oscar* when he states that 'Wilde was perverse in much more than a sexual sense, and his sexual, social and artistic perversities are deeply interrelated' (xi). Noting that the impetus for his play came from the fact that several of his Oxford students did not know that Wilde was Irish, Eagleton writes: 'if I have tried to avoid writing a "gay" play about [Wilde], this is not only because as a heterosexual I am inevitably something of an outsider in such matters, but because it seems to me vital to put that particular ambiguity or doubleness back in the context of a much wider span of ambivalences' (x–xi).[4] Among which, of course, we must include a degree of national ambivalence.

* * *

'[I]t is the mark of the ambivalence of the nation as narrative strategy,' writes Homi Bhabha in 'DissemiNation,' 'that it produces a continual slippage into analogous, even metonymic, categories, like the people, minorities, or "cultural difference" that continually overlap in the act of writing the nation' (292). Picking up where he left off in such important essays as 'Of Mimicry and Man,' 'Signs Taken for Wonders,' and 'Representation and the Colonial Text,' Bhabha here applies the notion of 'ambivalence,' which he had previously invoked to describe the colonial discourse of 'mimicry,' to 'the Janus-faced discourse of the nation' ('Introduction,' *Nation and Narration,* 3). Bhabha uses the term, both linguistically and culturally, as a sign of doubleness, of indeterminacy, 'a temporality of representation that moves between cultural formations and social processes without a "centred" causal logic' ('DissemiNation,' 293). Such an understanding of ambivalence, when applied to national narratives, forces a recognition that despite the authority and conviction with which historians like Benedict Anderson write of the 'origins' of nationalism and the nation-state as emblematic sign of cultural modernity, the 'margins of the modern nation' (to allude to Bhabha's subtitle) – through the incorporation of new peoples, the generation of other meanings, and the formation of local sites of resistance in relation to the central body politic – have from the beginning been in the process of inscribing a much different national narrative, one whose temporal and spatial reconfiguration of boundaries is at once anti-national, post-national, and trans-national in dimension.

In 'DissemiNation,' Bhabha seeks to articulate a methodology for the writing of a national narrative that will accommodate the lived experiences of minority peoples, to theorize the basis for a hybridized, non-pluralistic politics of 'cultural difference.' In so doing, he rejects the standard metaphoric temporality of representation – which erases difference in the horizontal movement of a 'homogenous [*sic*] empty time' – in favour of what he calls 'a metonymic, iterative temporality' (306) – which allows for the non-sequential inscription of oppositional discourses and subjectivities within the often 'ambivalent and chiasmatic intersections of time and place that constitute the problematic "modern" experience of the western nation' (293). Bhabha, 'modularly adapting' Anderson (who is, in turn, borrowing from Walter Benjamin), labels this supplementary space of cultural signification 'the "meanwhile,"' a place 'where cultural homogeneity and democratic anonymity make their claims on the national community,' and where 'there emerges a more instantaneous and subaltern voice of the people, a minority discourse that speaks betwixt and between times and places' (309).[5]

Bhabha's postcolonialist concept of 'national ambivalence' finds an interesting queer theory analogue, I would argue, in Jonathan Dollimore's term 'sexual dissidence.' In attempting at least a partial answer to the question of 'why in our time the negation of homosexuality has been in direct proportion to its symbolic centrality; its cultural marginality in direct proportion to its cultural significance; why, also, homosexuality is so strangely integral to the selfsame heterosexual cultures which obsessively denounce it' (28), Dollimore formulates a complex theory of 'perverse dynamics' and 'transgressive reinscriptions,' whereby otherness is at once contained within and produced by its 'proximate' (i.e., temporal and/or spatial; cf. Bhabha, above) relation to sameness (33). According to Dollimore, the 'dissident dialectic' operating 'betwixt and between' (to re-inscribe Bhabha's phrase) dominant and subordinate cultures, groups, and identities – especially *vis-à-vis* desire – produces a series of 'displacements which constitute certain repressive discriminations,' but which also '[denote] certain instabilities and contradictions within dominant structures which exist by virtue of exactly what those structures contain and exclude' (33).

Needless to say, the 'aesthetic of transgressive desire' performed throughout Oscar Wilde's oeuvre figures in Dollimore's eponymous book as a primary – if not *the* pre-eminent – example of sexual dissidence (11 and *passim*). And, as Sedgwick has demonstrated in her analysis of *The Picture of Dorian Gray*, at least one key text by Wilde can also be read in terms of what Bhabha describes as a narrative of national ambivalence (see 'Nationalisms,' 241–3; *Epistemology of the*

Closet, 171–6). In the remaining sections of this chapter, I want to suggest that Timothy Findley's fictions perform a similar ambivalent/dissident function within contemporary Canadian literature, particularly in relation to discourses of nationalism and sexuality. In choosing to evaluate Findley's work in this manner, I hope to develop an approach to (national) ambivalence and (sexual) dissidence that takes into account not only how the terms operate 'diacritically' inside the text, but also how they are experienced 'dialectically' across a broad spectrum of intertextual contingencies (the 'chance' operations of language and narrative) and extratextual exigencies (the historical specificities of writing and reading). Situating the concepts of ambivalence and dissidence within such a spectrum, to paraphrase Kobena Mercer, 'not only underlines the role of the reader, but also draws attention to the important, and equally undecidable, role of context in determining the range of different meanings that can be produced from the same text' ('Skin Head Sex Thing,' 170). Like Mercer, in his (re)reading of Robert Mapplethorpe's photographs, I thus feel compelled to outline some of the 'crucial changes in context' that frame my own highly ambivalent (and increasingly dissident) readings of Findley's work over the past decade or so, three different 'temporalities of representation' (each roughly four years apart) that I have attempted to (re)iterate in what follows.

* * *

1985: Mississauga, Ontario. Grade 12 English class. Reading The Wars *for the first time. There is something in the text, and particularly in the character of Robert Ross, that I find both connective and oddly discomfiting. On page 169 of the tattered Penguin edition that I am handed at the beginning of term someone – a previous high school conscriptee, no doubt – has pencilled the words 'read between the lines' in the margin near the bottom of the page. I read the lines of the novel immediately adjacent this boldly underlined injunction. All of them are made up of a single, simple sentence:*

> *Robert stood in the middle of the room.*
>
> *He wanted a clean shirt.*
>
> *He wanted a clean pair of underwear.*
>
> *He wanted a pistol. (169)*

I try to heed my predecessor's advice and 'read between the lines,' but I am too literal-minded and find myself focusing on the blank spaces in between the typeset text, half-expecting a secret message encoded in invisible ink to reveal itself under the glare of the classroom's fluorescent lights. So I read the lines of text immediately above instead: 'His assailants, who he'd thought were crazies, had been his fellow soldiers. Maybe even his brother officers. He'd never know. He never saw their faces' (169). Next to this someone else has added – in ink this time – the word 'FAGGOTS!'

In a recent article on *The Last of the Crazy People*, Barbara Gabriel has convincingly delineated 'the Wildean traces' (188) in Findley's first novel, demonstrating how the character of Gilbert Winslow, in particular, inhabits a 'stigmatized' site of homosexual figuration and quasi-martyrdom. Citing the example of *De Profundis*, in which Wilde draws overt parallels between his own suffering in prison and the crucifixion of Christ, Gabriel argues that, paradoxically, Gilbert's 'death-by-fire in a car suicide does not render him a perfect martyr-Christ ... If he remains a sacrificial figure like Christ, he is not innocent, but one who has *betrayed* innocence himself' ('Staging Monstrosity,' 191).

De Profundis, originally written as a long letter to Lord Alfred Douglas during Wilde's last months at Reading Gaol, was first published in 1905 – albeit in rather abbreviated form – by Robert Ross, a young Canadian man who in 1886, at the age of seventeen, became the Irish writer's first male lover, thereafter remained his closest and most loyal friend, and was subsequently designated his literary executor (see Ellmann, 275–8). On 1 April 1897 Wilde wrote to Ross informing him that he was dispatching the text of the Douglas letter to him under separate cover, stating that 'if you are my literary executor, you must be in possession of the only document that really gives any explanation of my extraordinary behaviour with regard to Queensberry and Alfred Douglas' (*Selected Letters*, 240). In actual fact, the manuscript was kept aside by the Prison Commission and handed back to Wilde upon his release from Reading Gaol on 18 May. Two days later, having taken the night boat from England to France, Wilde conveyed it directly into the hands of Ross on a pier at Dieppe (Ellmann, 528). The coincidence of characters' names notwithstanding, this last detail from Wilde and Ross's 'real-life' narrative would almost certainly not have been lost on Findley in his 'fictionalized' documentary account of (an)other Robert Ross – this one a nineteen-year-old Canadian soldier who undergoes his own ordeal by fire and displaced martyrdom in First World War France (see my second epigraph, above).

However, according to Lorraine York's reading of *The Wars*, it is the literary-historical figure of Siegfried Sassoon, and not Oscar Wilde, who 'looms over the entire novel' (*Front Lines*, 46).[6] Interrupting Juliet d'Orsey's first transcript, Findley's anonymous archivist-narrator decides that '*this is probably as good a place as any to point out that Lord Clive Stourbridge, Juliet and Barbara's eldest brother, was one of the Cambridge poets whose best known work – like that of Sassoon and Rupert Brooke – has its roots in the war*' (103). But it is also an equally good place for the attentive critic to point out that this parenthetical aside occurs in the midst of a long rumination by Juliet on the homosociality inherent both in her brother Clive's relationship with Jamie Villiers and in Robert's relationship with his ill shipmate, Harris, whom Robert visits daily at the Royal Free Hospital in London: 'Robert, though he never said so, loved Harris. It was clear in the way he dealt with his death and in the way he spoke of him afterwards to me. The war was part of it too' (103).

The war was indeed part of it. As Paul Fussell notes in *The Great War and Modern Memory*, the First World War poems of Sassoon, Brooke, and Wilfred Owen, among others, display a 'unique physical tenderness,' coupled with a 'readiness to admire openly the bodily beauty of young men' and 'the unapologetic recognition that men may be in love with each other' (279–80). According to Fussell, these homoerotic elements are not found in the poetry of the Second World War, at least not to the same degree, because later soldier-poets had become more self-conscious of matters relating to homosexuality, partly as a result of the increasingly widespread popular dissemination of psycho-sexual treatises by Krafft-Ebing, Freud, and others.[7] (In other words, 'homosocial desire' becomes transformed and re-articulated as 'homosexual panic,' evidenced in the routine purges of suspected gays from the 'fraternal' ranks of national armies post-1945.)

An earlier remark made by Juliet (who, incidentally, counts among her favourite novels *The Turn of the Screw* and *The Picture of Dorian Gray* [154–5]) during the same transcript, however, attests to the fact that the spectre of Wilde still necessarily haunts such male-male attachments: 'Barbara said that Clive had undermined Jamie's morals and she called them *Oscar* and *Bosie* and ultimately settled her affections elsewhere' (102). As York remarks, 'This sexual intolerance does not bode well for Barbara's relations with a young man of more cosmopolitan sympathies – especially one who shares the name of one of Oscar Wilde's closest and most constant lovers, one who stayed faithful to him throughout his trials' (*Front Lines*, 39). It is, of course, Robert Ross who also provides the historical link between Wilde and Sassoon, having befriended the latter in the years leading up to and during the First World War (in addition to a similar sexual orientation, Sassoon would eventually come to share Ross's pacifist politics). At any rate, according to York, Lady Barbara d'Orsey's aggressive pursuit of sexually ambivalent soldiers like Robert, Jamie, and Eugene Taffler 'rivals, even parodies, the progress of the war in France' (39). This is in keeping with her reading – a reading with which I am in substantial agreement – of *The Wars* as a doubly encoded narrative, one that recounts not only Robert's entry into 'the male enclave of the army,' but also his 'wholesale conscription into heterosexuality' (38).

For Frank Davey, the 'inverse' is true. In a chapter included in his recent book, *Post-National Arguments*, he claims that the First World War, as represented in Findley's text,

> marks Canada's full entry into a huge trans-national arena in which official heterosexuality masks a violent homosexuality which drives almost all activities – business, sports, courtship, and war. All considerations of nation, family, region, ethnicity, or race, on which a national polis might be argued – in fact all social and political considerations – are erased here by this monolithic, ubiquitously textualized force of *misdirected sexuality*. *The Wars* can see no social/textual alternative to this force. (126; my emphasis)

The primary textual examples which Davey uses to support his assertions are, of course, the 'sado-masochistic' sex scene between Taffler and the Swede which Robert witnesses in a brothel in Alberta, and Robert's rape by his fellow soldiers at the insane asylum in Desolé.

While I agree with Davey that Findley's text 'condemns the phallic authority on which nearly all the "official" transactions of that culture are conducted' (124), I take issue with his configuration of the discourses of nationalism and sexuality in outlining this condemnation. Indeed, in my mind Davey has gotten everything 'backwards.' It is not 'a violent homosexuality' which 'drives almost all activities' in society; neither does it figure in *The Wars* as a 'monolithic, ubiquitously textualized force of misdirected sexuality.' Rather, in both cases, it is the patriarchal discourse of 'compulsory heterosexuality' which prescribes that all sexual relations, regardless of the gender(s) of the persons involved, be structured, if not commodified, as violent possession or rape. Echoing York, Diana Brydon notes that in *The Wars* 'male friendship is idealized; heterosexual relations are portrayed as destructive and predatory' ('A Devotion to Fragility,' 82). Consider, in this regard, Juliet's description in her journal of

Robert and Barbara having sex: 'Barbara was lying on the bed, so her head hung down and I thought that Robert must be trying to kill her. They were both quite naked. He was lying on top of her and shaking her with his whole body ... Robert's neck was full of blood and his veins stood out. He hated her' (156).

Within the libidinal economy of Findley's text, then, the operative word in the homosexual rape of Robert at Desolé is not 'homosexual'; it is 'rape.' Indeed, one could go so far as to claim, along with Lee Edelman in his critique of Frank Lentricchia's reading of a Wallace Stevens poem, that 'what distinguishes this enabling seizure or rape of one male by another is its determining *hetero*sexuality – its participation, that is, in a psychic economy that defines itself *against* the historically available category of the "homosexual"' (39). Foregrounded within both texts, then, is not so much a narrative of same-sexuality as a further instance of the 'martialling of men' about which Robert voices 'doubts' at the beginning of Findley's novel (*The Wars*, 13),[8] a playing out to their fullest extreme of the authorized codes of an 'embattled male heterosexuality' (Edelman, 40), a way of 'redeeming,' or resurrecting, the *phallus* as locus of institutional power while at the same time disavowing the *penis* as locus of bodily desire. This heteronormative (and normatively hetero) scenario will, as we shall see, be enacted even more viscerally in *Not Wanted on the Voyage*, with Noah and Japeth's use of the unicorn's horn to rape Emma.

Likewise, it is not the S/M sex between Taffler and the Swede – which is, after all, presented as consensual and performative ('He'd never even dreamed of such a thing – of being hit and *wanting* to be hit. Beaten. Or of striking someone else because they asked you to'; 'The one who *played* the horse was bucking' [44; my emphasis]) – that is so problematic, but rather Robert's 'panicked' and violent reaction to it, especially in the wake of his own failure 'to perform' adequately with the prostitute Ella: 'He picked up a boot and held it in his hand. Its weight alarmed him and the texture of its leather skin appalled him with its human feel. He threw the boot across the room and shattered the mirror' (45). One need not be a strict Lacanian to perceive the symbolic significance of this gesture; but it is important to note that the crisis of masculinity recorded therein stems as much from Robert's uneasiness about the socially sanctioned terms of a prescriptive and pre-scripted 'heterosexuality' as it does from the 'homosexual' scene of surveillance which displaces these terms and rewrites this script.

Moreover, far from depicting homosocial/sexual relations as programmatically violent, I believe that *The Wars* can, and does, 'offer [a] social/

textual alternative to this force.' For example, in claiming that 'there are no instances of even remotely fulfilling ... homosexual relations' in the text (124), Davey curiously glosses over the strong bond established between Robert and Harris, which, as we have already seen via Juliet's perceptive analysis, was a kind of 'love – yes' (103):

> The thing was – no one since Rowena had made Robert feel he wanted to be with them all the time. If what he felt could be reduced to an understanding – that was it. 'I have to get over there and see him,' Robert would think every morning when he woke up. He also wanted to be there if Harris spoke. Harris said the strangest things – lying on his pillows staring at the ceiling. Strange and provocative. Robert didn't know, sometimes, what to do with Harris's sentences; where to fit them in his mind, or how to use them. He only knew they went somewhere inside him and they didn't come back out. (95)

Just as the sexually dissident impulses recorded in Sassoon's poetry provided a basis for his subsequent post-national pacifism (read: ambivalence), so does Robert's initial ambivalence regarding Canada's involvement in the First World War (he enlists less out of any sense of patriotic duty than to escape the domestic 'wars' of his family, and specifically memories of his sister Rowena's death), combined with his increasing experience of (homo)sexual dissidence (Taffler and the Swede, his relationship with Harris, even his rape), contribute to his defiance of the misdirected nationalisms (i.e., 'us' versus 'them') fuelling the carnage all around him. In attempting to save the horses, on whom the warring factions of England/Canada and Germany surely have no 'national' claim, Robert is struggling to 'do' something with the 'strange' and 'provocative' sentences of Harris, who swam repeatedly with schools of whales off the coast of Nova Scotia, just as Robert ran night after night with the coyote on the prairies in Alberta. This 'will-to-action' necessarily involves a sexual component as well. As Findley has remarked in conversation with Graeme Gibson, 'the blessed relief of action' is 'almost like orgasm in a funny way': 'It's a terrible striving for a necessary climax without which we do go insane ... [A]nd that's what I mean by "orgasm" – it's to do that thing that simply must be done' (144–5). Robert, who 'wished with all his heart that men could embrace' but 'knew now they couldn't' (*The Wars*, 171), embraces instead an animal that symbolizes both 'the sexuality he fears' (Taffler being 'ridden' by the Swede)[9] and 'a way of life that is under threat from the machine' (Brydon, 'Devotion,' 82).

Davey's commodification/conflation of identities (both national and sexual) in his reading of *The Wars* ignores the ways in which Robert's 'necessary climax,' his gesture 'against despair,' derails the (re)productive locomotive of (hetero)sexual desire and redirects traditional male-male attachments in transnational, capitalist, and patriarchal economies of power. In this regard, he is at odds with Richard Dellamora, who, in his reading of Mauberley's 'heroic gesture' in *Famous Last Words*, argues that Findley 'subverts the doxa of [A]nglo-Canadian culture while passionately affirming homosexual difference' (197).[10]

* * *

1989–90: Toronto. Final year of undergraduate study at University of Toronto. Completing an honours thesis entitled 'Clarity of Gesture, Clarity of Mind: Action and Insanity in Timothy Findley's Fiction' as fulfilment of a degree requirement towards a B.A. in English and history. Without ever having read Foucault's Madness and Civilization, *I produce a highly competent thematic analysis of the 'will-to-action' inspired by various forms of 'madness' in Findley's novels and short fiction. My adviser, in his assessment of the fifty-four-page essay, writes that what impressed him most about the effort was 'the candidate's ability to undertake and complete the project with only the minimum of supervision on my part.' The anonymous second reader wishes that I had engaged more fully 'in a discussion of the relation between the issues raised by the paper and Findley's own homosexuality.' No doubt because I am wrestling with my own ambiguous sexuality at the time, poised precariously on the verge of 'coming out,' this latter comment troubles me a great deal. In the end, however, my still predominantly New Critical sensibilities enable me to put it out of my mind, if only temporarily. After all, the essay has been judged worthy of an A+ grade. And I soon receive notice that it has won a competition sponsored by University College for best graduating essay.*

Commenting on the '(homo)erotic' collaborations between John Addington Symonds and Havelock Ellis, and between T.S. Eliot and Ezra Pound, Wayne Koestenbaum argues in *Double Talk* that the texts which resulted from these respective partnerships – *Sexual Inversion* (1897) and *The Waste Land* (1922) – reflect 'the violence that modernists will wreak on their Wildean precursors: he-men, they will subdue homosexual writing tendencies (the "literary" values of symbolism and Uranian verse) in an effort to be scientific' (50). At the same time, however, Koestenbaum goes on to acknowledge that in submitting his '"scrawling, chaotic poem"' before Pound for scrutiny, Eliot's 'male modernist anus ...

achieves a weird flowering ... Pound penetrates Eliot's waste land, and fills the hollow man with child' (123). In seeking to 'cure' *The Waste Land* 'of its hysteria,' as Koestenbaum points out, 'Pound's gestures are paradoxical; he denounces instances of linguistic effeminacy, and yet the very act of intruding commentary is homosexually charged ... The act of queerying – critiquing, editing, collaborating – has suspicious overtones of queerness, inferences which Pound highlights and denies' (124).

Building upon Koestenbaum's analysis, Richard Dellamora has recently noted the extent to which Findley further 'queeries' this collaboration between Eliot and Pound in *Famous Last Words*, where 'an exaggeratedly masculine Pound plays the role of the intellectual or artistic male who has nurtured the talent of the ephebe' (190). In Findley's revisionist account, however, the ephebe is not T.S. Eliot, but rather Hugh Selwyn Mauberley, the disaffected title character from Pound's eponymous poem, written two years before *The Waste Land.* Like Eliot, Mauberley approaches Pound – his surrogate 'father' – for literary guidance.[11] At the outset of *Famous Last Words*, we learn that Pound duly 'become[s] his mentor,' predicting that 'Hugh Selwyn Mauberley would become the greatest writer of his time.' In Mauberley's case, however, Pound 'was wrong' (4, 5).

That Findley's Mauberley fails to achieve the same literary apotheosis as Pound's Eliot reflects in part postmodernism's ambivalence towards modernist master narratives (national and/or sexual), as well as Findley's own more dissident attempts to un-/re-cover the Wildean traces latent in those narratives, to expose their doubly coded (again national and/or sexual) and repressed lines of authorship/discipleship. In this regard, it is entirely appropriate that the ephebe in Findley's text is also rather effete, that the Prufrockian, sexually neurasthenic tendencies Pound sought to excise from Eliot's *The Waste Land* should come back to haunt him in *Famous Last Words* in the form of his own poetic creation. The man who in Pound's poem is simply 'out of key with his time' ('Hugh Selwyn Mauberley,' l.1) becomes, in Findley's novel, 'the type of a generation of closeted homosexuals born shortly after the Wilde trials of 1895' (Dellamora, 177), a 'flit' who inhabits 'the world of white linen suits,' which Pound 'cannot bear' (Findley, *FLW*, 82).[12]

'Bashing back' in this manner, at least metafictively speaking (see Ingham), Findley is, I would argue, seeking 'to find a new channel for the violence' perpetrated historically 'against my kind' (Findley to Benson, 113), to recreate a minority narrative of national ambivalence and sexual dissidence both within and without, both inside and outside, the homoerotic/homophobic regimes of fascism and modernism. As Dellamora puts it, Findley's 'novel opens new possibilities for writing both as a gay and a Canadian,' creating imaginative spaces of identification that place an emphasis on 'self-reflexive change': 'becoming conscious of and responsible for one's sexuality, becoming conscious of oneself as the subject of a national experience which is not contained within the limits of relations to imperial powers' (173, 174). Ironically, in *Famous Last Words* this process of 'self-reflexive change,' of coming to (sexual and national) consciousness, would appear to be mobilized by 'retrograde' behaviours and ideologies, in particular Mauberley's apparent willing submission to fascistic and masochistic impulses.

Drawing on the work of film critic Joan Mellen, Barbara Gabriel, in another recent Findley article, this one on *The Butterfly Plague*, has commented on how Italian neo-expressionist films 'such as Luciano [*sic*] Visconti's *The Damned* (1968) and Bernardo Bertolucci's *The Conformist* (1970) configured the personality type most susceptible to Fascism in structures of homoeroticism and sadomasochism' ('Performing the *Bent* Text,' 228).[13] In fact, as Gabriel notes, such filmic representations are necessary 'misreadings, their theatrical framings at odds with the darker, as well as more accurate, picture of the fate of homosexuals under National Socialism' (228).[14] Indeed, it is not simply that homosexuality has occasionally flirted with fascism (cf., for example, the early drawings of Tom of Finland; the writings of Yukio Mishima; and the fetish wear of 1970s Fire Island, as described by Larry Kramer in *Faggots*),[15] but rather that fascism has historically *courted* homosexuality. As George Mosse points out in *Nationalism and Sexuality*, the German national cult of *Männerbund*, later to be superseded by *Männerstaat* under the direction of Heinrich Himmler and the Nazis, consciously drew upon the aesthetic codes of classical Greece in constructing the male body as site/sight of (homo)erotic spectacle (see 58–62 and 153–80). In this sense, fascism (or at least German National Socialism) needs homosexuality, if only as an absolute 'Other' against which to exorcize the homosociality inherent in its rituals of male beauty and fraternal bonding.

However, despite all of this, in *Famous Last Words* Findley, seemingly stealing a page from Visconti and Bertolucci, makes it clear that part of Mauberley's attraction to fascism is sexual and, moreover, masochistic. Following his impromptu lunch with Diana and Edward Allenby in Venice, during which the fall of Ethiopia to Mussolini's army is announced, Mauberley fantasizes about a young Blackshirt passing his table: 'I turned in my chair and watched that young man going away. And I went away with him – in my mind. And knelt before his strength. And his victory'

(91). Interpreting this scene within a classical Freudian scopic regime, Stephen Scobie claims that 'this passage defines, more clearly than anything else in the novel, the nature of Mauberley's attraction to Fascism. It originates in his psychological need to compensate for his father's abdication of male power, and it takes the form of a masochistic compulsion to replay ... his own sense of powerlessness while watching his father's suicide' ('Eye-Deep in Hell,' 216). Moreover, according to Scobie, the 'physical humiliation which [Mauberley] fantasises at the hands of the Blackshirt' is later enacted, 'even more drastically, in the scene where Harry Reinhardt forces him to lick Sir Harry Oakes's blood from his murderer's hands' (216). I want to argue, however, that Scobie's equation/conflation of these two fantasmatic scenes is a serious misreading of the ambivalent/dissident nature of Mauberley's masochism.

In *Male Subjectivity at the Margins*, Kaja Silverman, following from and building upon Freud's somewhat problematical Oedipal insights in '"A Child Is Being Beaten,"' distinguishes between two different, although related, categories of male masochism: 'moral masochism' and 'feminine masochism.' The former category, according to Silverman, occurs at the level of ego-identification, with the morally masochistic male subject turning 'away from the paternal ego-ideal to the maternal one, and from identification with the father to identification with the mother.' By contrast, she says, the feminine masochistic male subject 'literalizes the beating fantasy, and brings this cruel drama back to the body' (195). In both cases, however, 'the father is left holding the whip at the level of the unconscious fantasmatic' and, as such, the male masochist 'not only prefers the masquerade of womanliness to the parade of virility, but he articulates both his conscious and his unconscious desires from a feminine position' (212–13). Scobie's reading of the masochism displayed by Mauberley in *Famous Last Words* as stemming from his father's 'abdication of power' is already at odds with the Freudian schema outlined by Silverman, where the father is 'left holding the whip.' But things get even more complicated if we analyse Mauberley's passive-aggressive behaviour in terms of a third category of masochism, one that Silverman introduces in her chapter on T.E. Lawrence.

As Silverman astutely notes, the commitment to Arab nationalism expressed by Lawrence in *Seven Pillars of Wisdom* is clearly dependent on the author's homosexuality and, what's more, his masochism. They are all part of the same libidinal economy, albeit each in differing degrees of (de)sublimation. In adopting local Bedouin attitudes, customs, and dress, that is, in 'seeking to imitate the Arabs to the point where they might be prompted to imitate him back' – what Silverman labels a 'double mimesis' – the Lawrence of *Seven Pillars,* according to Silverman, 'both inverts and doubles the classic colonial paradigm' (312). This (re)inversion and doubleness is also characteristic of Lawrence's masochism, which (before the episode at Deraa, at any rate) articulates itself in terms of a 'dual identificatory relation' to 'the contradictions inherent in masculinity' (Silverman, 327, 326). Silverman labels this kind of masochism 'reflexive masochism,' a 'pathology' which allows the male subject to '[suffer/enjoy] pain without renouncing activity,' to occupy 'at the same time both an active and a passive position' (324, 325). Thus, reflexive masochism, much more so than feminine masochism, for example, retains an element of agency, 'the agency which performs the assault, and that which suffers it' (Silverman, 326).

It is worth pointing out, in this regard, that in an earlier draft of *Famous Last Words,* Findley, in addition to Charles Lindbergh, the Duke and Duchess of Windsor, and a host of other historical personages, 'also had T.E. Lawrence in the book' (Findley, 'The Marvel of Reality,' 6). Lawrence was eventually dropped from the text, but one of his fellow British officers, Edward Allenby – whom Lawrence identifies in *Seven Pillars* as '[coming] nearest to my longings for a master' (582) – remained. And, I would argue, so did Lawrence's peculiar blend of masochism, which gets transformed and reinvented in the character of Mauberley, who is likewise made 'to suffer' under Allenby's 'cool' severity in Venice (*FLW,* 85). And yet, whereas Silverman detects in *Seven Pillars* a gradual progression by Lawrence from reflexive to feminine masochism (culminating in his torture and 'rape' at Deraa), I want to suggest that the 'inverse' is true of Mauberley in *Famous Last Words.* While it is possible to read Mauberley's fantasy about fellating the Blackshirt as an instance of feminine masochism, his subsequent licking of Sir Harry Oakes's blood from Reinhardt's hands must not be construed, as Scobie would have us believe, as the same thing. Rather, it represents the culmination of a process of 'self-reflexive change' (cf. Dellamora, above) within Mauberley, and, more specifically, his movement from feminine to reflexive masochism. Moreover, the *sexual dissidence* recorded in this movement by Findley cannot be divorced from his simultaneous preoccupation with charting a specific trajectory of *national ambivalence.*

Sir Harry Oakes, at whose Bahamian estate Mauberley finds himself lodged in the summer of 1943, is the sole Canadian character in Findley's novel. And within him, as Dellamora points out, Findley 'inverts a number of the self-flattering clichés of anglo-Canadian culture' (182). An American by birth, Oakes's 'manner,' we are told by Mauberley, 'was appalling,' his 'rudeness and meanness ... legendary' (*FLW*, 331). When all of his millions – amassed from gold mines near Kirkland Lake, Ontario – failed to buy him a seat in the Canadian Senate, Oakes promptly went to England, where he 'was able to purchase a baronetcy': 'If Canada had slighted him, Canada would be sorry' (331). To this end, he makes another deal, absconding – along with his money – from his adopted homeland to the Bahamas, where '"taxes [are] next to nothing ... [and] death duties nil"' (332). Here the brash and vulgar Canadian forges an unusual neocolonial (i.e., mercenary) alliance with the Duke of Windsor, 'the epitome of all that is civilized, genteel, and respected' (332).

However, when the Duke, in his capacity as titular representative of the British government, proves unable to banish Oakes's son-in-law, Count Alfred de Marigny (whom Sir Harry suspects of having corrupted/seduced his son, Sydney), from the island colony, this alliance breaks down. And, moreover, when Oakes's ensuing crises of nationalism and sexuality threaten to disrupt the Duchess of Windsor's own plans for escape, Mauberley is forced to take action. In requesting of Reinhardt Sir Harry Oakes's murder, the one documented crime in the novel for which he is clearly responsible, Mauberley is, I would argue, moving from feminine to (self-)reflexive masochism: 'The realization I was alone with this horror drew me to my feet. It dawned on me what Reinhardt had in mind. This murder I had asked him for was to be mine completely, and when the authorities came it would be mine to pay for' (380).

Of course, whether or not this reflexively masochistic gesture, along with Mauberley's more passive acquiescence to the horrors around him, can likewise be recuperated as a moral one (especially in light of his subsequent written 'confession' on the walls of the Grand Elysium Hotel) is left open by virtue of the text's frame narration. Whereas Captain Freyburg thinks that Mauberley is trying to 'whitewash' the truth, Lieutenant Quinn insists that he is simply trying to '*tell*' it: 'About himself. Including the mistakes he made' (*FLW*, 154). But if, ultimately, Findley's exploration of nationalism and sexuality leans more towards ambivalence in *Famous Last Words*, the intersections and discontinuities between the two discourses receive a decidedly more dissident treatment in *Not Wanted on the Voyage*.

* * *

1993: Vancouver. First year in the Ph.D. program at the University of British

Columbia. Undertaking, as part of my course work, a directed reading on representations of masculinity in the recent fiction of Findley and South African writer Stephen Gray. Headhunter *has just been released, and for some reason reading it touches a nerve. I decide to ask a slightly polemical – and strategically essentialist – question of the author during his 'Out and Out' conversation with Jane Rule at this year's Writers and Readers Festival: Why are there so few positive representations of gay sexuality in your fiction? In the end, with Eleanor Wachtel having acknowledged my waving hand, and under the watchful gaze of no less than three Rogers Cable video cameras, I chicken out slightly and rephrase the question solely in relation to* Headhunter. *This is, nevertheless, enough to rile Findley, who informs me that the novel is deliberately dystopic and that if I am interested in reading its obverse, then I should pick up a copy of his latest work of drama,* The Stillborn Lover. *I do not tell him that I have already read the play and that it disappointed me even more than* Headhunter. *The next day I reread the text of Findley's 1987 address to the Philosophical Society of Trent University, which comprises the final section of* Inside Memory. *I pause over the following passage:*

> *If I am a hiding place for monsters – and I am – then I can also be a hiding place for harmony.*
>
> *Or, at least, I can imagine such a thing. (314–15)*

And I remind myself that if Findley hasn't imagined such a thing in Headhunter, *then at least he has done so in another, equally dystopic, fiction:* Not Wanted on the Voyage *contains perhaps his most positive representation of 'harmonious' gay sexuality – in the midst of unspeakable monstrosity – in the couple of Ham and Lucy.*

As the Prologue to Findley's fifth novel, *Not Wanted on the Voyage*, is set up typographically on the page, we first read the italicized quotation from chapter 7, verse 7, of the Book of Genesis:

> *And Noah went in, and his sons,*
> *and his wife, and his sons' wives*
> *with him into the ark, because*
> *of the waters of the flood...* (3)

What follows is Findley's immediate deconstruction of this passage, the first line of his narrative – 'Everyone knows it wasn't like that' (3) – informing us that the traditional version of the biblical flood story will be radically re-written, and at the same time drawing our attention to Findley's text as a highly self-conscious work of postmodernist fiction. Moreover, on the verso of this page, once again in italics, Findley (p)re-writes a portion of his own text, reproducing that section of the narrative in which Mrs Noyes discovers the blazing funeral pyre her husband has erected in their house prior to the ark's departure, which is, in fact, nothing more than a senseless slaughter of defenceless animals, those deemed unworthy of boarding the ark (4, 123–4).[16]

It is this spatial and temporal disunity at the beginning of *Voyage*, located in the very act of writing (or re-writing) a New World/nation, and thus reminiscent of Bhabha's/Anderson's 'meanwhile,' which points to the possibility of establishing a narrative of history (as opposed to a history of narrative), wherein cultural events can be re-contextualized and re-examined both inside and outside of the constraints of so-called marginality. Certainly Findley's use of such a narrative strategy points to his rejection of the mimetic tradition in literature, of the frequent 'link between historicism and realism, between the plausibility of linear order and coherence in history and the immediate evidence of the real in Literature,' which Bhabha sees as so characteristic of the representation of the colonial subject ('Representation,' 95).

Voyage is, therefore, deliberately anachronistic and ahistorical, or rather necessarily ambivalent with respect to iterative, or recursive, temporalities of representation (history may have a habit of repeating itself, to be sure, but never in exactly the same way). As we have seen with *The Wars* and *Famous Last Words*, Findley's awareness of history and fiction as contested markers of ideology makes it possible for him to reconfigure his own social positioning – as a gay man, as a (post-)national subject – in relation to 'critical moments' in time and space (floods, wars, etc.), to re-imagine *allegorically* the historical narratives of nations, for example, and the ways in which those narratives record minority experience. As such, *Voyage* not only 're-enter[s] the western episteme at one of its most fundamental points of origination' (Ashcroft et al., 104), that is, the *first* time the world ended, but also at a point in modern history known as the Holocaust, that period which perhaps bore witness to the *second* time the world (almost) ended. Diana Brydon is one prominent critic who argues convincingly for this kind of 'post-Holocaust, post-colonial' allegorical reading of *Voyage*. According to Brydon, like *The Butterfly Plague* and *Famous Last Words* before it, 'the novel may be read as a parable challenging the imperialist version of colonization as well as a warning against fascist eugenics and the impossible fascist quest for purity of any kind' ('Timothy Findley,' 587).[17] Likewise, York claims that *Voyage* 'is, in fact, every bit as much a retelling of the European Holocaust story as it is a nuclear-age revision of Biblical myth' (*Front Lines*, 107).

Indeed, at the level of the text, the ark, with its seemingly endless depths of animals crowded together and starving in perpetual darkness, is easily equated with a concentration camp, and Noah's blazing funeral pyre, with Nazi ovens. Similarly, the barring of the fairies from the ark, and their consequent drowning, refigures allegorically the fate of many homosexuals during the Holocaust. Moreover, both Yaweh ('he-way') and Dr Noyes ('no/yes'), with their categorical edicts and 'double-talk,' serve as excellent studies in demagoguery. The former's references to 'corruption,' 'contamination,' and 'monstrous perversions' in his impassioned speech on the 'Great Experiment' (soon to turn into a kind of 'Final Solution') when he first arrives at the Noyeses' house (89) echo similar anti-Semitic and homophobic pronouncements made by Nazi propagandists in the name of racial and sexual (i.e., national) purity.[18] In this regard, Noah's status as a putative member of the medical profession, along with his own frequent 'experiments' on Mottyl's kittens and his savage murder of the physically deformed Lotte-children, perhaps does more to establish him as a kind of Dr Mengele figure. At any rate, his presence at the helm of the ark does not bode well for Lucy, who claims that she joined the human race 'in order to survive the holocaust in heaven. In order to prevent the holocaust on earth' (110).

But if, at one level, Brydon sees Findley's re-writing of Genesis in *Voyage* functioning as an allegory of the cultural genocide enacted by Nazi Germany during the Second World War, so, at another level, does she interpret the text as a kind of *national* allegory, a postmodernist fable – to transpose the title of one of her articles – about 'inventing Canadian beginnings,' a 'dream of Tory origins.' Reading *Voyage* against the grain of George Grant's 1965 *Lament for a Nation: The Defeat of Canadian Nationalism*, Brydon argues that 'Findley doesn't simply turn Biblical narrative on its head; he advocates change as a return to lost origins ... To what extent this technique works as a strategic claiming of formerly conceded ground and to what extent it undermines itself by excessive lamentation for what has been lost is an open question' ('The Dream of Tory Origins,' 40).

The status of allegory as a contested narrative structure within national literatures of the postcolonial diaspora (see JanMohamed) took on added significance in academic circles when Fredric Jameson boldly asserted in the pages of *Social Text* that 'all third-world texts are necessarily ... allegorical, and in a very specific way: they are to be read as what I will call *national allegories*' ('Third World,' 69). To be sure, such a sweeping generalization necessarily raised the ire of several prominent critics. Not only is Jameson's theory of textual production 'grounded in a binary opposition between a first and a third world,' according to Aijaz Ahmad, but it also valorizes nationalism as 'the necessary, exclusively desirable ideology' (5–6). Likewise, Stephen Slemon prefers to shift Jameson's 'modality of critical access away from the determining structure of the first-world/third-world binary into the problematics of what might more accurately be called the conditions of post-coloniality,' a move which also allows for the identification of an 'interventionary, anti-colonialist' allegorical impulse within 'those colonising/settler societies such as anglophone Canada or white Australia and New Zealand' ('Monuments of Empire,' 9–10, 11).

I recognize that the critical caveats made by Ahmad and Slemon are integral to any reading of Findley's 'second-world' text as allegorical. But, like Sara Suleri in her analysis of the 'necessary misreadings' of Jameson and Ahmad, I am unwilling to dispense completely with 'the situatedness of nationalism in the colonial encounter' (*The Rhetoric of English India*, 14). Echoing Bhabha's comments on national narratives, Suleri calls for a 'provisional' 'collapsing of the idea of nation into the structure of allegory,' and a 'reading of the narratives at hand for their revision of the more precarious question of the complicities of memory *between* a colonial and a postcolonial world' (14; my emphasis). Add to this Christopher Lane's more recent assertion that, in the case of British colonialism at the turn-of-the-century at any rate, it was quite often homosexuality that performed 'the figurative and allegorical work' of the nation, dramatically 'transforming' and 'encoding' British subjectivity (7, 8), and we begin to see how co-implicated and cross-identified are these most basic of social formations and cultural rhetorics.

A 'provisional' reading of the postcolonial/-national allegories operating in *Voyage* reveals them to be profoundly ambivalent ones. Writing between two worlds, Findley is attuned to the one-step-forward-two-steps-backward march of time (in this regard, Lucy, herself caught between two worlds – heaven and earth – can be seen as incarnating Benjamin's 'Angel of History'), and to what Bhabha, following from Ernest Renan, has called the nation's 'syntax' of remembering and forgetting, or 'forgetting to remember' ('DissemiNation,' 311; see also Renan, 'Qu'est-ce qu'une nation?'; and Benedict Anderson, 204–6). 'It is this forgetting – a minus in the origin,' writes Bhabha, 'that constitutes the *beginning* of the nation's narrative' ('DissemiNation,' 310). And yet, Findley is also conscious of another temporality of representation shaping his story. That is, he recognizes that a national narrative, which is in essence a 'new world' narrative, 'can not be written evangelically' (Benedict Anderson, 205); it cannot exist *a priori*, like the Bible. Rather, it can only be endlessly re-written, making visible in the process all of the discontinuities and cultural differences that compose it. As Brydon remarks, 'Findley shows the narrative of origins as the site of a power struggle. He redefines Noah's new order, not as a divinely sanctioned origin for a new world but as a strategically grasped beginning' ('The Dream of Tory Origins,' 39).

Unlike George Grant, then, Findley does not 'lament' what has been lost in this power struggle; however, neither does he speculate overly long on what might have been gained. Indeed, in *Voyage*, I would argue, Findley subverts the notion of creating a New World in any way different from the Old by removing the central topos necessary for any utopian representation of cultural alterity, namely Mount Ararat, that symbol which Northrop Frye identifies in *The Great Code* as the New World 'type' to the Old World 'anti-type' figured in Mount Parnassus.[19] To the extent that post-diluvial diasporas and post-Holocaust nationalisms function in Findley's text as potential allegories for the processes of colonization and decolonization, their effect, as with most allegories, is thus principally rhetorical, identifying narrative closure or end-time as something to be *resisted* rather than *consecrated*. With his temporally disjunctive re-writing of the traditional Genesis story, Findley offers an ironic postcolonial, post-national twist to an old myth – re-creation as simulacrum – at the same time as he exposes the potential beginnings of a new one – difference as sameness (as encapsulated in the national metaphors of Canadian pluralism and multiculturalism, for example).

But if, to paraphrase Stephen Slemon, *Voyage* 'inhabit[s] the site of allegorical figuration' in order to subvert 'the social "text" of [nationalism]' ('Monuments of Empire,' 11), then this process also involves a reclamation of certain disavowed 'subtexts' of sexuality. And, again to paraphrase Slemon, 'the ways in which [Findley's text] performs this counter-discursive activity are inherently differential and diverse' (11). First, by locating the novel's moral consciousness in Noah's long-suffering wife, Mrs Noyes, and her blind female cat, Mottyl, Findley offers his readers an alternatively gendered world-view to the dominant patriarchal discourse espoused by Yaweh and Noah. Moreover, at the level of individual speech acts, or utterances, Findley imbues these characters with dissident/dissonant modes of discourse (Mrs Noyes's semiotic communication with the fairies, Mottyl's 'whispers'), private 'vernaculars' which are positioned in defiant opposition to the hegemony of Noah's 'oracular' pronouncements. However, it is the 'dissident vernacular'[20] disseminated by the cross-dressing angel, Lucy, which provides the most serious challenge to Noah's authority. And it is my contention that this particular counter-discourse is articulated in Findley's text through camp stylistics.[21]

In her article on *The Butterfly Plague*, Barbara Gabriel argues that 'though an over-determined *allegory of a plague of dreams of perfection* governs the narrative strands of the novel dealing with both Hollywood and Nazi Germany, transgressive meanings around gender and sexuality repeatedly break up this frame, providing a textual underground of *dissident meanings*' (228–9; my emphasis). According to Gabriel, 'the most pervasive of these [dissident meanings] operates in the performative register of camp, providing a subversive reading of the dominant narrative cinema of Hollywood that operates within the codes and conventions of gay spectatorship' (229). So, too, with *Voyage*, I would argue. In his sexually dissident re-reading of the biblical flood myth, Findley uses camp simultaneously to operationalize and destabilize his (post-)national allegory of origins. Through this supplementary temporality of representation, he is able to record a minority (counter-)discourse, or vernacular, inscribed 'betwixt and between' the unwritten and the endlessly rewritten spaces of cultural difference.

Camp, for many decades regarded, along with drag, as one of the worst identificatory manifestations of internally homophobic and misogynist gay men, has, in recent years, been re-politicized by contemporary queer criticism.[22] To this end, Carole-Anne Tyler, in a recent article, has noted that not only 'femininity' but even 'macho masculinity' is starting to come under the purview of camp and, as such, of the potentially subversive. Tyler cautions that it is important to read camp as an interpretative discourse that participates in the production of meaning and, therefore, 'the re-production of subjectivity,' contextually and 'symptomatically': 'In whose eyes is what chic radical? This is the difficult question theorists need to ask themselves when considering the function of camp, which is not ... the same thing to everybody' (33–4). Echoing Bhabha on 'colonial mimicry,' Tyler concludes that 'camp (like mimicry) functions complexly by dragging in many differences articulated with phallic narcissism in a symbolic which is really a white, bourgeois, and masculine fetishistic imaginary' (62).

Dollimore, who likewise associates the (counter-)discourse with mimicry, prefers to drag camp's differences 'out,' situating them 'in relation to other strategies of survival and subversion, especially the masquerade of femininity, and the mimicry of the colonial subject' (312). In so doing, he emphasizes not only camp's inherent 'dissidence,' but also its peculiar 'ambivalence':

> What it [camp] might be found to share with the first [masquerade] is a simultaneous avoidance and acting out of the *ambivalence* which constitutes subordination, and a pushing of that *ambivalence* to the point of transgressive insight and possibly reinscribed escape. As for the colonial context, Homi Bhabha argues that here mimicry is both a strategy of colonial subjection – an appropriation, regulation, and reform of the other – and, potentially, a way of menacing colonial discourse in and through an inappropriate imitation by the native, one which reveals the normative structure of colonial control. (312–13; my emphasis)

Dollimore's invocation of the concept of 'strategy' here is, I believe, important, and is consistent with a number of other recent queer re-evaluations of the discourse (see Bergman; Denisoff, '(Re)Dressing One's Self'). In examining how camp functions in Findley's text, I likewise want to make a distinction between camp as parodic, imitative excess and camp as a kind of tactically deployed, politically resistant self-styling. Like Dollimore, I see the former definition of camp as corresponding with psychoanalytic theories of masquerade, as well as Bhabha's notion of 'colonial mimicry,' both of which are enacted through an appropriation of the symbolic imaginary of the Other.[23] By contrast, I am suggesting that camp, when conceived of as resistant self-styling, as a 'transgressive reinscription' of the 'perverse dynamics' of 'sexual dissidence' (to allude once again to Dollimore), functions analogously not only with Foucault's discussion of sexual aesthetics/ascetics/ethics in the later volumes of *The History of Sexuality*, but also with postcolonial theories of national hybridity, practices, or 'technologies,' of self-disciplining and self-invention both actualized and resisted through the body.[24]

To the extent that bodies are also texts, camp thus legitimates not simply a way of *being* in the world, but also a way of *reading* the world, one that admits the aesthete, the sexual nonconformist, the decadent liar 'into [its] charmed circle,' one that deems truth 'entirely and absolutely a matter of style' (Wilde, 'The Decay of Lying,' 301, 305). For Eve Sedgwick, camp, when viewed as a kind of hermeneutics of reader response, 'involve[s] a gayer and more spacious angle of view': 'the sensibility of camp-*recognition* always sees that it is dealing in reader relations and in projective fantasy (projective though not infrequently true) about the spaces and practices of cultural production' (*Epistemology*, 156).

In such a realm of projective fantasy, at least as it is constructed in Findley's text, it thus becomes possible not only to recognize a camp sensibility operating within the character of Lucy, but also within her/his seeming antithesis, Japeth. Indeed, it would appear that Japeth and Lucy – in their respective self-stylings as hyper-masculine and hyper-feminine – occupy opposite poles on the 'camp continuum.' According to Martin Humphries, 'exaggeratedly masculine men are "camp,"' if for no other reason than that 'the shift to machismo has redirected our attention to ourselves as objects of desire and this results in a radical reversal of the self-image of many gay men' (79, 72).

It is just such a radical reversal of self-image that Japeth – the 'sexual ignoramus ... and virgin to boot,' the person who 'did not even know what "perverted" meant' (77) – is looking for at the beginning of *Voyage*:

> About two weeks ago – driven to distraction by Emma's refusal to sleep with him and by his own inability to force the issue – Japeth had taken off along the road, heading for the Cities. His leaving was not unlike the stories told in fairy tales of lads who, unhappy at home, set off to conquer the great world as dragon slayers and giant killers. Japeth's quest was to find his manhood once and for all – and, returning, to slay the dragon of Emma's virginity and kill the giant of his shame. But things had not worked out that way. Japeth had crept home, naked and blue and almost silent. (23)

Implicit in Japeth's encounter with the Ruffian King on the road to Baal and Mammon (read: Sodom and Gomorrah) is an allegory (or '*fairy* tale') of homosexual – and, what's more, sado-masochistic – awakening and denial: 'in spite of having made the necessary reconciliation between the horror he could not imagine and the horror he had known – [Japeth] was still unable to confront the central event without feeling ill' (79). Moreover, Japeth's resulting discolouring works counter-discursively to turn this scene into a specific instance of 'camp-recognition.' For Japeth, as 'Blue Boy,' not only evokes recollections of Thomas Gainsborough's 'femmey' 1770 painting, but also alludes to one of the oldest magazines of gay male pornography, which goes by the same name, and which is renowned for its pictorials of 'innocent' young boys.[25]

Japeth's anxiety about his own masculinity translates into an extreme fascination with that of another dragon slayer in the text, Michael Archangelis, who is camped by Findley as a specific gay fantasy type: 'Japeth had his mind on Michael Archangelis – a figure of glory unlike any he had ever dreamed could exist. The great angel's height – his strength –

his golden hair – and his armour presented the most dazzling images of manhood that Japeth had ever encountered' (75). Of course, these descriptions of 'homosocial desire' at the outset of *Voyage* are part of a larger discursive continuum that also includes a specific instance of 'homosexual panic' towards the end of the text: in 'decapitating' the Unicorn's horn (the instrument used by Noah to rape Emma), Japeth is able to displace symbolically the 'castration' enacted upon him by the Ruffian King, and thereby reaffirm his own masculinity and virility.

Yet, whereas Japeth sees a great warrior worthy of emulation in the 'Supreme Commander of All the Angels' (86), Lucy sees her brother as nothing more than 'a bore' (108). Notwithstanding the fact that angels have long been associated with a particular homosexual iconography (from Caravaggio to Kushner), the confrontation between Michael, the 'golden boy,' and Lucy, the 'rogue' whose 'star has fallen' (108), reads like pure camp spectacle, a '*Wonderful* scene' as Lucy describes it to her brother, whom she refers to as 'ducky' (106):

> 'What do you hope to accomplish by all this?' Michael asked.
>
> 'All what?' Lucy shook out her frail skirts and lifted her hand to her hair.
>
> 'Well – dressing as a woman to begin with. *And* a foreigner.'
>
> 'Nothing wrong with dressing as a woman. Might as well be a woman as anything else. And what, may one ask, do you mean by "a foreigner"?'
>
> 'Someone not of these parts,' said Michael, as if he was quoting from a book of rules for border guards.
>
> 'The slanted eyes, et cetera? The black, black hair – the white, white face? You don't like it? I *love*.' (107)

While it is possible to identify in this passage several stylistic or syntactical elements of what we might call a particular 'camp rhetoric' – the exaggerated emphasis of certain words ('*Wonderful* scene,' 'I *love*'), the linguistic repetition ('black, black hair,' 'white, white face'), the use of epicene epithets and pronouns ('ducky,' 'may one ask') – what I find most significant here is that Michael (the 'border guard') sees Lucy as transvesting not just across genders ('dressing as a woman to begin with'), but also across cultures ('*And* a foreigner').

According to Marjorie Garber, 'a transvestite figure in a text ... indicates a *category crisis* elsewhere, an irresolvable conflict or epistemological crux that destabilizes comfortable binarity' (17). Garber defines 'category crisis' as 'a failure of definitional distinction, a *borderline* that becomes permeable, that permits of *border crossings* from one (apparently distinct) category to another: black/white, Jew/Christian, noble/bourgeois, master/servant, master/slave' (16; my emphasis).[26] In the case of Findley, one might add to this list of criss-crossed categories human/angel, as well as Occidental/Oriental. Indeed, Findley's deliberate 'Orientalizing' of the transvestite figure in his text, his use of make-up, costume, gesture, symbol, and stylization traditionally associated (at least in the minds of Western readers) with Chinese opera and Japanese kabuki theatre, adds another element of 'national ambivalence' to Lucy's already evident 'sexual dissidence.'[27] As in David Henry Hwang's *M. Butterfly*, 'crises of nationalism and sexuality [are] troped on the transvestite figure' (Garber, 239). Hwang's similar deployment of a 'transvestite figure borrowed from *both* Chinese and Japanese stage traditions,' according to Garber, 'functions simultaneously as a mark of gender undecidability and as an indication of category crisis'; as she goes on to point out, in *M. Butterfly* Hwang seems to be '[preoccupied] with the transvestite as a figure not only for the conundrum of gender and erotic style, but also for other kinds of border-crossing, like *acting* and *spying*, both of which are appropriations of alternative and socially constructed subject positions for cultural and political ends' (238–9).

Of course, the 'gay-affirming and gay-occluding orientalism' – to borrow a phrase from Sedgwick ('Nationalisms,' 242) – inherent in Findley's depiction of Lucy's 'foreignness' also provides a further intertext with Wilde, in particular his *Salome*, not to mention the vaguely Japanese drawings by Aubrey Beardsley that accompanied the original 1894 English translation of the play. Garber reads the Dance of the Seven Veils at the centre of the Salome myth, and Wilde's play, as 'a transvestite dance,' another instance of 'border-crossing' (342). As she puts it, 'gender undecidability,' rather than mere exoticized sensuality, 'is the taboo against which Occidental eyes are veiled. The cultural Imaginary of the Salome story is the veiled phallus and the masquerade' (342). (So too, I would add, with Lucy's last-minute stand-in as Eve in Noah's production of 'The Masque of Creation': 'Lucy ... made her appearance – clothed in a long, transparent gown and wearing a crown of golden hair that fell to the ground all around her, gracefully hiding every bit of sexual evidence' [*Voyage*, 98].) However, in noting that Wilde, an Irishman, originally wrote his play in French – responding in part to earlier versions by Huysmans and Flaubert – Garber points out that 'the veils drawn aside have been national as well' (342).

Garber supplements her reading of *Salome* by alluding to 'an amusing and disconcerting photograph' (343) contained in Richard Ellmann's biography of Wilde, a photograph which Ellmann identifies with the cutline 'Wilde in costume as Salome' (428ff). Having no apparent reason to dispute Ellmann's assertion, Garber ruminates on what she assumes to be the 'transvestite masquerade' operating in the photograph, offering a final catalogue of Wildean personae: 'Wilde the author, Wilde the libertine, Wilde the homosexual, as Salome' (343). In fact, recent archival evidence has 'uncovered' that the Salome depicted in the photo is *not* Wilde, but rather a 'real' woman, 'an opera singer named Alice Guszalewicz' (Macdonald, 'Oscar's Grandson,' 6). Not that this at all changes the 'category crisis' implicit in the image. For the iconographic readings of Ellmann and Garber, among others, have so shifted the focus of our gaze – at least with respect to Wilde in this specific context – that it is now only ever possible to read this particular Salome as a kind of Victor/Victoria, that is, a woman masquerading as a man masquerading as a woman: a form of 'gender undecidability' and 'cultural espionage' with which the border-crossing Wilde and his successors – among them Findley and Hwang – would undoubtedly approve.

Of course, as Lucy well knows, and as Mrs Noyes and Hannah intuit, dominant culture will continue to see only what it wants to see, to interpret only what it wants to interpret: a volcanic ash storm in the middle of August it will call a 'blizzard' (21); friendly dolphins, marauding 'pirates' (235); a paper rainbow, a 'symbol of the Covenant' (351); 'Lotte-like-children,' a shameful 'secret' (160); and a 'seven-foot woman ... dressed for a foreign court,' a 'rogue,' a spy, a freak (60). Which is why the semiology of camp, troping as it does on the arbitrary divisions between inside and outside, surface and depth, artifice and reality, is such an effective counter-discursive strategy. And which is why it is Lucy, with her ambiguous sexuality, her hybrid human-angel status, her 'foreign' dress and appearance, and her camp vernacular, who most obviously disrupts the 'comfortable binarity' of this world (male versus female, human versus animal, upper orders versus lower orders, Old World versus New World), and who launches the most formidable challenge against Noah's 'apparently axiomatic significatory system which has in*vested* itself with absolute authority over those it has constructed as "Other"' (Ashcroft et al. 103; my emphasis). For it is Lucy whose magic is as powerful as Noah's, who leads the rebellion of the Lower Orders, who befriends the demons and the bees, and brings them top-side, and who, after removing her white face make-up (a sign in Japanese theatre, according to Garber, 'of the ideal white complexion of the noble, who can afford to keep out of the sun' [243]), wig, and kimono towards the end of the novel, starts a 'rumour' of 'another world,' where 'darkness and light are reconciled.' '"I don't know when it will present itself,"' she tells those assembled around her on the deck, her face streaked with running mascara and rain, '"I don't know where it will be. But – as with all those other worlds now past – when it is ready, I intend to go there"' (284).

The irony is that, within the aporetic space of Findley's text, Lucy's 'rumour' remains just that – a rumour, gossip, speculation, a further example of camp vernacular. For, to reconfigure once again Slemon's phrase, *Voyage* 'inhabit[s] the site of allegorical figuration' in order to articulate the relation between the unrepresented and the unrepresentable, between dominant discourse and the marginalized subjects inscribed with/in it. As such, Mrs Noyes seems to offer the only possible answer to Lucy's 'que(e)ry' about 'another world.' In 'pray[ing] for rain' (352), she is enunciating (from a minority position; cf. Bhabha, above) both an act of resistance and a gesture of despair.

Findley's revisioning of the biblical flood myth, like Wilde's retelling of the Salome myth, is thus decidely anti-mythic. Indeed, both writers – as ambivalent national allegorists *and* dissident gay genealogists – seem to be suggesting that myth (national, sexual, or otherwise) can only be exposed as myth, as a process that all too easily allows dominant culture to 'forget to remember' (and to remember to forget), when it becomes culturally removed, defamiliarized, alienated. In the case of the two writers profiled in my next chapter, Patrick Anderson and Scott Symons, this process of cultural removal involved a physical displacement as well, their respective self-exiles from Canada, much like Wilde's from Britain, putting the lie to certain myths of national and sexual pluralism. For Findley, who has himself recently decamped from Cannington, Ontario, for the south of France, the demythologization of myth is perhaps best accomplished through metafiction, where its discursive scaffolding can be assailed and its cultural baggage unpacked through still more creative ways of knowing and fantastical modes of storytelling. By writing neither at the end of one world, nor at the beginning of another, but rather in the 'projective fantasy' of spectacle and 'camp-recognition,' Findley effectively employs just such a Wildean methodology. In so doing, he positions himself and his story aslant of history rather than directly parallel to it, at an angle to the dominant narratives of nationalism and sexuality recorded therein – an angle decidedly 'gayer and more spacious' than the critical perspectives encountered by Anderson and Symons in the Canadian literary communities of the 1940s and 1960s.

3

Critical Homophobia and Canadian Canon-Formation, 1943–1967: The 'Haunted Journeys' of Patrick Anderson and Scott Symons

> Even our literature cannot embrace
> and comfort them
> we have few poems for naked sixteen-year-old boys
>
> Patrick Anderson, 'Y.M.C.A. Montreal,' *A Visiting Distance*, 131

> We are well into a literature of depravity and a culture munificently complicit with psychic deprivation. And given the wave of 'lady oracles' as current vogue, one might readily predict the next 'with-it-lit,' for the 1980's: – sado-masochistic homosexuality! A natural kick-back.
>
> The simple and overriding and unstated fact that we are confronted with is this: people who have done no living can do no writing.
>
> Scott Symons, 'The Canadian Bestiary,' 16

In 1943 A.J.M. Smith, then professor of English at Michigan State College, published *The Book of Canadian Poetry*. In his introduction to the anthology, Smith states that 'the main purpose of this collection is to illustrate in the light of a contemporary and cosmopolitan literary consciousness the broad development of English-Canadian poetry from its beginnings at the end of the eighteenth century to its renewal of power in the revolutionary world of today' (3). This early reference to 'a contemporary and cosmopolitan literary consciousness' points in turn to one of Smith's more contentious critical claims, made near the end of his introduction. In assessing modernism's impact on Canadian poetry since the 1920s, Smith distinguishes between two different, although related, poetic schools or traditions: the 'native' tradition, marked by 'the simplification of style and the emphasis upon the harsher aspects of reality' (29), includes E.J. Pratt, W.W.E. Ross, Raymond Knister, Earle Birney, Dorothy Livesay, and Anne Marriott; by contrast, the 'cosmopolitan' tradition, verse whose 'allusiveness of imagery and directness of language are characteristic features of metaphysical poetry' (30), lays claim to F.R. Scott, Robert Finch, A.M. Klein, Patrick Anderson, P.K. Page, Margaret Avison, and, of course, Smith himself. Although Smith goes on to assert that these 'new' poets, unlike their predecessors, '[were] not much concerned' with questions of nationalism (31), his implicit valorization of the 'cosmopolitan' tradition nevertheless succeeded in creating a new *national* canon of modern Canadian poetry. As Dermot McCarthy suggests, Smith's introduction 'can be said to inaugurate the second stage of Canadian literary history,' representing 'both a continuity and a break with [the] Romantic-nationalist tradition' consolidated in late nineteenth- and early twentieth-century anthologies and critical texts compiled by the likes of E.H. Dewart, W.D. Lighthall, Roy Palmer Baker, J.D. Logan and Donald French, and Lionel Stevenson.

To be sure, the fledgling Canadian modernist movement, then centred in Montreal, was by no means wholly united behind Smith, as the title of John Sutherland's 1947 anthology, *Other Canadians*, attests. In *his* introduction, Sutherland insists that 'Bishop' Smith's 'Eliotian' critical sensibilities have produced a false binary in Canadian poetry, in which the established cosmopolitan tradition must be seen to triumph over the upstart native tradition: 'If cosmopolitan Good is to be victorious in the accepted manner, then a devil – i.e. the native tradition – must be conjured up to challenge it: the hoax must be perpetrated, even though Mr. Smith knows it is utter nonsense to talk about a "tradition" of Canadian poetry' (8). While this passage might at first glance suggest otherwise, Smith and Sutherland were actually not so far apart in their respective views of Canadian poetry (the two would briefly work together on *Northern Review*), a fact that Sutherland comes close to admitting when he surmises that what Smith really meant by the 'native' tradition was poetry approved by the Canadian Authors Association: 'I can only regret that [Smith] has never referred to the C.A.A. by name, not just because it is healthy to call a spade a spade, but because a consideration of the C.A.A. can help to clarify the question of the national or native tradition in Canadian poetry' (6). In contrast to Smith's cosmopolitan (and, Sutherland suspected, far too 'clerical') corrective to this influence, however, Sutherland argued that only socialism could provide the necessary counterbalance to the 'literary colonialism' then infecting Canadian poetry (see *Other Canadians*, 14–20). Of course, just as his penchant for 'calling a spade a spade' would repeatedly land him in hot water, so too would Sutherland, following his own 'Eliotian' conversion to Roman Catholicism in 1954, eventually repudiate this position.[1]

Responding in part to Sutherland's criticisms, Smith noted in his introduction to the revised 1948 edition of *The Book of Canadian Poetry* that the gulf between the 'native' and 'cosmopolitan' schools was 'neither so fundamental nor so wide' as many supposed, and, indeed, that 'the most significant tendency of recent Canadian poetry has been the merging of these two traditions in the work of Birney, Livesay, Klein, Page, and, possibly, Anderson' (viii). Of the poets mentioned in this list, only Page and Anderson are included in Sutherland's *Other Canadians*. This is itself somewhat ironic, given that later the same year both Page and Anderson (along with Smith and a host of other Canadian literary luminaries) would resign in protest from the editorial board of *Northern Review*, of which Sutherland was managing editor. The origins of this dispute once again date back to 1943, and reveal something of the interplay between discourses of nationalism and sexuality in mid–Second World War Canadian literature and, perhaps even more significantly, Canadian literary criticism.

At the time of the publication of the first edition of Smith's *The Book of Canadian Poetry*, Patrick Anderson – British expatriate, Oxford and Columbia alumnus, Canadian landed immigrant, Labour Progressive Party member, pacifist, and homosexual – was editor of *Preview*, an influential avant-garde literary magazine in Montreal, which published writers like A.M. Klein, F.R. Scott, and P.K. Page. His main 'rival' in the Montreal 'little magazine' scene was none other than John Sutherland, editor of *First Statement*, which counted among its stable of contributors the 'triumvirate' of Canadian 'social realist' modernism: Louis Dudek, Raymond Souster, and Irving Layton (who were all featured prominently in *Other Canadians* and who, together, would go on to launch *Contact* magazine and press in 1952). In the June 1943 issue of *First Statement*, Sutherland printed an article of his own entitled 'The Writing of Patrick Anderson,' in which Anderson's homosexuality, his shameful childhood secret, is read as a sign of his poetry's inherent lack of honesty:

> ... while I have no desire to make an exposé of Anderson's personal life, I surmise that the distinction between the 'frightened boy' and 'the hero who sings of joy' [in the poem 'Montreal'] could be traced back to some period in the writer's childhood, when there occurred a sexual experience involving two boys, one of whom was frightened and the other demonstrated his

> joy. *Whether or not this deduction is completely correct, I do know that something of the kind occurred in Anderson's childhood.* The point that I wish to make is that, in the lines quoted from 'Montreal,' some sexual experience *of a kind not normal* has been twisted and forced into its present shape in the poem, where it wears *the false aspect* of some universal fact, or has to be accepted as a general mood in which people today participate. Surely these lines alone would signify the *falsity* of the poet's medium and his habitual distortion of content. (4; my emphasis)

Needless to say, Sutherland's homophobic speculations reveal more about his own 'panicked' response to 'Montreal' than they do about the poem's author.[2] Objecting to having been positioned – against his will, to be sure – as a passive participant in a 'homotextual' seduction, and, what's more likely, to having been seduced, Sutherland shifts the focus of discussion to authorial intention, suggesting that the sexually dissembling Anderson is using the 'false aspect' of his verse to beguile naïve and unsuspecting readers into acquiescent acceptance, if not wholehearted embracement, of a way of life 'of a kind not normal.' 'Falsity' is of course also here a synonym for 'un-Canadian-ness.' To this end, in 'The Great Circle,' an unpublished 'George Jones' (Sutherland's favourite literary persona) sketch that documents Sutherland's ongoing 'literary war' with *Preview,* Anderson's sexual 'perversion' is read as a sign of his poetry's national dissimulation (and vice versa):

> George wrote an article that attacked his opponent on literary grounds. The poem published by the rival editor was inadmissable [*sic*], because it did not grow out of Canadian soil. It could not be Canadian because George could not understand it, and if he could not understand it, he was sure no one else could. Not being as plain as the nose on your face, it must come from a perversion in the writer's character. What the poor fellow was doing was not giving you a peep into his communistic world of the future, but a peep into his sexual aberrations: whatever he said had a double meaning, and the thing to be criticized was his complete unawareness of it. George did not object to sex in poetry – in fact he was [in] favour of it – but he argued that anyone so unconscious of his real subject matter could only produce an abortion. He also said more than once that he was attacking his rival on literary and not on personal grounds. (Quoted in Fisher, 10–11)

Nevertheless, as Robert K. Martin points out, this 'ostensibly literary' critique carried with it some very 'personal' consequences, both for Sutherland and for Anderson: 'Faced with the possibility of a libel suit, Sutherland was forced to print a retraction in the following issue of *First Statement*, but the damage was, in large part, done' ('Sex and Politics,' 110). Martin is referring, most immediately, to the fact that Anderson's poetry, which had appeared in four of the first seven issues of *First Statement*, 'was not published there again until the final issue in 1945' ('Sex and Politics,' 110). Over the course of these two years, the feud between the two editors (Miriam Waddington retails Sutherland's retraction, not as a vindication for a talented poet accused of 'sexual deviation,' but rather as an unfair 'humiliation' for a promising 'young critic' [11])[3] had abated enough for Anderson's first collection of poems, *A Tent for April*, to be accepted for publication by *First Statement*'s press. Soon after, in 1945 (the year Anderson became a Canadian citizen), *Preview* and *First Statement* actually combined their resources, merging into *Northern Review*. Coexistence at the new magazine was far from amicable, however, and tensions came to a head over the August/September 1947 (vol. 1.6) issue.

The source of controversy was yet another vicious, *ad hominem* attack initiated by Sutherland, this time against Robert Finch. Once again the underlying tenor of the attack was homophobic. Reviewing Finch's *Poems*, which won the 1946 Governor General's Award for poetry, Sutherland derides the book's 'excessive self-consciousness,' its tendency towards 'coy and distressing confession,' its 'naked and embarrassed' tone, its 'decorative nature pieces.' In short, Finch's poetry is not 'manly' enough for Sutherland; 'the would-be pedestrian moralist' in Finch gives way to nothing more than a 'dandified versifier' (Review of *Poems*, 39). As with Anderson, Finch's 'cosmopolitan' style becomes, in Sutherland's mind, symptomatic of a deviant sexual disposition.[4] The review cost Sutherland dearly, at least in terms of editorial staff: in addition to those of Anderson, Page, and Smith, resignations were tendered by Neufville Shaw, F.R. Scott, A.M. Klein, and Ralph Gustafson, all of whom wished to make it clear that the vituperative opinions expressed in Sutherland's review in no way reflected their own. The *détente* between the *Preview* and *First Statement* groups, and, in particular, between Anderson and Sutherland, was sundered for good.[5]

In 1946 Anderson published his second collection of poetry, *The White Centre*, with Ryerson Press. The following year, with his marriage to American artist Peggy Doernbach crumbling (Patrick Campbell describes the union as a mistake from the beginning, 'a "propagandist marriage" that went right against Patrick's sexual proclivities' [96]),[6] Anderson retreated to England, where he 'met the man with whom he would spend the rest of his life ... Orlando Gearing' (Whitney, 'From Oxford to Montreal,' 44). In 1948 Anderson was back in Montreal, however, to take up a lecturing post in modern poetry at McGill University recently vacated by A.M. Klein. Two years later, he was offered a tenure-track assistant professorship by McGill's English Department, but Anderson declined the offer, departing instead for a temporary appointment in Singapore at the University of Malaya, an experience which eventually formed the backdrop to *Snake Wine* (1955), the first of Anderson's three autobiographical prose works (which also include *Search Me* [1957] and *The Character Ball* [1963]). By 1953 Anderson and Gearing were more or less permanently settled back in England, and Anderson, although still a citizen, was not to return to Canada for another twenty-one years. In 1953 McClelland and Stewart also published *The Colour as Naked*, Anderson's third poetry collection; included among the book's final poems is one (to which I will shortly return) in which Anderson offers the following enigmatic assessment of a country he called home for more than a decade:

William, as I sail away
from a country where the good
lies reflected in your eye –
crewed by these half-naked boys
corridors that smell of school
nose anxiety and fog,
rainbows flutter down the waves,
hours of waiting food and tea
find me in this bleak saloon,
as when Sunday black and drab
wanders oceans of ennui
and the funnies drift away. ('Leaving Canada,' 86)

After the appearance of *The Colour as Naked*, Anderson all but abandoned the writing of poetry, and it would be twenty-three years before Borealis Press, in Ottawa, would publish his next volume of new and selected poems, *A Visiting Distance.*

Given the long gap between his third and fourth Canadian literary imprints, not to mention his prolonged physical absence from the country, Anderson's relative obscurity in the annals of modern Canadian literature is perhaps to be expected. And yet, Anderson was by no means idle during this time, a period which witnessed the publication of no less than eight volumes of his memoirs and travel sketches, primarily with the British publishing house Chatto & Windus; as for choosing to live abroad, this does not seem to have had a negative impact on the career of another writer first published in the pages of *Preview*, namely Mavis Gallant (although recognition of her work in Canada was initially slow in coming). In fact, the sustained marginalization of Anderson's work from the aggressively masculinist and heterosexist canon of Canadian literature, and particularly modern Canadian poetry – despite his having published in 1946 'Poem on Canada,' a long verse narrative to rival any of E.J. Pratt's 'national epics' in terms of breadth and historical detail – cannot simply be attributed to passive acts of critical omission. Rather, in successive literary-historical accounts published between 1949 and 1976, it was through an actively intentional 'appeal to a virile nationalism ... that Anderson could be excluded from Canadian literature' (Martin, 'Sex and Politics,' 111). This appeal to virility has a long history in Canada, extending back well into the nineteenth century, and is profoundly sexist as well as homophobic.

Leading the crusade against Anderson we find, not surprisingly, John Sutherland. In a long article published in *Northern Review* in 1949, Sutherland attempts something of a 'reassessment' of Anderson's poetry, claiming that he will 'evaluate [Anderson's] achievement and indicate his promise' (8). Having learned his lesson, Sutherland sticks close to the specific poems under consideration this time, offering a not altogether unconvincing textual analysis of the dialectic of 'motion' and 'stillness' at work in Anderson's recurring symbol of 'the white centre.' Towards the end of the article, however, particularly in his examination of 'The Self Is Steep' (from *A Tent for April*), Sutherland steers his argument in a somewhat different direction, suggesting that this dialectic is indicative of an even more fundamental dualism in Anderson's poetry: 'We have reached the tentative conclusion that the stillness and motion of this centre are two images or projections of the self that operate in the creative process' (26). Far from signalling Anderson's poetic achievement, however, this dualism embodies the main '"problem" of Anderson's poetry' (26), that is, the conflict between social 'action' and psychological 'sleep,' or what Sutherland calls Anderson's inability 'to objectify his own personal emotions or conflicts in terms of social significance' (27). This is strangely at odds with Patricia Whitney's more recent construction of Anderson as poet and political activist, roles which she sees merging most successfully in Anderson's contributions to *En Masse*, the obscure 'cultural magazine' he edited briefly for the Labour Progressive Party in 1945, and which he sought to establish as 'both a vehicle for political change and a document of artistic merit' ('*En Masse,*' 76).[7] Ignoring such extra-textual considerations altogether, Sutherland maintains that the poetic 'cul-de-sac' in Anderson's work emerges from a third preoccupation, what Sutherland refers to as Anderson's depiction of Freudian narcissism, which, in Sutherland's estimation, necessarily militates against the revolutionary impact of any professed Marxist poetics: 'At bottom [Anderson] adopts revolutionary politics in obedience to a certain ideal of aggressive action, or of masculinity, which he hopes to beguile with proletarian subterfuges: nevertheless, he cannot discard his Christian inheritance, or change an almost obsessive idealism that springs from something puritanical and feminine in his nature' (26).

This construction of Anderson as 'feminine' and effete, a 'foreigner' whose close ties to the sexually suspect socialism espoused by British poets like Stephen Spender and W.H. Auden precluded his full participation in the national project of 'writing a masculine, virile "poetry of [Canadian] experience"' (Francis, 27), was to predominate for the next quarter century. Referring to Anderson as 'Audenesque in appearance and mannerisms,' Wynne Francis suggests, in her 1962 article 'Montreal Poets of the Forties,' that Anderson was poetically impotent, unable to come to grips with Canada in his verse, 'that he had failed, that Canada had somehow won. His leave-taking was more like a baffled retreat and he retained the hope that he would return some day to the land that he wanted to call his own' (27, 28). By contrast, Francis concludes, *First Statement* poets like Dudek and Layton '[scorned] the artifice of metaphor and symbol ... preferred to shout huzzahs and hurl insults, to fight, spit, sweat, urinate and make love in their poems, and did so in deliberate defiance of *Preview*' (27). In *The Making of Modern Poetry in Canada* (1967), Michael Gnarowski extends this critical perception, stating that the 'young, gauche and raw' poets associated with *First Statement* 'were obviously destined for the greater achievement,' and that the 'loss of interest and influence on the part of those associated with *Preview*' produced 'a more virile grouping among the poets of Montreal' ('The Role of "Little Magazines,"' 220, 221). Neil Fisher, in his 1974 'assessment' of the 'celebrated rivalry' between *First Statement* and *Preview,* likewise succumbs to these by-now-entrenched categorizations of effete dilletantism and manly purpose: '*PREVIEW* was a literary newsletter; *FIRST STATEMENT* was an aggressive magazine ... *PREVIEW* was a hobby; *FIRST STATEMENT*, a vocation' (8).[8] Writing in the second edition of the *Literary History of Canada* (1976), Munro Beattie claims that the description of Anderson as '"a kind of tea-drinking Dylan Thomas"' is an apt and even 'perceptive' one (283).

He then goes on to admit that while Anderson's 'obsession' with 'the appearance and sensations of teen-aged youths who are less conscious of their budding sexuality than their observer is' often proves 'troublesome,' 'it has also been the inspiration of some of his most satisfying poems' (284). Throughout this twenty-seven-year period, Christopher Ringrose, while completely eliding the issue of sexuality, was at the very least one of the few critics willing to champion Anderson's poetic voice as 'authentically' Canadian. 'If Patrick Anderson ever does return to Canada,' Ringrose concludes in a 1970 article, 'he would be justified in demanding a reassessment of his poetry, or at least that we abandon the current clichés about his work' (23).

At long last, such a reassessment seems to have begun, with articles by Robert Martin, Justin Edwards, and David Leahy, among others, trumpeting 'Anderson's importance in Canadian modernism' (Edwards, 81). Old habits die hard, however. In another recent, and supposedly 'disinterested,' attempt at critical revisionism, Brian Trehearne succeeds in dismantling the cliché surrounding the apparent 'weakness of the *Preview* aesthetics and the promise of *First Statement*' (23); nevertheless, with respect to the magazines' two editors, he likewise persists in unconsciously reproducing a familiar binaristic discourse of 'masculine' self-aggrandizement and 'feminine' self-loathing, 'heterosexual' swagger and 'homosexual' abjection. While, as Trehearne points out, Sutherland's successive critiques of *Preview* and its circle were largely personal polemics, he is at least portrayed as an *active* agent of a distinctly new Canadian poetics, however negatively that poetics may have originally been defined. Anderson, by contrast, is depicted as the *passive* recipient of Sutherland's bombast, 'with a tendency to internalize criticisms received and to allow [himself] to be partially defined by them' (42). Moreover, according to Trehearne, Anderson's later attempts at offering 'a factual corrective' to this accepted critical narrative (and the positioning of himself within that narrative) '[come] off poignantly, a mixture of defence and self-blame dominating his useful reminiscences' (22). And yet, it seems to me, that there is nothing at all defensive, or poignant for that matter, in Anderson's very 'useful' recognition that the 'virile' rhetoric used repeatedly in accounts of the Montreal poetry scene of the 1940s masked nothing so much as a latent misogyny. As Anderson puts it in a 1973 rejoinder to his critics,

> I always think recourse to virility as a value-judgement is dangerous, especially where women are concerned (*their* manly Miriam Waddington versus *our* languishing Patricia Page); it smacks of the Hemingway-Callaghan fight

> and makes me want to match Bruce Ruddick, who used to roll naked in the snow and was one of the most belligerant men I have met, against, say, the undoubtedly ebullient Irving Layton. ('A Poet Past and Future,' 18)

By this time, Anderson had already returned to Canada once (in 1971) and was about to make a second, extended visit: 'Baffled for so many years by what he felt was Canadian critical indifference to his work, [Anderson] was discovering that his reputation as a Canadian poet was not so moribund as he had feared' (Campbell, 93). Evidence of this came in a most unusual form, specifically a copy of a 1953 review of *The Colour as Naked* by Northrop Frye, one of the foremost arbiters of literary taste in Canada at the time. Professor Frye found the book 'delightful to read' and 'recommended [it] without reservation' (quoted in *The Bush Garden*, 24). This was a decidedly – and perhaps necessarily – New Critical antidote to the 'intentional phallacies' perpetrated by Sutherland and his ilk. Unfortunately, as Anderson points out in the preface to the 1977 McClelland and Stewart edition of his 'Selected Poems,' *Return to Canada* (Anderson's last book, published two years before his death), 'it took nineteen years for Northrop Frye's enthusiastic review ... to reach me' (9). Throughout this time, Canada was nevertheless to remain for Anderson 'a sort of "country of the mind,"' one which 'had released [his] imagination and which was still ... a place [he] was glad to have adopted' ('A Conversation with Patrick Anderson,' 72).

* * *

Just over two decades after Sutherland's attack on Anderson in 1943, Scott Symons was similarly savaged in print over the 1967 publication of his first novel, *Combat Journal for Place d'Armes.* The intervening years had of course witnessed a fervent growth in Canadian nationalism and a concomitant solidification of the literary canon in this country, impulses which were only heightened in the frenzied build-up to Expo 67 and Canada's centenary celebrations. Indeed, as Dermot McCarthy notes, Smith's *The Book of Canadian Poetry* can also be said to have helped pave the way for the third and 'most powerful version of Canadian literary history ... the displaced Protestant teleology of Frye's "Conclusion"' to the first edition of the *Literary History of Canada* (31–2). It was just such a 'displaced Protestant teleology' that Symons was reacting against in the hyper-Catholicism of *Place d'Armes.* Hugh Anderson's penitential entry into Notre Dame Cathedral to receive Holy Communion at the end of the novel – and his subsequent post-coital 'embrace' of the square outside – reflects not only a celebratory loss of his (and, by extension, Symons's) 'male maidenhead' in the asshole/'assoul' of the French-Canadian hustler, André; it also signals the successful defeat of the English-Canadian 'Blandmind' mentality, which Symons claims always wants to '"square" the Gothic medieval cathedral' (interview with Gibson, 312), eschewing any bodily connection with it: 'This is the definitive Canadian disease. That we've all been Norrie Fryed! That we've all been bitten by such a little WASPerie! ... The brute fact is that the Methodist-Presbyterian Canadian culture is against us being civilizedly articulate and sentient and sensual, if you wish, and palpable' (interview with Gibson, 316).

The added irony, of course, is that Symons was himself scion and hitherto favourite son of just such a Methodist-Presbyterian WASP culture, born into a prominent family from Rosedale, then 'Heart of Pan-Canadian Snobland,' as Symons puts it in *Civic Square* (1969), 'Residence-Royal of the Family Compact' (11). And, for most of his first thirty-two years, Symons did his best to live up to his oligarchic heritage, graduating from the University of Toronto's Trinity College and from King's College, Cambridge, with a flurry of degrees and awards, marrying an heiress from a wealthy Toronto family, and becoming assistant curator of the Royal Ontario Museum's Canadiana collection. In reality, however, during this time Symons was growing increasingly disenchanted with the state of his personal life, his choice of career, and what he saw as the crumbling infrastructure of English-Canadian society. By the late autumn of 1965, Symons had resolved 'to smash the impasse of his marriage, his creativity and his nation' (Taylor, *Six Journeys*, 211). He did so, significantly, by boarding a train for Quebec.

This trip, which saw Symons spending three weeks in a cramped hotel room adjacent Montreal's Place d'Armes, and which subsequently became the basis for his novel of the same name, was not his first visit to the city; nor was he arriving completely ignorant of Québécois culture. In 1960, soon after returning from Paris (where he had been studying French literature at the Sorbonne), Symons joined the staff of *La Presse*, quickly publishing over the next six months a series of twenty-five articles examining the sources of the political and intellectual ferment in the province and, in effect, prophesying the future: 'At a time when English Canada remained largely ignorant of the challenge that was about to be mounted in Quebec, Symons had predicted the Quiet Revolution' (Taylor, *Six Journeys*, 203–4). The articles won Symons a National Newspaper

Award, as well as honorary 'French Canadian citizenship' among his Québécois peers (see Taylor, *Six Journeys*, 204). But what was missing from this earlier attempt at cultural immersion was a sexual conversion of the sort described so hyperbolically in *Place d'Armes.* It is not enough to 'know' French Canada; one must 'Know' it as well. And, as Hugh puts it in *Place d'Armes*, in the midst of his back-to-back 'tricking' with Yvon and Pierrot, 'only the Biblical "Know," with its capitalized "K" describes for me this kind of knowledge' (38).

Along with Cohen's *Beautiful Losers* (1966) and Aquin's *Trou de mémoire* (1968), texts I discussed in chapter 1, and which bracket the publication of Symons's own, *Place d'Armes* can be said to have helped inaugurate Canadian literary postmodernism. All three books are highly metafictional (not to mention extemely misogynistic). *Place d'Armes* alone is composed of at least five different 'personal narratives,' most distinguished by their own typeface (10-point roman, 12-point roman, italic, boldface, etc.). The book opens with a third-person frame narrative, in which protagonist Hugh Anderson, about to leave Toronto, determines to write 'a short novel on La Place d'Armes in Montreal' (3). In order to accomplish this task, Hugh begins to keep a 'Novel Notebook' for 'his own private edification,' as well as '[a] kind of revenge against the restrictions of the Novel itself – a sort of intimacy. The intimate privilege of the first person' (4). However, on Day 2 of the journey the reader soon discovers that Hugh is keeping another first-person diary, this one a record of his 'assault on reality,' a 'log-book' of impressions, opinions, and rants which he calls his 'Combat Journal': 'Between my notebooks, my Combat Journal and what I manage to write of my novel, the picture should be complete. As complete as I can make it. And if I succeed, then I'll have my novel from it. Then the rest can be set aside' (23). On Day 7 Hugh finally begins his novel, *Place d'Armes*'s fourth narrative layer. Yet, immediately a fifth layer is introduced when Hugh's main character, Andrew Harrison, begins his own first-person diary. At this point separate storylines become hopelessly enmeshed and deliberately confused, something which Hugh remarks upon in his 'Combat Journal': 'by allowing my protagonist, Andrew, to write directly of his adventure, into his Diary (which then becomes me! weird, that), by presenting the rationale of it, his Diary becomes my Novel, becomes my Adventure, becomes me now – and my Novel, being merely his Diary is reduced, and what I am living becomes merely my Novel' (97). By the end of Symons's text, this is in fact what happens, with Andrew's diary merging not only with Hugh's novel, but also with Hugh's 'Combat Journal': 'as I [Andrew] type this diary now I realize that my novelette is in fact some deeper assault on reality than I cared to admit. It is war ... between reality and me – I'll call this diary a Combat Journal: That's it – my Combat Journal – I'll stick a label on the front cover' (265–6). Hugh has become his own main character, the writer writing as well as being written: 'Suddenly I [Hugh] have it ... have it all – the novelette – the story ... absurdly clear – even the name of the man: Hugh Anderson!' (267).

Like Cohen and Aquin (both of whom appear in *Place d'Armes*, Cohen as himself, 'a member of that fraternity of exile[d]' Jewish writers [140], and Aquin as the revolutionary novelist Jacques Prévost, a man 'who rejected his youth – killed his mother in revenge – went sterile – and took his revenge, again ... in politics,' and who, moreover, inscribes a copy of his book '"À mon ami Hugh Anderson ... ce livre qu'il a mieux senti que la plupart de mes amis Canadiens-français"' [117]),[9] Symons is also attempting, in the midst of all this metafictional subterfuge, to re-articulate – in part by re-eroticizing – his relationship with Canada, to provide 'a vision of a sexualized nationalism' by focusing on the 'figure of a doomed visionary whose thwarted sexuality mirrors that of a nation' (Martin, 'Cheap Tricks,' 199). As Hugh notes in his journal at the end of Day 13, 'better, by far, to be a pédéraste than a "féderaste" ... trust the French Canadian to find le mot juste for the gelded Canadian who makes a career out of his self-castration in the Ottawa Pork Barrel. All féderastes are of course pédérastes manqués' (141). Whereas this strategy earned for Cohen and Aquin critical accolades and Governor General's Awards (both refused), it earned for Symons only enmity and scorn. *Place d'Armes* was almost without exception savaged by reviewers when it first appeared, reviled for being sexually prurient *and* nationally seditious. As Charles Taylor notes in *Six Journeys: A Canadian Pattern*, 'most of the critics not only attacked the book for its literary faults; they also emphasized its homosexual passages, and were explicitly offended by the author's broadsides against English Canadian society' (217). Spearheading the attack was Robert Fulford. In a review published in the *Toronto Star* under the headline 'A Monster from Toronto,' Fulford concluded that Hugh Anderson 'may well be the most repellent single figure in the recent history of Canadian writing' (quoted in Taylor, *Six Journeys*, 217). This blatantly homophobic construction of *Place d'Armes*'s protagonist – and, by extension, its author – as monstrous has persisted in eclipsing the novel's significant technical achievement, so that in successive critical studies of Canadian literary postmodernism which claim Cohen and Aquin as precursors (Hutcheon's *Narcissistic Narrative* and *The Canadian Postmodern*,

Söderlind's *Margin/Alias*, to cite the main titles mentioned in chapter 1) Symons is consistently left out of the picture.[10]

Soon after the publication of *Place d'Armes*, events in Symons's private life colluded in solidifying his disreputable public image. Having fallen in love with a handsome seventeen-year-old from a prominent Toronto family, Symons was forced to flee the country for Mexico when his lover's parents sought the intervention of the Toronto police department's morality squad. For almost a year, Symons and his lover were on the run, evading both Canadian embassy officials and Mexican *Federales*. As Symons commented on his situation, 'I face the absurd reality of being some mere latter-day Oscar Wilde! – only possible in a still Victorian Canada' (quoted in Taylor, *Six Journeys*, 219). Symons was only able to return to Canada without fear of immediate arrest when it was announced that *Place d'Armes* had won the Beta Sigma Phi Best First Canadian Novel Award. Three years later, however, he felt compelled to escape Canada again, this time to Morocco.

Like Anderson before him, then, Symons's outsider status, the perception of him as both a national and sexual outlaw, made a voluntary form of exile appear if not inevitable, then certainly desirable. And while Symons's 'returns' to Canada have been more regular and prolonged, the work of both writers has to a large measure remained exiled from the canon of Canadian literature. However, as Robert K. Martin has noted (see 'Sex and Politics' and 'Cheap Tricks'), recent developments in gender theory and postcolonial studies offer productive ways in which to reread and reposition this work, not to mention the entire narratives of Canadian literary modernism and postmodernism, which, as I have attempted to suggest here, as well as in chapter 1, are themselves queerly ripe for reassessment. One such way is to view Anderson and Symons not merely as poet and novelist respectively, but also as travel writers.

* * *

Patrick Anderson's most sustained critical examination of the place and function of homoeroticism and homosexuality in Western literature can be found in his introduction to *Eros: An Anthology of Friendship*, the volume he co-edited with Alistair Sutherland in 1961. As Anderson remarks therein, the subject of the book is 'any friendship between men strong enough to deserve one of the more serious senses of the word "love"' (8). Thus, included among the pieces collected in the anthology are excerpts from Homer celebrating 'the heroic comradeship' between Achilles and

Patroclus, one or two of Shakespeare's homoerotic sonnets, a couple of Whitman's 'Calamus' poems, several English public school stories, and so on. Commenting on this broad spectrum, Anderson intones none too modestly that he does 'not think it is the job of an anthologist to be too firm about his categories, at least when the collection is something of a pioneer' (12). Still, he is firm enough in his literary self-convictions to place his own work within the historical parameters of this homoerotic tradition, including among the 'Exotic Encounters' section a passage from *Snake Wine.* It is, I think, significant that Anderson chose to anthologize his prose in this context, rather than his poetry. For, while much of Anderson's early poetry is clearly preoccupied with eroticizing male friendship, it nevertheless helps, I would suggest, to read this work through the lens/prism of his subsequent prose, particularly his 'Oriental' and 'Mediterranean' travel writing. Indeed, as I hope to demonstrate, such a move not only provides a much-needed corrective to the virile nationalist dismissal of Anderson's verse, but also helps to expose, to 'bring out' if you will, its homosexual lines of filiation, especially in the case of literary precursors like Hart Crane and Lord Byron.

Of Byron, it has recently been argued that, in addition to being one of the most popular and influential writers of his time, he also 'invented a new form of "travel poetry"': in '*Childe Harold's Pilgrimage* a recognizably new attitude to travel is given narrative form, and a new kind of traveler is delineated in the form of the romantic rebel' (Porter, 126). In *Byron and Greek Love,* however, Louis Crompton wonders whether the poet's bisexuality might better 'explain the psychology of the so-called Byronic hero' (8). For Crompton '[a] dawning awareness of his bisexual nature ... was important in inspiring [Byron's] first trip to Greece and Turkey' during 1809–11 (12), just as his later exiled return there in 1816 was in large part attributable to prevailing attitudes of 'Georgian homophobia' in England. Certainly his strong appeal to Anderson, both as a biographical subject to analyse and as a poet to emulate, would seem to stem in equal measure from Byron's role as 'travel writer' *and* 'sexual nonconformist.' In both *Dolphin Days* (1963), his 'Notebook of Mediterranean Pleasures,' and *Over the Alps* (1969), a book of 'Reflections on Travel and Travel Writing,' Anderson devotes whole chapters to Byron's treks through Greece (the latter book also includes a chapter on another 'notorious' homosexual traveller exiled from England, William Beckford), documenting in detail the poet's successive relationships there with Nicolo Giraud and Loukas Chalandritsanos: 'In some such waters Byron and Nicolo bathed. Despite their whirlpools and dreary depths, we cannot ignore the physical exaltation and intellectual sympathy which the two must have experienced as they re-entered "*le paradis des amours enfantins* [*sic*]"' (*Dolphin Days*, 135). Moreover, in *First Steps in Greece* (1958), Anderson admits that his own childhood fascination with the country had 'something to do with The Body,' as well as the fact that 'Lord Byron had concluded a disreputable life by dying for it' (11). Byron's influence on Anderson is even reflected, I would argue, in the above-cited passage from 'Leaving Canada,' the pathos of which can also be found in Childe Harold's decision to abandon his 'fellow bacchanals' and his 'native land' for 'scorching climes beyond the sea':

> And now Childe Harold was sore sick at heart,
> And from his fellow bacchanals would flee;
> 'Tis said, at times the sullen tear would start,
> But Pride congealed the drop within his ee:
> Apart he stalked in joyless reverie,
> And from his native land resolved to go,
> And visit scorching climes beyond the sea;
> With pleasure drugged, he almost longed for woe,
> And e'en for change of scene would seek the shades below. (Canto I, vi)

However, much more of a poetic presence in 'Leaving Canada,' and, arguably, within Anderson's entire oeuvre, is Hart Crane, 'a favourite American whom ... [Anderson] had discovered ... in his own Caribbean landscape during the Christmas of 1939' (*Dolphin Days*, 35–6). As in Crane's 'Voyages,' the celebrated sequence of six lyric love poems that he wrote for Emil Opffer in 1926, and in which he 'attempted his most sustained literary inscription of homosexual relations as the incarnation of "the Word made Flesh"' (Yingling, 91), the sea provides for Anderson a 'flood / of romantic imagery' with which to describe male friendship (*Colour*, 86). In particular, the second stanza of 'Leaving Canada' seems to contain several echoes of Crane. For example, not only does Anderson's 'silk and simpleton the dream' (86) recall Crane's 'silken skilled transmemberment of song' in 'Voyages III' (*Collected Poems*, 104), but Anderson's subsequent evocation of William's 'cousin's suicide / leaped beyond the rim of good / in the midnight' (86) can in part be read as an allusion to the American poet's own death by drowning after jumping from the deck of the *Orizaba* into the Gulf of Mexico 250 miles north of Havana on 27 April 1932.

'[P]ast midnight' is, of course, the point at which Crane's 'Voyages' – in sequence V, specifically – are 'overtaken' by the 'slow tyranny of moonlight,' the lovers unable to 'deflect this tidal wedge' of time and change (*Collected Poems*, 107). Only at this point – separation – does Anderson's own poem begin: in the opening stanza, the speaker is already 'sail[ing] away' from William and 'a country [Canada] where the good / lies reflected in your eye' (*Colour*, 86). However, despite the 'icy and bright dungeons' of the sea in 'Voyages VI' (*Collected Poems*, 109) and the 'icebergs smelling of dead fish' in the final stanza of 'Leaving Canada' (*Colour*, 88), both Crane and Anderson conclude their respective poems with a transcendent vision of the 'still fervid covenant' of bodily desire transmembered into something more spiritual, and therefore 'unbetrayable' (Crane, *Collected Poems*, 110): in 'Voyages VI' this vision is accomplished through 'the imaged Word' (*Collected Poems*, 110); in 'Leaving Canada,' through the 'ordering look' of memory (*Colour*, 88).[11]

Elsewhere in *The Colour as Naked*, Anderson concludes another 'nautical' poem, 'Voyage to Saguenay,' with an oblique reference, not only to Crane, but also to the 'favourite American's' most famous poem:

> Was there ever fitted fine and spry
> ship such as ours to cock and peak the brow
> and set the sealegs with a nautical tilt
> along the strange sweet summer, soft and low,
> between the island flats and channel narrows
> pricked out with buoys and dredge's sultry smudge
> and *crane* above reflection black and gauche,
> as evening comes and the talented orchestra
> appears our only engine, and we move
> to strangers, ships in the night,
> tomorrow's appetite,
> and Murray Bay and golf and *bridge* and love? (30–1; my emphasis)

Anderson had previously displayed a debt to Crane's 'The Bridge' in writing his own national epic, labelling section IV of 'Poem on Canada' 'The River.' For both Crane and Anderson, the river in question is at once an actual body of water (Crane's Mississippi versus Anderson's St Lawrence) and a metaphor for the railway snaking its way 'West [across] the land. And North' ('Poem on Canada,' *The White Centre*, 42). Anderson's *Dolphin Days* likewise ends with an extended meditation on the 'balance between earth and angels' achieved in Crane's 'last, and perhaps best poem,' 'The Broken Tower' (223–4).

Although the immediate destination of the speaker at the end of 'Leaving Canada' is England, Anderson himself left the country in 1950 for a two-year sojourn in Singapore, an 'episode' that provides the basis for *Snake Wine*, as well as several of the poems included in *The Colour as Naked*. In the latter text, it is possible to trace the same kind of self/other dialectic that Sutherland saw operating at the 'centre' of Anderson's earlier poetry, this time played out in terms of the distance (both physical and psychical) travelled between the 'intense cold,' 'rose of ice,' and 'white turn' of Canada and the t(r)opical pleasures of Singapore/Malaya, whose 'strange birds,' 'jacarandas,' and 'sensuous technicolour'[12] feed but do not fully sate '"the deeper, more complex needs of the northern soul,"' as Anderson, quoting from Thomas Mann's 'Mario and the Magician,' puts it in the opening section of *Snake Wine* (58). Commenting later in that text on some 'other reasons why Canada should appear over the edge of the balcony' of his house in Singapore, Anderson writes: 'the tropics demand their opposite, palms call forth images of ice and snow, and this not only because the modern mind enjoys a paradox and likes to see different kinds of experience wrestling together; rather because behind the difference there lies a dreaming similarity' (226).

An interesting theory. In practice, however, Anderson's own neo-Adornian poetics preclude such easy synthesis. His 'negative dialectics' make of Canada, as utopian ideal, as 'white centre,' a mere unreal semblance of harmonious unity (as, indeed, politically it always has been), while the defamiliarized and unreconcilable shapes and sounds and sights of Singapore – its 'canon of prohibitions,' to use Adorno's term (*Aesthetic Theory*, 53) – only point out the necessary failure of any attempt at poetic syncretism. (It is perhaps no coincidence, then, that after his stay in Singapore, which culminated in the publication of *The Colour as Naked*, Anderson largely abandoned the writing of poetry altogether and, moreover, only returned to poetry when he started thinking about Canada again – and, concomitantly, when Canada started thinking about him again.) Thus, in Canada, out of 'the lovely negativity of ice / pleasures alight in flocks upon the ponds,' 'summer and winter [stroll] hand in hand,' and 'the bell / of dark' is kept at bay ('Sestina in Time of Winter,' 20). In Singapore, however, the poet's 'ghostly ... projected soul / panic[s],' and his 'amputated' other seems 'separate and grey,' reminding us that in 'Plato's cave' 'when illusion died / ... man and lens were left outside' ('A Monkey in Malaya,' 68). Whereas in Canada 'a poem hardly makes a shadow' and is 'a thing of light' ('The Candles: Dorchester Street,' 33), in Singapore

The poet must be devoured

by his terrible image. The stuffed bird going black
on the flowered wall, the stillness caged like a condor
holds face from lace, the cupboard place from the parlour,
mice behind golden picture, dark from dark,
O into a mirror
flies my face, in a metaphor I am altered,
and the bird in the glass and the bird in the word strikes back.
('The Strange Bird,' 84)

What Anderson is here confronting in his 'consideration of the Orient,' according to Roland Barthes, is nothing less than 'the possibility of a difference, of a mutation, of a revolution in the propriety of symbolic systems' (*Empire of Signs*, 3–4). Whereas Canada remains for Anderson a fixed symbolic system, where poetic images signify stasis, containment, causality, and where in 'the lovely negativity of ice' there is still a white centre out of which 'pleasures alight in flocks upon the pond,' Anderson's Singapore, like Barthes's Japan, manifests itself as a void, a black hole ('dark from dark'), an empire of perpetually inscrutable and endlessly proliferating signs, where 'the bird in the glass' is also 'the bird in the word,' and where 'the *inside* no longer commands the *outside*' (Barthes, *Empire*, 62).

Of course, Somerset Maugham had, in *The Casuarina Tree* (1926) and *Ah king* (1933), already captured the Western colonial perspective on the 'chaos' of Malaya, warning of the dangers of 'running amok' in its uncentred spaces.[13] In *Snake Wine* there is never really any question of Anderson succumbing to the 'darkness' of Singapore, of the poet himself wanting to 'go black,' and thereby 'plunder [his] European self' (72) – at least, certainly not to the extent that a similar process of 'going native' was possible in Canada (that is, the Canada that Anderson saw or was permitted to see), where elisions of race and class then appeared more easily negotiable. Indeed, in *Snake Wine*, as the empire begins both to strike and to write back, the reader finds Anderson quickly abandoning his wartime Canadian socialist principles and eagerly assuming all the trappings of colonial privilege: 'Ever since London, where my friends were so amusing on the subject, the idea of having a servant has been almost an obsession with me, as a symbol of luxury, a challenge to my imagination and tact, and an opportunity to get into direct relation with the East' (43). To be sure, in the case of Anderson and his newly acquired 'Boy,' Ah Ting, it soon becomes difficult to tell 'which ... is really the master' (43); indeed, in this domestic *ménage* Ah Ting is in part Anderson's jailer, a dialectical image reinforced by the ubiquitous presence of Ah Ting's key chain. Throw homosexual desire into this admixture of racial and class differences and one can potentially understand Anderson's uneasy and disquieting fascination with the 'dark margins' of Singapore, 'a crazy world of flaring lamps, far too much beer, and children whose business was to flirt with Europeans for money' (281), 'a place where the evocative cry *Boy!* with its connotations of Ganymede, Giton and the interests of some of my London friends, echoed from every corner' (32). Anderson's textual regulation of these competing differences forces him to transform the beguiling boy in the cachou tree with whom he shares 'a smile of complicity' in *Snake Wine* (72) into a well-scrubbed public school martyr, of the likes described by Hopkins or Housman 'with [their] tightlipped art,' in a poem included some twenty years later in *A Visiting Distance* (103).

Anderson ruminates upon this dialectical process of rendering the 'primitive' boy 'in terms of classical art' at greater length in *Search Me*, an 'autobiography' of his years in Canada, Spain, and the Black Country of England. Commenting on a 'game' he liked to play, in which 'two boys repeated, if in rather exaggerated ways, the two types of friend I had sought when I was myself young,' Anderson distinguishes between what he calls the 'brown' boy, who is 'rather brutal-looking' and whose body emphasizes 'the mere possession of flesh,' and the 'fair' boy, who is 'the pretty type, slim and delicately built,' 'content to be passive' (106, 107). He then goes on to claim that 'much of my childhood seems to me now the attempt ... to reach completion through ... friendship with a fair one, although this was likely to be such a rare occurrence that brown substitutes had often to be found' (108). It would appear that Anderson continued to seek out 'brown substitutes' as an adult as well, both in his prose and in his poetry. For the description of Toto's gypsy dance at the end of *Search Me* (216–17),[14] or Terrence's Carmen Miranda routine in *Snake Wine* (60–1, 70), or the 'unorthodox but dramatic photographs' of Paul, George, Mike, and Evangelos at the 'Rock and Roll' bar in *First Steps in Greece* (110–23) are all of a piece with Anderson's depiction of Timofyey, the 'twelve year old with the mouse fringe,' who is 'neither male nor female,' who wears 'neither a shirt nor a dress,' in *The White Centre* ('Boy in a Russian Blouse,' 57), and the 'wide boy,' the 'Ganymede kid' who 'sit[s] in the nightclub so sulky,' in *The Colour as Naked* ('Spiv Song,' 77, 78), and the 'sailor picked up somewhere near the Zoo' who 'had a train to miss' and a 'warm wet gravel of [a] kiss' in *A Visiting Distance* ('Strangers Brought Home,' 97). The connection that I am making here between Anderson's early 'Montreal' poems and his later 'foreign' prose has much to do with the fact that although he eventually became a citizen of the Canadian *nation* (in 1945, as mentioned above), Anderson remained for the most part a *sexual* tourist in Quebec.

In his 1989 memoir of Anderson, Patrick Campbell notes that 'if Greece had been the epicentre of Patrick's old world, rediscovered in the fifties long after the ritual steeping in the classics at Sherborne and Oxford, then Canada had previously occupied that position during the forties' (93). More specifically, I would argue, it was *Quebec* that occupied the position of Greece for Anderson during the 1940s. And, perhaps even more particularly, Montreal. (Anderson concludes his 1974 interview with Seymour Mayne by stating that 'I guess I *am* a Montrealer' [79].) The metaphorical equivalency established between Quebec and Greece in Anderson's writing, it seems to me, is less a geographic than an erotic one, mapping the desire, rather than the distance, between two fantasies of otherness. As Robert K. Martin has persuasively argued, 'English Canadian writers who have wished to attack their own culture for its Victorianism, its Puritanism, and its moral rigidity have turned to Quebec with the same ambivalence that the late Romantics regarded Italy or Greece' ('Two Days in Sodom,' 28). Anderson, the so-very 'English'-Canadian writer, the 'tea-drinking Dylan Thomas' gradually coming to writerly awareness of his sexuality, could hardly then have avoided becoming occasionally Byronic in his poetic descriptions of his new city, as indeed Byron would later figure so prominently in many of Anderson's travel memoirs. Thus, in a poem like 'Montreal,' 'the frightened boy utter[ing] his tedious soliloquy' and the 'other hero [who] sang of joy like a tenor' do not harken back 'to some period in the writer's childhood,' as John Sutherland would have us believe ('The Writing of Patrick Anderson,' 4); rather, they 'belong to [another] theatre [Anderson] knew' ('Montreal'), namely, the legendary same-sex love affairs (Zeus and Ganymede, Apollo and Hyacinth, Sylvanus and Cyparissus) performed in classical mythology and restaged by successive generations of poets, including the Romantics. In the end, of course, Byron's Romantic vision of Greece was also a political one – exemplified no better than in his own death. So, too, with Anderson's vision of Montreal, where 'the terraces of class run down to our nationhood,' where 'the broad street of the Jews / lay open between the twisted fascist alleys,' and where the 'people's armies' are composed of 'French and English, / Jew and not Jew, artist and public' ('Montreal').

The 'infinite consanguinity' (to borrow a phrase from Crane's 'Voyages') of sexual and national politics infusing Anderson's writing on Quebec finds further expression in two chapters in *The Character Ball*, chapters that trace 'interior' journeys – 'exteriorized,' respectively, in a late-night cruise of the city and a tranquil summertime 'idyll' in the countryside – to which Anderson would return, in poetic form, in *A Visiting Distance*. In the case of the opening of the chapter entitled 'The Teeth of the Lion,' Anderson was actually returning to a setting first explored in 'Night Out,' a poem included in *A Tent for April*. Both works describe the casual fraternity experienced in a Montreal tavern, yielding enough textual clues to suggest that, in each case, the tavern in question is in fact a gay bar: in 'Night Out,' 'soldiers opaque with purpose / [drink] gymnastically on death's edge,' 'the evening opens to an endless prospect / of male and easy city,' and dawn brings with it 'transformed identities' and 'logical breakfasts' (*Tent*); in 'The Teeth of the Lion,' the Peel Tavern is a place where 'no women are allowed,' where 'eyes must be kept to themselves,' and where 'degenerate intimacies,' though discouraged, are nevertheless possible (*The Character Ball*, 161). One such 'degenerate' intimacy comes closer to fruition for Anderson when he is joined by Jacques, a handsome blond Québécois 'tough,' who 'strutted and rolled his shoulders like the hero of a Western' and was 'the essence of youthfulness' (161). Jacques, a former pro baseball player, has turned to 'a life of crime' (162), suggesting that his character might also have served as the basis for Anderson's 'wide-boy' in the poem 'Spiv Song.' Suffering from a painful toothache, Jacques immediately enlists Anderson's aid in accompanying him to the dentist. What follows is a brief tour through the seedy streets of Montreal's underworld, where doctors keep offices above strip clubs, that culminates in a drunken confrontation in Anderson's apartment. Throughout the comic sketch, Anderson offers glimpses of both local colour – 'There is a superstition in Quebec that if you bury your teeth in the garden you are more likely to breed boys' (164) – and sexual tension: 'Jacques turned round, grinning. "You got any girls in this house?" he asked. The dusty light from the small bulb over the sink romped in his hair. Then he swung forward into the dark of the hall. In the shadow his swollen face seemed all the more flushed, gay, contemptuous. "Don't bother to answer," he added' (165).

Returning to the poem 'Night Out' via this story, we notice that the changes Anderson makes to the version included in *A Visiting Distance* (retitled 'Night Out: Montreal Tavern') consist mainly of adding extra elements of *québécité*, of introducing into the homoerotics of place symbolized by the tavern a measure of national alterity as well:

enter *le gang,*[15] *les boys,*
Sweet Caps inhaled into theatre-red lungs
which move the furry pectorals below
pindot and check and stripe,
then pouted out from powerful gargoyle lips
the adult signatures deforming in the air,
pants hitched, brought forward
the curious nakedness of human hands
too big, like animals for hurt, escaped
from somewhere's dim *paysage,* the shoulders hunched
to bury them on the freckled wooden moon
of an evening's pleasure. (*A Visiting Distance,* 35)

The speaker of the poem is at once inside and outside this scene, content to be a silent observer 'when friend denounces friend,' but also recognizing that the urinal 'that weeps and prays all day, / for all of us all day,' is 'familiar as a cave,' an altar 'where we confess ourselves and write our names' (*A Visiting Distance,* 35, 36).

Questions of inside and outside, figure and ground – especially as they relate to nationalism and sexuality – are also paramount in 'At Baie St. Paul,' a prose sketch that 'documents' an 'idyllic' summer holiday spent by the fictionalized Anderson and his wife, 'Mary,' in Quebec's Laurentians. Even though there is a war on, and even though the province is gearing up for a plebiscite concerning its participation in that war – '*Votez Non* for conscription on every wall' (*The Character Ball,* 110) – the Andersons are initially loath to abandon their metropolitan condescension regarding the essential 'vitality' of the rural *habitants* and *paysage*: 'Mary and I, who felt so tender towards the landscape ... felt that, whatever the politics, there must be innocence and lyricism and gaiety underneath' (111). Only the arrival of 'the deserter' jolts Anderson out of his colonial complacency, forcing him to acknowledge that to the Québécois townspeople he and his wife are very much '*les Anglais,* the imperialist oppressors and therefore in league with the police' (119). Watching the young man hide his Army greatcoat in the river, Anderson realizes that, despite his political sympathies ('leftist supporter of the war,' 'proponent of a Second Front'), he will 'do nothing about it' (117). Instead, the incident provokes 'sudden sympathies' within Anderson, a recognition of 'mutual hiding': 'as I identified myself with the deserter, something in me deserted too' (121).

Two earlier Baie St Paul sketches, both published in *Preview* in 1943, make no mention of the episode with the deserter, but nevertheless provide clues regarding Anderson's deeply ambivalent attachment to the region and its inhabitants. The first, entitled 'Notes from My Journal: Baie St. Paul,' focuses on a local boy, Pierre, and his 'fiches,' a collection of tracts that formed 'a kind of encyclopedia of Catholic thought' (10). While dubious of the claims made by Pierre's fiches, Anderson is reverent in his appreciation of Baie St. Paul itself: 'I had seldom been so attracted to a place as I was to Baie St. Paul. Its people were kind and hospitable, and I felt that I could understand and sympathise with their grievances and loyalties, just as I could sympathise with the Boers or the Irish' (11). In 'Further Notes from Baie St. Paul,' Anderson introduces his readers to the conjuror Brother Maurice, a mysterious Mannian figure (featured prominently in the final published version of 'At Baie St. Paul') who seems to cast a pall over Anderson's vision of the landscape and of himself: 'I was, I suppose, over ready to detect the sinister and strange, especially since this countryside symbolised many confused haunting preoccupations of my own – this place that was so lovely and so wrong, so much minority-land, rich in grievances, frustrations and out-moded faiths' (7–8).

The identification between Quebec as national minority and Anderson as sexual minority that runs throughout all three stories is made much more explicit in the poem 'Remembering Baie St. Paul.' Returning to the landscape 'after thirty years to salvage a sketch or a poem,' Anderson realizes that his 'heart's minority was saying No' to bourgeois heterosexuality in much the same way that 'Quebec said No to conscription':

Obsessed with our
propagandist marriage, too nervous to be hurt,

we took years to cry out the two considered No's
that broke us up (*Visiting*, 149)

Thus, in both prose and poetry, Anderson's peregrinations in 'minority-land' (be they in Malaya, Greece, or Quebec) enable him to capture something of the paradox at the heart of sexual travel *and* domestic nationalism – the separateness of sameness – at the same time as they 'must make him doubt the utility of a common front that allows no place for difference' (Martin, 'Sex,' 113).

* * *

That no similar writerly epiphany seems to have occurred to Scott

Symons in the nearly twenty years between the publication of *Place d'Armes* and his most recent novel, *Helmet of Flesh* (1986), suggests something of the way in which his 'textual nationalism' is complicit with a kind of 'sexual imperialism,' the way in which, in order to rewrite 'homosexuality' (identity) as 'mansex' (mere activity), Symons repeatedly transforms all other differences (national, cultural, class, even architectural!) into fetishes. In *Place d'Armes*, for example, Pierrot's rotten teeth, like Jacques's in 'The Teeth of the Lion,' are 'indelibly Canayen ... like rotted patates frites,' the 'life-giving dirt' of his body suggestive of 'a lusher, richer wine. Pourriture noble' (38). In *Helmet of Flesh*, moreover, Symons repeatedly puns on the novel's title, remarking at one point that Marrakech is 'like a cathedral with a hard-on,' its hordes of beautiful brown boys like 'Roman candles, sparklers, detonating where they stand' (276, 42). Thus, paradoxically, in employing French-Canadian hustlers and Moroccan boys as textual representations of *national* alterity, Symons also requires of these characters an absence of signification other than the purely *sexual*. They are simply a metaphorical means to an equally metaphorical end: the shattering of the English-Canadian writer's 'male maidenhead.' (It is surely no coincidence that 'Keb,' the diminutive York Mackenzie bestows upon his Moroccan lover in *Helmet of Flesh*, is also short for '*kebab*' – 'dark meat' on a skewer – nor that it rhymes with '*zeb*,' the Arabic word for penis.) The folkloric and eager-to-please 'foreign' boys that populate Symons's fiction tax neither the hearts nor the minds of his protagonists, and whatever image of the 'other' we are permitted to glimpse in their lithe, pliant, and frequently malnourished bodies perforce remains a composite one: in *Place d'Armes*, Yvon-Pierrot-André are more or less interchangeable; in *Helmet of Flesh*, York distinguishes between the young men he meets with names like 'Blue Boy' and 'Blondboy,' but remains unable to describe his lover, Kebir, in any terms other than absence ('couldn't think about Kebir, because Kebir then vanished' [42]; 'Couldn't think what Kebir was, only what he wasn't!' [117]).

If ever there were a candidate in Canadian letters for the sobriquet of 'Byronic hero,' it might well be Scott Symons. Like Byron's Childe Harold and Don Juan, Symons's Hugh Anderson and York Mackenzie, *Helmet of Flesh*'s putative hero, compose 'personal narratives' of their travels (and sexual conquests), 'combat journals' outlining their disaffection from their 'federastic' birthplaces, which simultaneously double as *Baedekers* to the 'pederastic' pleasures awaiting them in 'foreign' lands (in the case of Symons, Quebec and Morocco). Yet, as Robert Martin has recently pointed out, it is 'important to examine some of the premises on which

Symons casts himself as revolutionary hero,' particularly the ways in which his 'search for a more hospitable gay place may involve the appropriation of the other for what amounts to a kind of sexual tourism' ('Cheap Tricks,' 198). Focusing on *Place d'Armes*, 'a travel journal that wants to rewrite the conventions of travel writing,' Martin demonstrates how Symons's 'remapping' of Montreal as 'a city of male desire' – a textual strategy materially reinforced by the annotated maps, postcards, newspaper clippings, and souvenir brochures included in the manila pouch on the inside front cover of the 1967 first edition[16] – constitutes an example of what Mary Louise Pratt has termed 'anti-conquest' literature, that is, literature in which colonial guilt is attenuated and national virtue accentuated through the eroticization and fetishization of otherness (see Martin, 'Cheap Tricks,' 202, 203; and Pratt, *Imperial Eyes*, 38–68). And yet, while Pratt's representation of the 'protagonist' of anti-conquest travel writing as the 'seeing-man,' the 'male subject of European landscape discourse ... whose imperial eyes passively look out and possess' (7), easily relates to Hugh Anderson, it even more aptly describes York Mackenzie.

As Joseph Boone has recently noted, 'the number of gay and bisexual male writers and artists who have traveled through North Africa in pursuit of sexual gratification is legion as well as legend' ('Vacation Cruises,' 90). Think of André Gide and Oscar Wilde meeting in Algeria in 1895 (a desert 'encounter' delineated by Jonathan Dollimore at the beginning of *Sexual Dissidence*, 3–18). Think of the perverse pleasures and sexual escapades of Gustave Flaubert and Lawrence Durrell in Egypt, or those of Sir Richard Burton and T.E. Lawrence in 'Arabia,' or those of just about everybody else – including Paul Bowles, William Burroughs, Tennessee Williams, Truman Capote, Gore Vidal, Allen Ginsberg, Joe Orton, Jean Genet, Ronald Firbank, Michael Davidson, and Roland Barthes – in Morocco. It is thus hardly surprising that Scott Symons, exiled from the 'Canadian Bestiary,' the 'world's most succesful anaphrodisiac,' should also eventually find his way to this libidinal paradise – a place that 'is everything Canada ain't' (*Helmet*, 72) – and, what's more, that he should choose to make it the setting of his third 'confessional' novel.

In many respects, *Helmet of Flesh* picks up where *Place d'Armes* leaves off, opening with a sensuous description of a crowded city square alive with music and dance: 'The street dissolved, and he was standing in an immense open square. A sound like tambourines exploded about thirty yards away, and curious he hastened towards it' (11). Just as the cathedral spires of Notre Dame symbolize male plenitude in *Place d'Armes*, so does the tower of the ancient Koutoubia mosque incarnate the 'phallic liturgy of Marrakech' in *Helmet of Flesh* (271). Like Hugh, York fashions himself as a fugitive from his own culture, an 'escapee' of 'the whole fucking Canadian Protestant plausible Gliblib gynarchical' regime, a sexual adventurer who has travelled to Morocco in order 'to look orgasm in the eye,' that is, to reaffirm his masculinity, and thereby his national identity (*Helmet*, 22, 21). Also like Hugh, York keeps a notebook or diary, recording his impressions of and experiences in this new land.

A sense of perspectival doubleness thus pervades *Helmet of Flesh*. Not only are Canada and Morocco repeatedly juxtaposed, but the narrative itself is constantly shifting: diegetically between the third-person frame and the interior first-person commentary of York's diary; temporally and spatially between Marrakech and Osprey Cove, Newfoundland; stylistically between lush participial romanticism and biting declarative satire. As a result, it is often very difficult to distinguish between what is 'reality' and what is 'fantasy' in the text, between those events York has actually experienced and those he has imagined, or even hallucinated (such as the 'magic carpet' tea ceremony with Karim in chapter 8). This process is exacerbated by the competing emotional pulls York feels towards Kebir, the young Marrakshi boy he meets on his first day in Morocco, and John, the Canadian lover waiting for him in Osprey Cove. In York's mind, the two men become fused as one: York even gives Kebir John's two-headed falcon talisman to wear for the duration of his stay in Marrakech.

As Peter Buitenhuis has remarked, the novel's plot structure is also doubled, 'consist[ing] of two great and dizzy loops': 'The first takes York through and beyond the Atlas mountains to a remote oasis and back; the second takes him to a sheikh's mansion in the interior near Demna before returning him to Marrakech and his departure for Canada' (64). Accompanying York on his first trip into the sub-Saharan interior are two British men he meets at the Grand Hotel Fauzi: James Goodison, an apparently upper-class Oxbridge type conducting research on the Glaoui, 'the last great warlord of North Africa' (38); and Anthony Napier, a retired army colonel and 'perambulating zebophile,' who is conducting certain investigations of his own under the burnouses of local Moroccan lads (148). What starts out 'like a *Boy's Own Annual* escapade, or *Chums*' (89), soon turns into a frightening journey into Africa's 'heart of darkness,' culminating in what York's sensory-overloaded mind registers as a bloody sacrifice in M'Hamid.

The British gentlemen – who, it turns out, are not really gentlemen at all, the one merely 'imitation,' the other disgraced (187) – are themselves contrasted with the vaguely aristocratic French decadents whom York meets at 'le tout Hôtel des Amis' upon his return to Marrakech: Monsieur Claude, 'Grand Master of All Ceremonies,' a painter who is forever finding angels in the faces of the boys who sit for him (258); Richard, who, like 'an endless subjunctive clause ... out of Proust,' has come to Marrakech to die (299); and Bertrand, a 'fallen satyrling' addicted to heroin and his own beauty (270). At an allegorical level, of course, both sets of castaway characters can be seen to represent the two 'founding nations' of Canada. While the Grand Fauzi and Hôtel des Amis groups never interact directly in the text, English and French (not to mention Canadian and Moroccan) are brought together symbolically in the novel's final chapter at the dinner party hosted by Herbert and Rebecca, a 'volubly normal' British couple (311), for the Hôtel des Amis 'boys': here the common enemy becomes the American tour party that invades the restaurant and takes over the dance floor. York, while fascinated by the European expatriates he meets in Morocco, is also at great pains throughout the text to distance himself from them. This takes the form of his repeated insistence that he is neither gay, nor a tourist. For, according to York, the 'gay world is a predicate of phallic failure,' and tourists 'parasite a culture' (261, 260).

The problem with such an assessment is that it completely elides the economics of York's relationship with Kebir, which York not only places outside the Third World 'tourist trade in boys' (see Boone, 99), but also Occidental 'instalment plan' sex: 'K. only gives what he already holds. The opposite to debit-loving, expense account sex (play now, pay later)' (*Helmet,* 118). And yet, while York, unlike most sexual tourists in Morocco, may not have to pay Kebir for sex, this does not mean that their relationship is completely non-exploitative. In this regard, it is important to note that Kebir is not just York's lover; he is also York's guide: 'Keb's task in life still was – to be Kebir. To be the person he was: the splendour of their voyage through the mountains, song of that high valley, endless dance of Morocco' (252). As in *Place d'Armes,* the body of an autochthonous other ('manscape') becomes synonymous in *Helmet of Flesh* with the indigenous landscape; it is unexplored territory (unexplored, but not necessarily virgin) to be charted and possessed, a 'whole nation lying rampant' under a colonizing eye/I (*Place,* 39): 'Black crepuscular landscape, mountains and valleys of Marrakshi named Kebir. And rising in that landscape, a giant red flower on a black stalk. Rich tulip of Kebir's cockhead' (*Helmet,* 57).

Robert Martin has convincingly documented Symons's debt, in *Place d'Armes,* to André Gide's *L'Immoraliste* (see 'Cheap Tricks,' 207). In *Helmet of Flesh*, with its North African locale, the debt to Gide's 1902 novel, as well as to his 1926 autobiography, *Si le grain ne meurt*, is even more pronounced. Like Michel in *L'Immoraliste*, *Helmet of Flesh*'s York undergoes a near-death experience on the edge of the desert; also like Michel, York's 'surrender to inner passions' is frequently 'projected outward onto the African landscape' (Boone, 101). But just as Anderson's *Snake Wine* finds an unlikely intertext in Barthes's *Empire of Signs*, so can Symons's *Helmet of Flesh* be read, it seems to me, against the grain of Barthes's posthumously published *Incidents*.

Both *Helmet of Flesh* and *Incidents* are, in their own way, travel books: the one a novel that maps a clear identitarian itinerary of exile and return, the other a journal documenting an international cruising circuit. Both are also what I would call highly 'ocular' or 'scopophilic' texts, in the sense that they are concerned with the power of observation, the defilement of perception, and the narcissism of the desiring gaze (in the body of the other might I catch a glimpse of my true self). Yet, whereas Symons casts York as a kind of 'Don Quixote who quails at a teapot' (*Helmet*, 329), the passive, all-seeing 'anti-conquest' hero shuffling nervously at the centre of the 'dervish dance that goes on all around him' (Buitenhuis, 65), Barthes's Moroccan impressions are invariably recorded at a slight remove, not to mention at a mimetically skewed angle. The semiology of Barthes's text is one of refraction rather than mere reflection, fleeting 'evanescence' rather than perpetual 'synaesthesia.'[17] Whereas York is constantly trying to make sense of Morocco, to plumb its depths for hidden meanings, to naturalize the landscape and its inhabitants syllogistically, Barthes's Moroccan diary is all about surface and the displacement of meaning, his writing deliberately aphoristic, appositional, allusive. For Barthes, language itself becomes the necessary measure of his desire for the other: 'I enjoy Amidou's vocabulary: *dream* and *burst* for *get an erection* and *have an orgasm*' (*Incidents*, 29).[18] Of course, ironically, both Symons's and Barthes's Moroccan texts can be taken as examples of what Martin has called an '*écriture gaie*,' a way of 'writ[ing] homosexually without writing homosexuality,' inspired in part by the corpus of Barthes's own works ('Roland Barthes,' 282). The masturbatory prose of *Helmet of Flesh*, for example, its almost apocalyptic *jouissance*, follows the 'productive' prescription made by Barthes at the end of *The Pleasure of the Text*; in turn, the fragmentary, epigrammatic, and voyeuristic style employed by Barthes in *Incidents* is of a piece with his later works, most notably *A Lover's Discourse*. The question remains, however, as to which text/style, in its bodily specificity, is better suited to the representation of cultural difference.[19]

Certainly Symons would appear to be more susceptible than Barthes (or Anderson, for that matter) to the totalizing gesture. Witness, for example, the opening and closing refrain of *Civic Square*: 'All cocks are beautiful.' Symons's limited edition second novel, 848 pages of unbound typescript loosely packaged in a mock Birks blue box, is, in formal terms at least, perhaps his most experimental; it is also, in my opinion, his least successful. Divided into three 'segments,' the novel is actually a series of thirty-five letters penned by 'Scott,' and addressed to 'D.R.,' or 'Dearreader.'[20] These letters are dated chronologically, spanning the period between 10–11 May 1966 and 21 April 1967, but are arranged in no particular sequential order: for example, letter #29, which starts on page 387 of the text, is followed by letter #7 on page 400; and letter #9 (pp. 451–85, 522–58, and 575–99) is interrupted by letter #31 (pp. 486–521) and letter #32 (pp. 559–74). Occasionally, 'D.R.' writes back to 'Scott,' as in letter #14, and the two 'characters' finally come/cum together in a phallic moment of 'psychic tumescence' at the end of the novel.[21]

Civic Square is thus partly structured as a nineteenth-century epistolary romance, a collection of love letters through which Symons gradually seduces us, his readers. Mostly, however, it is an extended rant, a litany of complaint. Writing in and of Toronto, his 'hometown,' and the city he has come to associate most with the 'Blandmind' mentality stifling English Canada, Symons is, for the first time, unable to offer any redemptive vision at the end of all his sermonizing. There is no Morocco or Quebec to supply the necessary ecstatic alternative. Compared to Montreal's Place d'Armes, and Marrakech's Djema-El-Fna, Toronto's Nathan Phillips Square is cold and passionless, its new city hall oppressively ugly and virtually panoptical in design. Again, like Anderson before him, Symons is here confronting that quintessentially Canadian paradox of inside and outside. Accustomed to his role as intrepid outsider, travelling to new lands and cultures in search of an exportable identity, Symons finds himself, once back inside the heart of English Canada, incapable of importing difference.

* * *

In *Haunted Journeys: Desire and Transgression in European Travel Writing*, Dennis Porter uses Freud's concept of the 'uncanny' or 'unhomely' (*Unheimlich*) to suggest that 'there is a sense in which our desire to leave a given home is at the same time the desire to recover an original lost home ... [T]here is a *déjà vu* of travel that is to be understood in part through the theory of the uncanny. The lands we pass through are haunted even if the ghosts do not always manifest themselves directly' (12). Of course, for Freud, the 'original lost home' is also the womb, a concept not without relevance to Anderson and Symons, both of whom had their own peculiar Oedipal fixations. In the final stanza of Anderson's 'Dear Son,' for example, the title character 'ride[s] the children's pony of his lust' within his mother's 'jolly tent' (*The Colour as Naked*, 27); for his part, Symons seems more intent on matricide in *Place d'Armes*, railing against Canada's 'New Mommy,' with her *vagina dentata*, 'eating all, everyone – thousands sacrificed to this new smotherlove' (155). Moreover, in *Helmet of Flesh*, York asserts that 'Gay world is Mommy's revenge, passed through Sonny-boy. Mommy's cunt-rule passed up dear Sonny's arse (eroticism of hate, from generation unto generation!)' (262). The irony here is that this 'eroticism of hate' is fully congruent with the 'virile nationalism' espoused by Sutherland and his successors in their critical attacks on Anderson, Symons's virulent misogyny the manifest sign of a deeply internalized homophobia. In both versions/visions of Canada, women are consistently left out of the picture, their sole apparent function to breed patriotic sons (who then eviscerate them in words, if not in deed), a point which will be investigated further at the beginning of chapter 5.

Immediately superseding the womb, then, is another home: the nation, an 'imagined community' capable of manifesting its own ghostly patterns of exile and return. As Charles Taylor puts it in *Six Journeys*, each of the subjects profiled in his book 'was forced into a life of loneliness and isolation. They felt compelled to escape their Canadian society, and to sharpen the edges of their identities in different forms of exile ... They journeyed into spiritual realms which modern Canada ignores or denigrates, yet none was an escapist: each was concerned to formulate a vision that would work in Canada, for Canadians' (v, vi). This is in keeping with Anderson's assertion in *Over the Alps* that the most successful traveller is the one who achieves 'that balance between inner and outer which suggests experience appropriated, a vision achieved' (32). Certainly his own 'desire not to lose faith with Canada' was repeatedly signalled by the inclusion of 'substantial pieces on [his] adopted homeland in every one of [his] early prose books' (Anderson, 'A Poet,' 10). Symons likewise admits to 'a nostalgia. For my land, and its people. I'm a romantic. A sin in this era of belated Canadian positivism' (*Place d'Armes*, 11).

But the sense of national longing that runs throughout so much 'travel writing' – including that of Anderson and Symons – is more often than not accompanied by an equally palpable element of sexual transgression, as Porter's study makes so abundantly clear, with its chapters on Flaubert, T.E. and D.H. Lawrence, Gide, Freud, and Barthes. This, too, is the subtext of Taylor's book, the foregrounded homosexuality in the concluding Symons chapter remaining the unspoken secret in the preceding two on Herbert Norman and Emily Carr. One can only speculate on how Canadian literary history – and, in particular, the narratives of Canadian modernism and postmodernism – might have been different, or differently written, had Anderson and Symons received a more sympathetic hearing from their contemporary critics. What the examples of Anderson and Symons do suggest is a somewhat different 'Canadian pattern' from the one proposed by Taylor, one whose every rewriting – in works by Colin McPhee (*A House in Bali*), Edward Lacey (*The Forms of Loss, Path of Snow*), John Glassco (*Memoirs of Montparnasse*), Stan Persky (*Then We Take Berlin*) – and rereading (in this chapter, for example) helps to reconceptualize 'the complex undercurrents of those fantasized geographies of male desire that depend on, even as they resist, the homoerotics of [a nationalist] discourse' (Boone, 104).

Of course, as the next chapter will attest, this 'pattern' – be it Taylor's or my own – is in many ways only applicable to English Canada. In Québécois literature and culture, where inside and outside frequently get reversed, and where the trope of exile is used repeatedly to designate Quebec's position *within* Canada (hence the political relevance of a slogan like 'Maîtres chez nous'), nationalist fantasies – at least as they have been represented on stage over the past two decades – seem to be far less resistant to homoerotic and homosexual encrypting. Much to the chagrin of someone like Hubert Aquin.

4

'Pour exprimer un problème d'identité': Michel Tremblay and His 'Bastard Sons'

Si je relève d'abord ... [le] sujet des variantes littéraires de l'homosexualité au Canada français, c'est que je reconnais ... une valeur sociologique. Aussi, ce déviationnisme sexuel me paraît l'explication la plus vraisemblable et la plus inavouable d'une littérature globalement faible, sans éclat et, pour tout dire, vraiment ennuyeuse ... Cette sorte d'inversion qui me paraît avoir contaminé sérieusement la presque totalité de notre littérature, n'est pas une inversion qui s'affiche ou qui cherche à scandaliser. Non, c'est une inversion profonde: donc, elle prend soin de se voiler elle-même par une thématique diversifiée ... Les catégories littéraires de l'inversion n'ont pas été systématiquement inventoriées jusqu'à ce jour, mais quelque chose me dit que ces catégories sont très nombreuses et contiennent une proportion majoritaire de stéréotypes qui, précisément, s'annoncent comme des cas de non-inversion. S'il est une situation humaine génératrice de dissimulation, c'est bien l'homosexualité.[1]

Hubert Aquin, 'Commentaire I,' 191

Je ne sais pas si j'ai beaucoup parlé d'homosexualité au théâtre! ... Les premières fois que j'ai utilisé des personnages homosexuels, c'était pour exprimer un problème d'identité. *La Duchesse* ... [et] *Hosanna* ne sont pas des pièces sur l'homosexualité. Non que je ne veuille pas en parler, mais je me servais d'eux pour d'autres raisons, pour leur volonté d'être quelqu'un d'autre, à l'image de notre société.[2]

Michel Tremblay, 'Il y a 20 ans,' 73

All right, it's confession time. Despite all my sophisticated theoretical posturing in the previous chapters, we now arrive at that point in the book where I must come out as a closet Canadian nationalist. I admit to voting 'yes' to the Charlottetown Accord in 1992, to being almost apoplectic with worry during the television coverage of the most recent (1995) Quebec referendum, pacing the apartment frantically, phoning my parents immediately after the narrow 'no' victory to verify that their house on the West Island of Montreal had not yet been torched by vengeance-seeking separatists. This is perhaps not the response one would expect from the typical British Columbian, whose dim view of Quebec-Ottawa political relations frequently betrays his or her own secessionist impulses (witness the furor over whether or not to recognize B.C. as a 'distinct' region worthy of its own constitutional veto). But then, unlike most residents of B.C. (the majority of whom would seem to me to be expatriates from Ontario), much of my youth and adolescence was inextricably bound up with the rise of the contemporary sovereigntist movement in Quebec.

My parents moved to Sherbrooke, Quebec, from New York City (my father, a Maritimer by birth, had a postdoc at Columbia) in 1975, a year before the unthinkable happened: René Lévesque's Parti Québécois won the provincial election. Je me souviens que/that while I was blissfully watching the precocious Romanian gymnast Nadia Comaneci win all her gold medals at the Montreal Summer Olympics, the Anglo exodus from la belle province – not to mention, the substitution of slogans on all motor vehicle licence plates – had already begun. Our family stayed put, however, at least for the time being. In 1977, in the middle of grade 3, we moved to Chateauguay, the part of Montreal's 'south shore' that is connected to the island by the infamous Mercier Bridge. (Chateauguay is also bordered by the Kahnawake – then Caughnawaga – Reserve, several of whose inhabitants would blockade the Mercier Bridge in sympathy with the Mohawk Warriors at Kanesatake in 1990.) We remained in Chateauguay for the next six years, long enough for my parents to be temporarily vindicated by the 'no' victory in the 1980 referendum on sovereignty-association, and for me to acquire the rudiments of official bilingualism through French immersion classes. Oh yes, and to fall in love with my best friend, who also happened to be named Peter (but that's another story entirely – or is it? – see Probyn, below).

In 1983 we were on the move again, this time to Ontario. Mississauga, to be precise, where I underwent an acculturation process so thorough that by the time I graduated high school I had lost most of my fluency in French. Just as I was about to begin my first year as an undergraduate at the University of Toronto, my parents moved back to the Montreal area, where they continue to reside. They are the only Anglos I know of who voluntarily headed back into the fray of Quebec separatist politics after making it to the apparent safe haven of life in the Toronto suburbs.

So there you have it: some of the reasons why my interest in competing Canadian and Québécois nationalisms is anything but academically dispassionate. The fact that my perapatetic parents live in Quebec, that so many of my friends and colleagues continue to make Montreal, in particular, their home, means that I have a personal stake – however small – in the future status of that province within the Canadian federation.

Nevertheless, when the occasion warrants it, I am not above taking a cold and calculated view of Quebec sovereignty, which, as I see it, is founded primarily on an antiquated and outmoded nineteenth-century concept of nationalism ill-suited to late-twentieth-century post-national globalism, what Michael Ignatieff, in a recent study, has referred to as 'blood and belonging.' Distinguishing between 'civic' and 'ethnic' nationalisms, Ignatieff notes that whereas the 'psychology of belonging' accompanying the former is based on a shared belief in certain political practices, government institutions, and legal rights, the definition of belonging attached to the latter maintains that what holds societies together is not common citizenship but common cultural roots, a common ethnic/racial/religious/linguistic heritage, in short, people 'of your own blood' (4–6). 'Belonging, on this account,' according to Ignatieff, 'is first and foremost protection from violence. Where you belong is where you are safe; and where you are safe is where you belong':

> To belong is to understand the tacit codes of the people you live with; it is to know that you will be understood without having to explain yourself. People, in short, 'speak your language.' This is why, incidentally, the protection and defence of a nation's language is such a deeply emotional nationalist cause, for it is language, more than land and history, which provides the essential form of belonging, which is to be understood. (6, 7)

The linguistic metaphor deployed in this passage is, I think, telling, especially in the context of Quebec nationalism, which, as the debates surrounding Bill 101 and French-only versus bilingual signs (Bill 178) have demonstrated, is repeatedly framed within a discourse of linguistic survival. Ignatieff's use of the term 'belonging' is, however, somewhat more problematic, in that he allows it to substitute for a general theory of national identity without at all taking into account how such an identity is articulated within and across multiple communities (of which the 'national' is but one); without, in other words, paying attention to what

Elspeth Probyn (following from Giorgio Agamben and others) has referred to as the local, the particular, the quotidian exigencies of 'being and longing' – be-longing in its 'so-what' singularity, its 'whatever' specificity (see *Love*, 45 and *passim*). In her monograph, *'Love in a Cold Climate': Queer Belongings in Quebec*, Probyn outlines a theory of belonging that returns the concept first of all to the body, that reconfigures community relations in terms of desire and power, and that encapsulates the tensions between a mode of individual existence ('being') and a fantasy of social interaction ('longing'): 'an ethical practice of belonging and a politics of singularity must start from where one is – brutally and immediately from one's belonging, modes of being and longing' (64). Above all else, according to Probyn, a queer, postcolonial, and feminist social theory of belonging must resist the compartmentalizing of different forms of community affiliation into different epistemological domains, and must instead consider the manifold ways in which identity categories like 'nationality and sexuality constantly rub against each other' (35). Writing as a Welsh lesbian academic who, at the time, was teaching sociologies of gender and sexuality at a francophone university in Montreal (she has since relocated to Australia), Probyn goes on to note that 'the sentiment that first moved me to write this essay was caught up in a lingering desire to experiment with, if not to prove, my belonging in Québec,' and 'to think through the particular piquance of sexuality and nationality that constitutes Québécois expressions of identity' (26, 27).

To be sure, Probyn, like Ignatieff, does not wish to separate the concept of belonging (both national and sexual) from its frequent associations with violence:

> [T]o speak of these images [of belonging] in terms of their 'so-what' singularity is not to condone their violence; it is not to be blasé in the face of the terror that they may bring. Rather, in refusing equivalence, it is to be moved, to be touched by the impact of this image, and this one, and this one. It is to be bodily caught up in ways of being a being-such, a being shorn of the trammels of identity as individual possession ... [I]t is to argue that [these images of belonging] seek to reproduce relations of a general order, the order of the same. As they graft certain relations of gender and sexuality they participate in the reproduction of the homosocial relations, of the nation as normal. (65)

Nowhere was the potential for violence in images of national belonging more evident than in the normalizing discourses of same-ness 'reproduced' during the course and aftermath of the 1995 referendum campaign, with Lucien Bouchard lamenting Quebec's comparatively low birth-rate among 'les races blanches,' and Jacques Parizeau's recriminations about 'les votes ethniques.'

For 'les gens de souche' and 'les Québécois pure laine,' psychic identification with the aspirations of political autonomy is thus perhaps best defined (in a reversal of Julia Kristeva) as 'nationalisms without nations.' Or to put this another way, Québécois nationalism, which is, as I have already indicated, essentially a linguistic nationalism (albeit one that can play the race card when it has to), has, since the Quiet Revolution of the 1960s, been, above all else, an attempt to reconcile the frequently divergent interests of 'nation' and 'state,' where the former is defined as 'a people' with a language, history, and tradition of their own and the latter as the 'institutional apparatus' of self-government. As Ignatieff puts it, 'francophone Quebecois identify Quebec as their nation, and Canada as their state, while English-speaking Canadians identify Canada both as their nation and as their state ... Quebec has never needed Canada as a nation. Now it is asking itself whether it even needs it as a state' (112). For Charles Taylor, Quebec sovereignty is most fundamentally a political desire to establish a link between nation and state in order to guarantee institutional control over the expression of the French language that is deemed intrinsic to Quebec national identity (see 'Why Do Nations Have to Become States?' 40–58).[3] The irony, of course, is that in the wake of the 1995 referendum on Quebec sovereignty, the rest of the Canadian provinces have caught up with Quebec in demanding a devolution of state control at the federal level in regional (i.e., provincial versus national) affairs, a mantra even Jean Charest has learned to take up in making the leap from the leadership of the federal Conservative party to that of the provincial Liberals in Quebec. Moreover, as support for a possible post-partition partition of Quebec grows within the province's non-francophone communities, the question may no longer be one of reconciling *nation* and state, but rather – in a return to Machiavelli's Renaissance Italy – *city* and state. This is especially the case in Montreal, Quebec's most 'cosmopolitan' and ethnically mixed metropolis, the overwhelming majority of whose population voted 'no' in the last referendum.

The comments by Bouchard and Parizeau point to the fact that Quebec nationalism's relationship with race and ethnicity is, to say the least, agonistic and historically complex (let's not forget Esther Delisle's and Mordecai Richler's separate exposés of the long legacy of anti-

Semitism in the province, made all the more bizarre by the Hassidic community's endorsement of Parizeau and the 'yes' campaign during the last referendum, and recently brought to the surface again with the furor over Lieutenant-Governor Jean-Louis Roux's swastika-wearing university days; and let's not forget either the constant effacement in the sovereigntist rhetoric of self-determination of similar struggles within the province's Indigenous communities, particularly the Northern Cree nation, which held its own referendum prior to Quebec's, and the Mohawk nation, which demonstrated just how far it would go in defending its land claims at Oka/Kanesatake in 1990).[4] Moreover, as Bouchard's comments further attest, Quebec nationalism's relationship with gender is still thoroughly inflected by the misogyny of the Catholic Church (the so-called 'revenge of the cradle' ideology).[5] It should come as no surprise, then, that Quebec nationalism's relationship with sexuality, and particularly *homo*sexuality, in many ways reflects an even more profound displacement of contemporary social anxieties within the province.

As my first epigraph from Aquin demonstrates, in the nationalist rhetoric of Québécois cultural criticism, homosexuality has frequently been characterized as the 'enemy within,' chief among a discursive taxonomy of 'categories of inversion,' a nefarious process of identitary dissimulation capable of 'contaminating,' for example, almost all of Quebec literature (see Schwartzwald, 'Fear of Federasty,' 186–7). At the same time, the second epigraph from Tremblay, no less a Quebec nationalist than Aquin, confirms that homosexuality has likewise been subject to repeated 'metaphorical, sometimes allegorical, often sentimentalized conscription [as a trope of decolonization] in Quebec popular culture' (Schwartzwald, '"Symbolic" Homosexuality,' 265). Robert Schwartzwald, whose work I have been following here, has, in a series of related essays, shown how thoroughly imbricated are the discourses of nationalism and homosexuality in Québécois cultural production. In one of his more recent articles on the subject, for example, Schwartzwald analyses the work of three contemporary Québécois social theorists – Jacques Lavigne, Gilles Thérien, and Jean Larose – in order to determine why 'the homophobic elements of [Quebec's] *learned* discourse on identity are largely inconsistent with both liberal legal discourse and popular attitudes' of tolerance of homosexuality in the province, and to assess what exactly such a situation can 'elucidate about discursive engagements between subject positions articulated around nationhood, on the one hand, and sexualities, on the other' ('"Symbolic" Homosexuality,' 266). Using Schwartzwald as my principal theoretical guide, in the remainder of this chapter I will be drawing upon the work of three contemporary Québécois dramatists – Michel Tremblay, René-Daniel Dubois, and Michel Marc Bouchard – in order to explore similar 'discursive engagements' between nationalism and sexuality in the production and reception of their plays, both inside and outside the province. The problem faced by each playwright is essentially the same: how to affirm a gay identity that is at once part of and separate from a cultural narrative of nationalist over-determination. How each playwright tackles this problem is another matter entirely.

* * *

In 1965 a precocious twenty-three-year-old writer from Montreal's east end began work on a play about fifteen married and single women, ranging in age from mid-teens to ninety-three, who gather together in the kitchen of Germaine Lauzon on the rue Fabre sometime during the post-Duplessis 1960s in order to help paste into books the one million trading stamps won by their hostess. Produced for the first time three years later at Montreal's Théâtre du Rideau-Vert, Michel Tremblay's *Les Belles-Soeurs* was an instant success, changing forever the face of drama in Quebec. In place of polite interpretations of the French classics, here was a rare example of an indigenous *Québécois* play: set amid the working-class district of francophone Montreal, focusing on the squalid and marginalized existence of the people who lived there, and, what's more, written entirely in their language – *joual* – a hybridized form of subcultural communication combining French and anglicized slang that frequently defies adequate translation. Not since Gratien Gélinas's *Tit-coq* premiered twenty years earlier had anything quite like it been seen on stage in Quebec; critics and theatre-goers alike immediately interpreted the play as a political statement.

Over the course of the next decade, Tremblay would write eleven more plays for stage and television, each of them set in the same social and geographical milieu of Montreal, each of them focusing on what the playwright himself has referred to as the 'fringes of society' (working-class women, gay men, prostitutes), each of them interpreted, at some level, as a national allegory about Quebec. With the production and publication of *Damnée Manon, sacrée Sandra* in 1977, and with his return from Paris after the PQ election victory, Tremblay declared that his '*premier cycle*' was now complete, and that he was temporarily withdrawing from writing for the theatre: 'I have written twelve Québécois plays. These plays constitute a saga or cycle: "The Saga of Les Belles-Soeurs" ... Having talked in my plays about the family and politics, about the fringes of society, about sex and religion, I have nothing more to say at the present time in drama' (*Stage Voices*, 285).[6] Of course, in just three short years, Tremblay would once again return to the theatre, writing *L'Impromptu d'Outremont*, which, as its title suggests, marked a notable change in setting for Tremblay's plays, reflecting perhaps the author's own upward move from the working-class Plateau Mont-Royal area of Montreal to the much tonier Outremont.

If Tremblay's plays, and those making up his 'premier cycle' in particular, are repeatedly read as allegories or fables of Quebec's colonized identity, this has much to do with their author's own widely disseminated and oft-quoted interpretations of them: 'If I choose to talk about the fringes of society it is because my people are a fringe society. We are six million French-speaking people in a North America of three hundred million people. So we form a fringe of society. And in this fringe of society in which I was raised I decided to make my point' (*Stage Voices*, 283). This view of the fringes of society would seem to extend to Tremblay's homosexual and transvestite characters as well, as evidenced by my second epigraph. As early as 1971, even before the first production of *Hosanna*, Tremblay maintained that although his plays featured 'gay' characters, they must not be seen as purely and simply 'gay theatre,' that his use of transvestism – or, more appropriately, *le travestissement*, which signifies not only cross-dressing, but also a more general sense of misrepresentation or disguise – as a symbol or metaphor encompassed national as well as sexual meanings: 'On est un peuple qui s'est déguisé pendant des années pour ressembler à un autre peuple ... On a été travestis pendant 300 ans' ('Entrevue avec Michel Tremblay,' 64; 'We are a people that has disguised itself over the years in order to resemble another people ... We have been in drag for 300 years').[7]

This is certainly in keeping with Marjorie Garber's view, discussed at the end of chapter 2, that the transvestite is a figure of 'category crisis,' a figure upon whom 'crises of nationalism and sexuality [are] troped' (239). And this is certainly in keeping with the by now standard interpretation of Tremblay's most famous transvestite character, 'Claude,' the hairdresser from Plaza St-Hubert / 'Hosanna,' the celebrated drag queen of 'La Main.' Again I quote from the playwright himself:

> Hosanna is a man who always wanted to be a woman. This woman always wanted to be Elizabeth Taylor in *Cleopatra*. In other words this Québécois always wanted to be a woman who always wanted to be an English actress in

> an American movie about an Egyptian myth in a movie shot in Spain. In a way, that is a typically Québécois problem. For the past 300 years we were not taught that we were a people, so we were dreaming about somebody else instead of ourselves. So *Hosanna* is a political play. (*Stage Voices*, 283)

Claude finally gets his chance to live out his dream of becoming 'Elizabeth Taylor in *Cleopatra*' when he learns that the theme of this year's annual Halloween drag ball will be 'great women of history.' But for Hosanna the dream turns into a nightmare when she discovers that she has been the butt of a cruel joke, arranged by a rival queen we never see, Sandra (who would eventually be given her own moment in the spotlight in *Damnée Manon, sacrée Sandra*), with the aid of Hosanna's own lover, Raymond/Cuirette: 'Hosanna v'nait de faire son entrée dans Rome, pis tout le monde était habillé comme elle! En plus beau!' (71; 'Hosanna had made her entrance into Rome, and everyone was dressed like her! Only better!' [95]).[8] In Tremblay's play, which is set in the hours immediately following Hosanna's humiliation, this scene occurs off-stage and is only related to the audience in flashback during a long and protracted monologue by Hosanna that takes up most of the second act. At the end of this monologue, Cuirette returns to the apartment, having fled Hosanna's recriminations about his part in her disgrace at the end of act 1. It is now his turn to rage and fulminate on stage, except that his anger, unlike Hosanna's, is not directed towards members of his own subcultural community, but rather towards those who police that community, specifically those 'pigs' who have put up searchlights in Parc Lafontaine, one of Cuirette's favourite spots for late-night cruising: 'On va vous faire ça dans'face, hostie! ... Ça fait qu'on va toutes faire ça ensemble, en pleine lumière, les culottes baissées, au beau milieu du terrain de baseball, sacrement!' (68–9; 'From now on we're gonna do it in public, goddamn it! ... So why don't we do it together, eh? We'll all get under the lights, drop our pants, and go to it right in the middle of the fuckin' baseball field!' [91]). Cuirette's defiant call to arms, 'his refusal to seek new shadows and relegate his desire to the realm of the hidden[,] sets the stage for Hosanna's own moment of enlightenment' (Schwartzwald, 'From Authenticity to Ambivalence,' 499). Having dispensed with the various accoutrements of her Cleopatra costume throughout the course of the play, Hosanna must now take the final, necessary step: she sits down at her vanity table, removes her wig and make-up, looks at herself in the mirror, and announces that 'Cléopâtre est morte, pis le Parc Lafontaine est toute illuminé!' (75; 'Cleopatra is dead, and the Parc Lafontaine is all lit up!' [102]). Then the newly revealed Claude gets up, takes off his underwear, and confronts his lover (and the audience) with his naked self: 'R'garde, Raymond, chus t'un homme! Chus t'un homme, Raymond! Chus t'un homme! Chus t'un homme! Chus t'un homme ... ' (75; 'Look, Raymond, I'm a man ... I'm a man, Raymond ... I'm a man. I'm a man ... I'm a man ...' [102]).

According to Tremblay, 'although *Hosanna* concerns two homosexuals ... it is really an allegory about Quebec. In the end they drop their poses and embrace their real identity ... [W]hen Hosanna kills Elizabeth Taylor and ... appears naked on stage and says he is a man[,] [s/he] kills all the ghosts around him as Quebec did' (*Stage Voices*, 284). And, indeed, this would seem to accord with most of the reviews by Montreal's francophone press of the original 1973 Théâtre de Quat'Sous production. Writing in *Le Devoir* soon after the play's opening, Albert Brie maintained that although 'Tremblay a écrit une pièce ayant pour thème l'homosexualité ... [n]ous autres, normaux, avons intérêt à voir "Hosanna"' (10; 'Tremblay wrote a play with homosexuality as its theme ... those of us who are normal would be advised to see "Hosanna"'). He then goes on to note that Tremblay and André Brassard, the play's director, 'nous invitent plutôt à réfléchir sur ce qui est un fait de la vie sociale et individuelle ... "Hosanna" n'aura peut-être pas le succès de scandale que certains prévoyaient mais restera un moment précieux dans l'évolution de la dramaturgie québécoise' (10; 'invite us instead to reflect on what is both a social and individual fact of life ... "Hosanna" may not be the scandalous success that some had predicted but will remain a precious moment in the evolution of Québécois drama'). And, in reviewing *Hosanna* in the French edition of *Maclean's* magazine later that fall, Jean-Claude Germain concluded axiomatically that 'le théâtre québécois est un théâtre politique' (52; 'Québécois theatre is a political theatre'). Moreover, literary criticism emanating from the Quebec academy has also tended to canonize the reading of the end of Tremblay's play as a quest for national authenticity. In an article included in the encyclopaedic volume *Le Théâtre canadien-français*, Jacques Cotnam echoes the author himself when he asserts that, with *Hosanna* and the other plays comprising the 'Belles-Soeurs cycle,' Tremblay 'est en train de créer une dramaturgie nationale authentique, qui reflète les frustrations accumulées depuis trois cents ans et la révolte qu'elles ont finalement provoquée' (367; 'is in the midst of creating an authentic national drama, [one] that reflects the frustrations accumulated over three hundred years and the revolt that they finally provoked'). As for Jean-Cléo Godin and Laurent Mailhot's reading of the ending of the play in their *Théâtre québécois II: Nouveaux auteurs, autres spectacles,* they maintain: 'C'est le *travesti* qui est en cause, le mensonge de l'identité d'emprunt. Le double travesti d'Hosanna, imitant Elizabeth Taylor en Cléopatre, montre admirablement cette absurde situation ... L'intérêt de cette pièce vient justement de ce que Hosanna, reconnaissant l'illusion, la brise' (178; 'It's the *transvestism* that is of concern here, the lie of a borrowed identity. The double transvestism of Hosanna, imitating Elizabeth Taylor in Cleopatra, admirably illustrates this absurd situation ... The interest of this play comes when Hosanna, recognizing the illusion, breaks it').

And yet, despite this critical consensus from within Quebec, indeed, despite the author's own repeated assertions (and here it is worthwhile pointing out that Tremblay's account of his play in *Stage Voices,* from which I have been quoting extensively, was first printed *in English,* and aimed primarily at an *English-speaking audience outside Quebec*), 'English speakers [outside the province] seem to have been almost invariably incapable of understanding the play's political content' (Martin, 'Gender, Race, and the Colonial Body,' 96). As Tremblay himself has put it, with ironic understatement, '*Hosanna* signifie au Canada anglais tout à fait autre chose' ('Michel Tremblay: Du texte à la représentation,' 214; '*Hosanna* signifies for English Canada something else entirely'). Make no mistake, however: this has less to do with any prevailing post-structuralist 'death of the author' critical methodology than with a trans*national* failure in trans*lation* of Hosanna's trans*culturation,* a refusal on the part of most anglophone critics and viewers to make the necessary link between national and sexual self-determination. As Jane Koustas has put it, while Toronto 'enthusiastically recognized the merits' of the first English-language production of John Van Burek and Bill Glassco's translation of Tremblay's play at the Tarragon Theatre in May 1974, 'it was also quick to claim Tremblay as its own at the expense of his theater's political drive and *québécitude*' ('From "Homespun" to "Awesome,"' 91).[9] Reviewing this production for the *Globe and Mail,* reporter Herbert Whittaker called the labelling of *Hosanna* 'a Quebec play' 'naive.' For Whittaker, the play had universal applications: 'Tremblay is not spending all this time on a mere homosexual anecdote. He is writing about a love affair turned sour, of the fading satisfactions of advancing age' (15). David McCaughna, commenting on *Hosanna* in the glossy Toronto arts magazine *Motion,* claimed that although Tremblay is 'a very political writer and all of his plays have dealt in one way or another with the condition of Quebec society,' 'it does not hit home that this is a play which has a great deal to say about the state of

Quebec' (48). As for the play's debut later that fall on Broadway, let us just say that *Hosanna* succeeded brilliantly in confounding New York's jaded theatre critics. Witness, for example, the following remarks made by Clive Barnes in the *New York Times*: 'It appears that [Tremblay's] play has a political purpose in trying to teach Quebec to be its own country ... The political symbolism is more well-meaning than meaningful. I doubt whether it will do much to raise Quebec's level of national consciousness, but the play itself is far from being without interest' (46).

Moreover, once again these reviews from the popular press would appear to be completely coextensive with academic criticism from English Canada. Renate Usmiani, in her 1982 book-length study of Tremblay, insists that '*Hosanna* will doubtless survive its political uses because its psychological and philosophical themes have universal implications' (96). To this end, she claims that 'on the level of psychological analysis,' *Hosanna* 'offers a gripping insight into the complex workings of a lovers' relationship, in which the fact that both happen to be male becomes irrelevant' (89). This reading of *Hosanna* as a play whose characters move from 'alienation' towards 'transcendence' is echoed, in much more homophobic tones, by John Ripley: 'Claude and Raymond are social deviants and will always be so; but marginality, they come to realize, need not imply alienation. Their recipe for relatedness requires as its key ingredient acceptance of, and respect for, one's own individuality' (53).

Pitted against each other, and occasionally playing off one another, for the past twenty years or so, these two dominant sets of readings of *Hosanna* – political allegory inside Quebec versus psychological drama outside – have ensured the play an almost mythical status in debates surrounding Québécois cultural production and English-Canadian cultural reception. However, what both sets of readings fail to take into account is the ultimately unfinalizable quality of Tremblay's text, its undecidability as a vehicle 'pour exprimer un problème d'identité,' either nationally or sexually. According to Yves Jubinville, in the 'transvestic space' of *Hosanna*, 'un paradoxe saute aux yeux ... à l'endroit des discours identitaires gai et nationaliste: en fondant l'identité (collective ou individuelle) sur l'affirmation d'une différence, force est d'admettre qu'on ne fait là que reconduire l'impératif de ressemblance' (116; 'a paradox jumps out at you ... in the intersection of gay and nationalist discourses of identity: in basing identity [collective or individual] on the affirmation of a difference, we are forced to admit that all we are doing is renewing the imperative of sameness'). This paradox of 'difference as sameness' was vividly enacted in a recent remounting of the play by Théâtre de Quat'Sous in

1991. Summarizing the many changes to the original script in this latest production, Schwartzwald writes that 'Hosanna removes neither her make-up nor her briefs in the closing moments, and her final line – "Chus t'un homme" – resembles less an affirmation than an interrogation charged with ambivalence' ('From Authenticity to Ambivalence,' 501). As Schwartzwald goes on to note, this new ending 'shifts the focus of the play's preoccupations with questions of identity away from sexuality [and, I would add, nationality] toward those of gender roles' (502). In this regard, it is significant, as Robert K. Martin points out, that this new production was directed by a woman, Lorraine Pintal (see Martin, 'Gender, Race, and the Colonial Body,' 95–7).[10] In her program notes, Pintal asks the audience to consider the multiplicity of identities that the play evokes, stressing that 'c'est pas clair d'être un homme ou une femme aujourd'hui, en 1991' (quoted in Schwartzwald, 'From Authenticity,' 508n; 'it's not clear what it means to be a man or a woman today, in 1991').

Seeking to account for a similar structural 'asymmetry' between masculine and feminine gender roles in Québécois literature, Patricia Smart, like Eve Sedgwick, develops a triangular model based on the 'exchange of women.' This she labels the 'patriarchal' or 'Oedipal' triangle, 'with the figures of the father, the son or suitor, and the woman-object constituting its three points' (*Writing*, 15). According to Smart, the woman writer must 'explode' this symbolic paradigm in order to acquire a subject position within literary discourse; the male writer, on the other hand, is quite capable of – and comfortable – working within it, rebelling against the castrating mother as a prelude to his displacement of the father at the head of the household. As Smart goes on to point out (190–203), this project of 'self-virilization' achieves its apogee in the revolutionary-nationalist texts of the 1960s, in which images of violence against women (rape, murder, mutilation) proliferate. As we have seen, with my brief discussion of *Trou de mémoire* in chapter 1, paradigmatic in this regard is the work of Hubert Aquin. While Tremblay, the gay playwright, 'clearly does not participate in the ritual violence that Smart shows is central to the nationalist novel,' Tremblay, the sovereigntist playwright, is nevertheless 'caught up in an equation that links masculinity with nationhood' (Martin, 'Gender,' 96). Commenting in a 1971 interview on the parodying of gender roles and the linguistic ventriloquism in *La Duchesse de Langeais*, the playwright emphasizes that 'comme on n'a pas d'homme au Québec, j'ai voulu faire le prototype de l'homme-femme, c'est à dire un homosexuel qui représente l'homme et la femme' ('Entrevue avec Michel

Tremblay,' 75; 'since we have no men in Quebec, I wanted to create the prototype of a man-woman, that is, a homosexual who represents both man and woman'). The Duchess and, subsequently, Hosanna, in their respective imitations of Hollywood icons, have since become Tremblay's 'man-woman prototypes.'[11] And if, according to Tremblay's dramaturgical logic, the feminine side of each character is associated with subservience to the colonial regime, then their acquisition of a 'true' national identity can only be achieved through a strong, forceful, and, above all, *physical* declaration of masculinity. Hence the unmasking and disrobing in the original script of *Hosanna* to the closing refrain of 'Chus t'un homme.' In this regard, the 'climax' of Tremblay's play is in keeping with the prevailing clinical (Lavigne), cultural (Larose), and semiotic (Thérien) view in Quebec – once again as summarized by Schwartzwald – of homosexuality and femininity as psychosocial phases of 'arrested development,' the one merely 'symbolic,' the other 'false,' a simultaneously homophobic and misogynist 'diagnosis' used to 'explicate the indentitary impasse of the Québécois subject-nation' ('"Symbolic" Homosexuality,' 267). The irony in the case of Tremblay, the gay dramatist of Quebec's marginalized fringes, is that this 'conviction that a "phallic deficiency" impedes the satisfactory resolution of the national question may dissimulate another, preconscious desire that the national question be resolved as a *precondition* to the "disappearance" of the problem of deviant sexualities' ('"Symbolic" Homosexuality,' 288; my emphasis), a point to which I shall return at the end of this chapter.

Pintal's updated production, in attempting to subvert the metaphorical equivalency of the colonized body as the feminized body and, concomitantly, the decolonized/national body as the masculinized body, thus has Hosanna remain in drag, an ambiguous representative, again to use Garber's terms, of 'gender undecidability' and 'category crisis.' In this scenario, Hosanna's necessarily ambivalent assertion of identity at the end of the play thus succeeds at once in sundering the masculinist/nationalist conflation and diverting our gaze to the other (nationally and sexually) cross-dressed character in the play, Cuirette.[12] In other words, turned into an open-ended interrogative, 'Chus t'un homme?' can be read as 'If I'm a man, what are you?' Moreover, as Jubinville has remarked, it is important to keep in mind here that inasmuch as Hosanna's final lines can be taken as a definitive statement of identity, Cuirette's final look ('R'garde Raymond'), the affirmation/negation of his/her self-same other, immediately calls into question the stability of this identity. For Jubinville, such contradictions are part of the expressive richness of Tremblay's text, and help explain the creative differences between André Brassard's original staging of the play and Lorraine Pintal's 1991 version. In the end, he maintains, the critical distance mapped in the almost two decades between the two productions reflects nothing less than a radical resituating of 'the problem of identity' itself:

> La première [mise en scène], d'inspiration moderniste, rallait émancipations homosexuelle et nationale autour de l'idée d'une identité retrouvée au terme d'un dur combat. Y triomphait cette liturgie de la libération, alors en vogue, qui n'allait pas sans un certain lyrisme et des accents utopiques. En 1990 [*sic*], soit près de vingt ans plus tard, la pièce donnera lieu à une réflexion sur la fragilité de l'identité à l'heure de la 'fin des utopies.' Là, point de *happy end*: l'affirmation de soi à l'heure de la postmodernité n'est jamais qu'un ouvrage inachevé. Quelle est la meilleure lecture? Au terme de cette réflexion, il faut sans doute les choisir toutes deux (quitte à dire qu'elles sont nécessairement partielles!), parce que la pièce travaille elle-même sur ces deux tableaux. (123)[13]

* * *

According to Pierre Lavoie, Michel Tremblay is 'le premier, sinon l'un des premiers, à avoir abordé le thème de l'homosexualité au théâtre [québécois]' ('Il y a 20 ans,' 73; 'the first, or one of the first, to have broached the topic of homosexuality in [Québécois] theatre'). As such, he has necessarily influenced a whole generation of gay male playwrights in Quebec who came of age – and came out – in the politically volatile 1970s, people like Normand Chaurette, Robert Lepage, René-Daniel Dubois, and Michel Marc Bouchard, each in his own way a 'fils illégitime de Tremblay' (see Dubois, 'Vivre de sa plume,' 11; 'bastard son of Tremblay'). While an analysis of the 'uses' of homosexuality in Chaurette's *Provincetown Playhouse, juillet 1919, j'avais 19 ans* (1982) or Lepage and Marie Brassard's *Le Polygraphe* (1988) would likely yield interesting results *vis-à-vis* a discussion of 'problems' in Québécois identity, in the remaining pages of this chapter I have nevertheless chosen to focus on Dubois's *Being at home with Claude* (1985) and Bouchard's *Les Feluettes* (1987), two plays that, like *Hosanna*, explore issues of (homo)sexuality and nationalism, but in much different ways, and with much different effects.[14]

I have made this decision for a number of reasons, not the least of which is the overwhelming critical success these two writers have achieved in Quebec during the past decade. In 1983 Dubois, was named, by a jury of his theatrical peers, 'Grand Montréalais dans le domaine du théâtre,' and in 1985 his play *Ne blâmez jamais les Bédouins* won the Governor General's Award for French-language drama. Bouchard has twice been nominated for the same award (in 1986 for *La Poupée de Pélopia* and in 1990 for *Les Muses orphelines*); in 1988 he won both the Grand prix littéraire du Journal de Montréal and the Prix du Cercle des critiques de l'Outaouais for *Les Feluettes*, repeating this double coup two years later for *Les Muses orphelines.* This success has also 'translated' somewhat into the rest of Canada, making *Being at Home* and *Lilies* (to use the English title of Bouchard's text) two of the more popular Québécois plays to be seen by English audiences in recent memory, and thus making a comparison of French and English reviews – as was done with *Hosanna* – somewhat easier. Finally, as playwrights, Dubois and Bouchard share many dramaturgical affinities with their celebrated predecessor, Tremblay. Like Tremblay, they both make frequent use of transvestism on stage: for Dubois, most notably in *Ne blâmez jamais les Bédouins* and *26bis, impasse du Colonel Foisy*; for Bouchard, repeatedly in *La Contre-nature de Chrysippe Tanguay, écologiste, Les Muses orphelines,* and, of course, *Les Feluettes.* Dubois has also experimented, in *Being at home,* with the use of *joual.* And just as Tremblay developed over a number of years his 'Belles-Soeurs' cycle of interconnected east-end Montreal psychodramas, so is Bouchard in the midst of putting together an equally impressive cycle of plays based on the fictional Tanguay family of the Lac Saint-Jean region of Quebec (the cycle is currently composed of four plays: *Dans les bras de Morphée Tanguay, La Contre-nature de Chrysippe Tanguay, écologiste, La Poupée de Pélopia,* and *Les Muses orphelines*).

The very title *Being at home with Claude* echoes the trials of 'gay domesticity' documented in *Hosanna,* at the same time as its inscription in English throws the 'nationalist' message of Tremblay's play into ironic relief. For what Dubois's play reveals, in my mind, is nothing less than an alternate ending to *Hosanna,* in which the reconciliation of counterpointed (national, sexual, masculine, feminine, etc.) identities, the resolution of difference into sameness, is replaced by an 'act of passion' which is, in fact, the negation of identity itself, the 'murder' of sameness: 'Mais mon frère, lui, mon semblable, mon reflet, lui oui, j'y ai fermé les yeux. Pis y est mort de plaisir. Sans jamais avoir eu à passer ses journées dans marde' (110; 'But him, my brother, my twin, my reflection, him, yes, I closed his eyes. And he died of pleasure. Without seeing his life go to ratshit' [432]). Inasmuch as this act contains within it an echo of Baudelaire's address to the reader at the beginning of *Fleurs du mal* – 'Hypocrite lecteur, – mon semblable, – mon frère!' – Dubois seems to be offering to unburden his theatre-going public of its sympathetically (hypocritically?) mis-/dis-placed identifications as well. Here the intertext is perhaps not so much Tremblay as it is Aquin, and specifically the Aquin of *Neige noire*, the murderous plot of which is not without certain Baudelairean resonances in its doubling, or 'twinning,' of characters and in its attempts to 'déconcerter en quelque sorte le spectateur' (157; 'disconcert the viewer to some extent' [*Hamlet's Twin*, 128]) – the 'viewer' who, in Aquin's script, is perforce also the reader.

Dubois's play, which, like *Hosanna* twelve years earlier, opened at the Théâtre de Quat'Sous in November 1985, has a simple enough plot: 'Him,' a young male hustler, having killed his lover, Claude, while making love to him, has now, three days later, called the police and confessed. He has also called a local newspaper and barricaded himself in the office of a prominent Montreal judge (who also happens to be one of his regular johns), presumably as possible leverage to buy his way out of an almost certain murder conviction. As with the drag ball in *Hosanna*, all of this action has occurred off-stage, and when the curtain goes up on *Being at home* we are already *in medias res*. In the wee hours of the morning, with the judge on his way, and with reporters and photographers waiting outside the door for an exclusive scoop, a harried and impatient police inspector is busy interrogating the suspect, going over the facts again and again, trying to piece together the story, as well as come up with a motive for the crime. The hustler, who is only identified by name – Yves – midway through the play, is not being deliberately coy or antagonistic in witholding information; he simply cannot understand what more the 'Inspector' and his fellow police officers (in particular, the 'Stenographer,' who sits quietly on stage for most of the play, transcribing the dialogue) need to know: 'Pourquoi vous voulez absolument mett' tou'es morceaux ensemble? Y'a quelqu'un qui est mort. Ça doit vous prend' un coupab'? Vous l'avez. Qu'est-cé qu'y vous faut d'pluss?' (72; 'Why do you insist on puttin' all the pieces together? Somebody was killed. It's your job to find the murderer? You got him. What more do you want?' [415]). Nevertheless, he attempts to fill in some of the pieces of the puzzle for the Inspector (and the audience) in an extraordinary closing monologue that comprises the final twenty minutes of the play. Once again the similarities with Tremblay become strikingly apparent.

What may be somewhat less clear, however, is how Dubois's 'gay play' also encompasses 'national themes.' The first clue to this equally complex puzzle, I would argue, can be found in the setting of *Being at home*. In the second of his 'notes' to the published text, Dubois states that 'au moment où la pièce commence, le 5 juillet 1967 à 10h30, l'interrogatoire dure depuis le matin du 4 juillet à 1h, sans interruption' (14; 'at the moment where the play begins, at 10:30 in the morning on 5 July 1967, the interrogation has been going on since 1:00 o'clock in the morning of 4 July, without interruption' [392]). Very shortly after the start of the play, we are further informed by the Inspector that 'l'autopsie dit qu'y [Claude] est mort le premier juillet ent' neuf heures pis onze heures' (37; 'the autopsy shows [Claude] died between 9 and 11, July 1st' [400]). Moreover, the Inspector goes on to reveal that Claude was a 'card-carrying separatist' (403), a 'membre du R.I.N. [Rassemblement pour l'Indépendance Nationale]' (42). The significance of these details, together with the fact that Him/Yves carries out his 'crime of passion' 'pendant la fin d'semaine d'la fête d'la Confédération, avec un quart de million de touristes en ville pour l'Expo [67]' (39; 'during Confederation Day long weekend, with a quarter of a million tourists in town for Expo [67]' [402]), that after having committed the murder he picks up an American surfer while working 'Dominion Square' (87–9; 422), and that he eventually ends up sitting on a fence in the wealthy Anglo enclave of Westmount looking at grand houses similar to the one his grandparents owned before 'ils ont perdu leur fortune' (28; 'they lost all their money' [397]), cannot, it seems to me, be underestimated. On Canada's one-hundreth birthday, in the middle of an international world's fair, a young Québécois hustler, who sells his body to visiting American tourists, kills his separatist boyfriend: surely the confluence of discourses of nationalism and sexuality is more than merely coincidental here.

But where exactly do Yves's – and, by extension, Dubois's (see below) – nationalist sympathies lie in this scenario? Or, perhaps more importantly, what precisely is the gestural significance of Yves's 'shocking' crime? For if Hosanna's divestiture and affirmation of his manhood in front of Cuirette at the end of Tremblay's play is an attempt to fuse national with sexual self-determination, then surely Yves's cutting of Claude's throat while fucking him attests to the impossibility of this emancipatory project. In the course of his closing monologue, Yves discloses that in the over four months they had known each other neither he nor Claude had bothered introducing the other to their respective circles of friends. Yves's reasoning for this is that he never thought the relationship would last. As for Claude, 'y avait pas envie de mélanger les affaires qui vont pas ensemble' (103; 'he didn't feel like mixin' up things that didn't go together' [429]): that is, the 'national' and the 'sexual' were meant to be kept apart. When, however, in the middle of their final dinner together, some separatist friends of Claude phone up in order to get him to 'aller à l'Expo crier chou pendant l'feu d'artifice' (101; 'go to Expo and boo during the Confederation Day fireworks' [428]), he is forced to make a choice. Apparently the Expo disruption had all been arranged in advance through Claude's girlfriend but 'y a changé d'idée en cours de route' (102; 'he changed his mind somewhere along the way' [428]). As Yves desperately tries to explain to the sceptical Inspector,

> ... pour la première fois, c'est pas le rêve que ses chums représentaient pour lui qui a été le plus fort, mais celui qu'je r'présentais, moi. Plutôt que d'embarquer su l'aut' terrain, pendant qy'y parlait au téléphone, y est resté avec moi. J'dis pas dans la cuisine, c'est sûr que c'est là qu'y était, c'est là qu'est l'téléphone. J'veux dire avec moi dans sa tête. Ça fait que y a pas eu à r'venir, comme un étranger, les aut' fois, pis à se réhabituer à moi. C'est l'contraire qui est arrivé. Il leur a parlé dans le même état qu'y était avec moi. Y leur a dit qu'y avait queuqu' chose de ben ben urgent à faire, en me r'gardant en pleine face. J'avais chaud. J'frissonnais. J'savais pus où m'mett'. Y leur a dit qu'y les appellerait le lendemain matin. (102)[15]

The apparent clarity and lucidity of Claude's decision – embracing the sexual rather than the national – is rendered forever murky and uncertain, however, by Yves's own subsequent actions, which are the result, not of conscious deliberation – indeed, according to Yves, in making his choice, Claude 'me d'mandait pas d'en faire autant. Y me d'mandait rien' (103; 'wasn't asking me to choose. He wasn't asking me to do anything' [429]) – but of an instinctive impulse to preserve the transcendent purity of the moment, to rescue the person he loved from the inevitable consequences of his apparently irrevocable choice: 'en même temps que l'couteau est arrivé, jus' le temps qu'ça pris pour que l'son s'fasse, on v'nait. Ensemble. Pas moi, pas lui, nous deux. Pis j'nous ai vus. Moi, r'partir chez mes clients ou bendon avoir à décider de pus y aller. Pis lui, êt' obligé de s'engueuler avec ses chums. Combien d'temps on aurait été capab'? Hein? Combien d'temps?' (106; 'when the knife hit the floor, in the time it took for the sound to register, we came. Together. Not him. Not me. Both of us. And suddenly I saw us. Me leavin' to meet my customers, or havin' to decide not to. And him, having to argue with his friends. How long could we have stuck it out? Eh? How long?' [430]). To be sure, Yves, in seeking to kill his lover so that he might be reborn – 'J'espère jus' que lui, y est jus' v'nu au monde. Pis qu'y a pas vu l'aut' bord d'la médaille'

(110; 'I just hope he was born, without seeing what was ahead. Without seeing the other side of the coin first' [432]) – does not reflect overly long on the political consequences of his mercy-killing. And yet, ironically, they are manifold. For in death, Claude has, despite himself, become something of a martyr to the nationalist cause. As the weary Inspector summarizes to the Stenographer at one point, between a murdered student radical, a male prostitute, an anxious judge, a separatist girlfriend who refuses to believe her boyfriend was queer and suspects a political frame-up, and a provincial cabinet minister who wants everything hushed up (57; 409), even 'une bombe à l'Expo' (55; 'a bomb at Expo' [408]) would have trouble competing with this story.

Although his sixth produced play, *Being at home* is the first in which Dubois employs the basic techniques of dramatic realism. Gone are the self-conscious role-playing, the intertextual allusions and language games, and the postmodernist foregrounding of the whole performative context that characterized *Ne blâmez jamais les Bédouins* and *Adieu, docteur Münch.* Instead, we are presented with the fairly conventional staging of 'une pièce policière.' Except that in this crime drama the 'crime' has already been solved, allowing Dubois to give full expression to the real 'drama' of the play: the conflict between homosexual desire and national (be)longing. In risking the link between homosexuality and criminality, between sex and death, Dubois is sending a message to the Quebec cultural establishment: that he is 'un [Jean] Genet d'ici et d'aujourd'hui' ('Vivre de sa plume,' 12; 'a [Jean] Genet of here and now'). Indeed, like Genet's romantic homosexual anti-heroes, by the end of the play Yves is even allowed to experience his own unique spiritual catharsis, 'de devenir une sorte de saint Sébastien,' in the words of Alexandre Lazaridès (Camerlain et al., 'Séminaire,' 73; 'to become a kind of Saint Sebastian'). To this end, in the 1988 remounting of *Being at home* at the Théâtre du Rideau-Vert, under Dubois's own direction, the force of the antagonism between the Inspector and Yves is toned down a bit. The Inspector, in particular, becomes more sympathetic to Yves's predicament, and 'la pièce se clôt sur l'image de la pietà. Le policier tient Yves dans ses bras ... À la dernière scène, il a enfin gagné, converti le policier' (Michel Vaïs, in Camerlain et al., 'Séminaire,' 73; 'the play closes on the image of the pietà. The policeman takes Yves in his arms ... By the last scene, he has finally won, having converted the policeman').

Yves may have won the cat-and-mouse game by the end of the play, convincing the Inspector that he killed out of love, that murder was the only way out of an identificatory impasse for both himself and Claude, but to what extent has Dubois converted his audience? For, as I see it, part of what Dubois is attempting to do with Claude's murder is sunder the uneasy allegorical alliance between nationalism and homosexuality in Quebec drama, to forestall the institutionalization of such an alliance within the historical animus of one stock character (as signified, for example, by the 'inc.' in the title of Jubinville's essay), and to force his audience either to accept or condemn Yves on the basis of his sexuality alone. The reference to Genet becomes even more telling in this respect. With it, Dubois is placing himself within a tradition of homosexual writing that resists the narrow confines of national borders. It is a personal position – a critical conviction – that has not won Dubois any extra friends in Quebec, several producers doing their best to ensure (or so the playwright maintains) that Dubois suffer 'un sort pire que celui qu'on a fait subir au premier du nom [de Genet] en France' (Dubois, 'Vivre de sa plume,' 12; 'a fate worse than the one who was stuck with the name [Genet] in France').

The 'neoromantic impulse' in *Being at home* – what Yves Dubé (following from Paul Toutant), in his preface to the published text, poses as the Wildean question 'Peut-on tuer parce qu'on aime trop?' (xii and *passim*; 'Can we kill because we love too much?')[16] – is certainly evident, and to a much higher degree, in Bouchard's *Les Feluettes*, with its staging of a tale of doomed homosexual love, its explicit foregrounding of Gabriele D'Annunzio's *The Martyrdom of Saint Sebastian* as a *mise en abyme*, and its elevated poetic language. Even the play's subtitle, 'la répétition d'un drame romantique,' makes Bouchard's strategies of literary recuperation clear.

The play, which premiered 10 September 1987 at Montreal's salle Fred-Barry, in a Théâtre Petit à Petit (Montréal) / Théâtre français du Centre national des Arts (Ottawa) co-production directed by André Brassard, begins with a prologue. It is 1952 and on the proscenium stage of an abandoned auditorium fifty-nine-year-old Simon Doucet awaits the arrival of Monseigneur Bilodeau, a former classmate of his at the Collège Saint-Sébastien in Roberval, Quebec. Simon has just been released from jail after spending over thirty years there for a crime he did not commit. He is now confronting Bilodeau for his role in this miscarriage of justice, as well as for the priest's complicity in the death of Simon's adolescent lover, le Comte Vallier de Tilly, also known as 'Feluette,' or 'Lily-White.' In order to help him do this, Simon has brought along several fellow ex-convicts who, for the duration of Bouchard's play, stage their own play, recreating the events in question that took place forty years earlier. This play-within-a-play thus becomes at once an extended theatrical flashback

(Roberval 1912) and a present-day trial of the Monseigneur (abandoned auditorium 1952), whose final judgment comes in the closing epilogue, when we are returned to the outer frame setting and Simon pronounces his verdict: 'Moi, je te déteste au point de te laisser vivre' (125; 'I hate you so much ... I'm gonna let you live' [69]).

Jane Moss is one critic who has discussed the trend towards a 'revival' of romanticism in recent gay drama coming from Quebec. According to Moss, playwrights like Bouchard, Dubois, and Chaurette have repeatedly sought to externalize the romanticism of their texts, resulting in what she calls 'hypertheatrical' productions, where the whole dramatic apparatus is foregrounded self-reflexively, and where 'the theatricalization of homosexual experience creates scenarios of passion, violence, madness, and impasse,' which in turn '[reflect] psychological fragmentation and patterns of obsessional repetition' ('Sexual Games,' 295). Her examples include Bouchard's *La Contre-nature de Chrysippe Tanguay, écologiste,* in which a gay couple and the social worker assigned to assess their fitness as prospective adoptive parents act out the theatrical fantasies scripted by the pre-operative transexual Louis, one of the would-be 'fathers'; Dubois's *26bis, impasse du Colonel Foisy,* in which 'Madame,' a Russian princess (to be played by a male actor), addresses the audience directly, her monologue interrupted by occasional interventions from 'la Voix de l'auteur' (xxvi); and Chaurette's *Provincetown Playhouse,* in which the thirty-eight-year-old Charles Charles obsessively replays in the theatre of his mind the experimental drama he wrote in 1919 to celebrate his nineteenth birthday, as well as the 'real-life' murder mystery that resulted from its performance.

Moss's analysis can also be extended quite easily to *Les Feluettes,* which contains not one but two plays-within-a-play, or, more accurately, a play (D'Annunzio's *The Martyrdom of Saint Sebastian*) within a play (Simon's 'petite soirée théâtrale' [23]; 'little theatrical evening' [13]) within a play (Bouchard's *Les Feluettes*). In this regard, it is once again worthwhile emphasizing Bouchard's subtitle, which, as Sara Graefe points out, 'contains a clever play on words: "répétition" implies both the rehearsal of a play, and the repetition of a previously performed drama' (166). No single word in English quite encompasses both of these senses, although translator Linda Gaboriau's choice of 'revival' does bring with it its own doubly encoded associations: the 'restaging' of an older period piece (*The Martyrdom of Saint Sebastian,* for example); and the 'resuscitation' of something or someone dead or dying, which 'in the context of [Bouchard's play] can take on several levels of meaning' (Graefe, 166).

The 'repetition' or 'revival' of romantic dramatic conventions is also intimately connected, I would argue, with gay self-expression and the foregrounding of homoerotic desire on stage. This is certainly the case in 1912 Roberval for Father Saint-Michel, whose production of D'Annunzio's homoerotic, sado-masochistic, and redemptive classic allows him to circumvent, however momentarily, the regulatory gaze of the Catholic Church: 'Au théâtre, on peut tout faire, vous savez. On peut réinventer la vie. On peut être amoureux, jaloux, fou, tyran ou possédé. On peut mentir, tricher. On peut tuer sans avoir le moindre remords. On peut mourir d'amour, de haine, de passion' (30–1; 'One can do anything in the theater, you know. One can reinvent life. One can be in love, jealous, insane, tyrannical or possessed. One can even lie and cheat. One can kill without feeling the slightest remorse. One can die of love, of hate, of passion' [17]). And this is equally the case in 1987 Montreal for Bouchard, whose plays represent an attempt to subvert the normalizing 'philosophie de banlieue' ('suburban philosophy') that says we must all be alike: 'La normalité n'est qu'une histoire de collectivité. Et à travers la masse on risque de disparaître. Donc je mets en scène des marginaux. J'essaie de montrer aux gens leur fascination pour ces individualités qui ne font pas partie des codes sociaux dominants' ('Tout plein d'émotions,' 12; 'Normality is nothing but a collective history. And you risk getting lost in the crowd. So I put marginal people on stage. I try to demonstrate to people their fascination for these individualities that are not part of dominant social codes').

As Robert Wallace has noted, Simon and Vallier's '"burning" passion is given literal representation' ('Homo Creation,' 219) at the end of Bouchard's play, with the young lovers exchanging rings and 'marriage vows' in the school attic as flames lick at the door they have barricaded against Bilodeau and the rest of Roberval. Finally professing the love for Vallier he had previously denied, Simon declares: 'Ast'heure, t'es mon amant, mon homme, mon amour. Seul, unique amour. Le soleil pis le lac sont nos seuls témoins ... à la vie, à la mort' (120; 'Now, you're my lover, my man. My one and only love. The sun and the lake are our only witnesses. For life, till death do us part' [67]). And 'while we can argue,' as Wallace goes on to point out, 'that the play's valorization of death represents a romanticization of homosexual love typical of the masculinist cultural imperative, visual signifiers overcome such an argument: we see desire rather than death depicted on the stage' (220). Moreover, for Wallace, 'in this epoch of AIDS, this statement – dying because of loving – is both radical and courageous, possibly one that only a gay man would dare to make' (221).

The question remains, however, as to whether romanticism in Bouchard's play is also connected with issues of Quebec nationalism. Margery Fee has demonstrated how the Indigene remains 'an important mythical figure' in contemporary English-Canadian literary romanticism, 'and its related political ideology – nationalism': 'A variant of mainstream nationalism [i.e., romantic nationalism] uses the First Peoples' position as marginal, yet aboriginal, to make a similar claim-by-identification for other marginal groups' (17). In this regard, according to Fee, 'the Native is connected to the Jew [in Richler and Cohen, for example] ... to the Mennonite visionary [in Wiebe] ... and to the *sexual nonconformist* [in Findley, Engel, and Maillard] ...' (17; my emphasis). Within the context of Fee's argument, as applied to *Les Feluettes*, it is important to keep in mind that 'Lily-White' Vallier, the 'sexual nonconformist,' has also, in his secret labour as a fishing guide to visiting tourists, become 'aussi sauvage qu'un Indien' (85; 'wild like an Indian' [49]). While la Comtesse de Tilly is dreaming of her eventual return to France, her only son is busy staking his autochthonous claim to a part of the New World that within a few generations would become a hotbed of Québécois separatism (as the Lac Saint-Jean area remains today).

According to Solange Lévesque and Diane Pavlovic, in Bouchard's play 'nous ne sommes plus en présence de l'univers homosexuel auquel nous avait habitués Michel Tremblay ... Si les homosexuels de Tremblay étaient mal dans leur peau et se perdaient dans un jeu constant de l'apparence, ceux de Bouchard, sans artifice et sans complexe, ne se préoccupent que de l'essence des choses' ('Comédiens et martyrs,' 155; 'we are no longer in the presence of the homosexual universe we became accustomed to with Michel Tremblay ... If Tremblay's homosexuals were ill at ease with themselves and lost themselves in a constant game of appearances, those of Bouchard, without artifice and without complexes, preoccupy themselves only with the essence of things'). Leaving aside the complete effacement of André Brassard – who directed the original productions of both *Hosanna* and *Les Feluettes* – in these comments, I want to suggest, counter to the 'essentialist' claims of Lévesque and Pavlovic, that any attempted nationalist reading of Bouchard's play perforce depends upon the Tremblayesque allegory of Quebec as a dysfunctional family.

Despite the plethora of male bodies on stage, Roberval in 1912 is quite literally fatherless:[17] Father Saint-Michel is dismissed early on by his Church superiors; Vallier's father is back in France, completely oblivious to his wife and son's financial predicament (or so we are told by the capricious Lydie-Anne); Simon's father, Timothée, is an abusive drunkard; and so on. As Solange Lévesque has elsewhere commented with respect to *Les Feluettes*, 'la France a longtemps été considérée ici [au Québec] comme une mère patrie' ('À propos,' 178; 'France has for a long time been considered here [in Quebec] like a mother country').[18] In Bouchard's play, France is represented, of course, by Lydie-Anne de Rozier and la Comtesse de Tilly, the one merely on 'vacation' from the mother country, the other in 'exile' but nevertheless still fantasizing about her triumphant return. In the middle of the play, during episodes 4 and 5, these 'deux Françaises prennent la vedette, l'une anachronique mais irrésistible, l'autre manipulatrice et brillante' (Lévesque, 'À propos,' 179; 'two French women take centre-stage, the one anachronistic but irresistible, the other manipulating and brilliant'). However, with the explosion of Lydie-Anne's aerostat, and with Vallier's burial of his mother at the end of episode 6, any lingering thoughts of returning to France on the part of either Simon or Vallier are also laid to rest. As the delusional Comtesse puts it, 'Assez parlé. Le dernier bateau pour la France va partir bientôt' (112; 'Enough talk. The last ship for France will be leaving soon' [63]).

This sets the stage for the return of the fledgling/foundling Quebec nation's absentee father, someone who will put 'straight' – that is, sunder – the unnatural acts (specifically, the 'marriage' between his sons, Simon and Vallier) that have transpired in his absence. On stage this symbolic return is signalled by the epilogue, with its temporal relocation of both players and audience(s) to the frame setting of 1952. Monseigneur Bilodeau is there, in all his ecclesiastical, patriarchal, and repressed homosexual glory, but lurking behind his robes is another Quebec 'father,' this one a political surrogate, charged with the task of bringing his electoral novitiates firmly into the twentieth century but ultimately responsible for twenty more years of '"la grande noirceur" in Quebec' (Graefe, 167). I am referring, of course, to Maurice Duplessis, iron-fisted 'chief' of the Union Nationale Party, and premier of Quebec during 1936–9 and 1944–59. Ironically, then, the death of the 'colonialist' mother and the return of the 'nationalist' father fails to bring Quebec's offspring 'à la maturité' (Lévesque, 'À propos,' 179), but rather leaves them orphaned, quite literally in the case of Duplessis's 'lost children,' many of whom are only now surfacing to tell their stories.[19] This idea of Quebec as 'un peuple orphelin' – represented to some extent by the presence of the forgotten prisoners in *Les Feluettes* – would be explored by Bouchard at greater length in his next play, the fourth in his Tanguay series: *Les Muses orphelines*.

While the francophone press in Montreal has been lavish in its praise of Dubois's *Being at home with Claude* and Bouchard's *Les Feluettes*, and has been quick to situate both playwrights in a dramatic tradition whose particular 'queerness' extends back to Tremblay, it has tended to shy away from this kind of overtly 'nationalist' interpretation of the two plays in reviews. Robert Lévesque's assessment of *Being at home* in *Le Devoir* is a case in point:

> Dans l'ensemble de l'histoire du théâtre québécois depuis le renouveau des années soixante, *Being at home with Claude*, de René-Daniel Dubois, rejoint les quelques pièces parfaitement senties ... qui donnent au théâtre d'ici son appui spécifique, sa valeur intrinsèque ... [Dubois] prouve, avec *Being at home with Claude*, qu'il est à la fois le plus esthète de nos écrivains de théâtre et, ce qui fait son génie à l'égal de Tremblay ... le plus viscéral des poètes dramatiques. ('René-Daniel Dubois,' 23)[20]

Similarly, in covering the premiere of *Les Feluettes* for the same paper, Lévesque noted that

> l'une des particularités thématiques du théâtre québécois, passée l'affirmation nationale, le réalisme familial, la poésie féministe, c'est l'homosexualité. Déjà un des moteurs du théâtre de Tremblay, l'amour et les conflits homosexuels ont donné au théâtre québécois des oeuvres majeures depuis dix ans. Qu'on parle de Normand Chaurette avec *Provincetown Playhouse* ..., ou *Pommiers en fleurs* de Serge Sirois, ou de *Being at home with Claude* de René-Daniel Dubois, les pièces homosexuelles ou les pièces sur l'homosexualité (il y a nuance) sont devenues l'un des champs d'introspection du théâtre québécois ... Michel-Marc Bouchard ... s'inscrit au centre de ce ring de la réalité homosexuelle. ('Michel-Marc,' C1)[21]

Of course, the subtle skirting of issues of nationalism in these two reviews – most notably in the second, where the 'theme of homosexuality' in Québécois theatre is catalogued separately from that of 'national affirmation' – may have something to do with a certain unease around the critical mass of romanticism achieved in Dubois's and Bouchard's respective plays: after all, 'Claude' didn't have to die at the end of *Hosanna*; he only had to get naked, and maybe not even that.[22] Or it may simply be perceived as overkill (excuse the pun), the apparent surfeit of 'gay plays' on the Montreal stage over the past decade leading several contributors in a recent special issue of the journal *Cahiers de théâtre jeu* (no. 54 [1990]) to bemoan the 'over-representation' of homosexuality in contemporary

Québécois theatre. Whereas once homosexuality, as in Tremblay's plays, was viewed by theatre critics almost uniformly as symbolic of 'l'expression de la collectivité québécoise' (Camerlain, 7),[23] it is now being treated as a sign of 'un grand malaise' (see Fréchette and Vaïs) and 'l'absence d'identification' altogether (Richard, 23). Lurking behind such sentiments is the increasingly widespread belief that Quebec theatre is perhaps getting 'too queer' for its (and Quebec's) own good. As Dubois has rather bitterly noted in an interview, even celebrated Tremblay interpreter André Brassard 'a refusé de monter *BEING AT HOME* parce que son public est "écoeuré d'entend' parler des tapettes"' ('Vivre de sa plume,' 12; 'refused to stage *Being at home* because his public was sick of hearing about faggots').

By contrast, the English-language critical reception of Linda Gaboriau's translations, *Being at Home* and *Lilies*, has been marked by a noticeable increase of nationalist interpretations in the press since the Toronto and New York debuts of *Hosanna*. This becomes most apparent at the dramatic level of each play's setting. For example, writing in the *Toronto Star* after the premiere of *Being at Home* at the Tarragon Theatre in April 1987, Robert Crew assures his readers that 'the setting – Quebec during Expo 67 and the upsurge of the separatist movement – gives [the play] a historical and political resonance, stretching beyond the immediate subject of intricate and difficult personal relationships' (D3). Such a reading, emanating as it does from an English Canada jittery about proposed new constitutional talks with Quebec leading up to the Meech Lake Accord, perhaps goes a distance towards explaining director Jean Beaudin and screenwriter Johanne Boisvert's decision, in the aftermath of the Accord's failure, to change the backdrop of the play to 1990s Montreal during the Jazz Festival in their subsequent film adaptation. Back 'at home' in Quebec, however, Dubois was merely chastised in the press for not having translated the title of the English version of his play into French (see Dubois, 'Vivre de sa plume au Québec,' 12).

The Toronto press's coverage of the premiere of Bouchard's *Lilies* at Theatre Passe Muraille in 1991 likewise made much of the play's setting, with reviewers going out of their way to contrast the Catholic Church–dominated region of Roberval in 1912 and 1952, as portrayed on stage, with the heavily separatist area of present-day Lac Saint-Jean, Bouchard's birthplace (as well as that of another famous Bouchard from Quebec).[24] The precise importance of this setting, along with nuances of language and class, tends to get lost in John Greyson's recent English-language screen adaptation of the play, although Bouchard seems to have fared somewhat better than Dubois in this regard *vis-à-vis* the critics. (The fact that the film won both the Telefilm Canada Prize at the Montreal World Film Festival and the 1996 Genie Award for Best Canadian Feature has of course helped.) At any rate, what the different critical responses to Dubois's and Bouchard's respective plays inside and outside Quebec – like those accompanying Tremblay's *Hosanna* a decade-and-a-half earlier – most clearly point to, according to Robert Wallace, is a 'problematic ... fundamental to translators challenged to create texts that are both "true" to their original sources and effective in their new incarnations' (*Producing Marginality*, 220). This problem of 'translation' (a problem I explore at greater length in the next chapter), this need for a kind of 'transvestic inqu(ee)ry' when approaching the texts of Tremblay, Dubois, and Bouchard, also extends, I would hasten to add, to the cross-cultural critic/reader/viewer. As Wallace goes on to remark, 'inasmuch as the whole process of inter-cultural production is a project in which one culture "translates" another into its own terms – whether by creating a production from a script or by (simply) viewing one that has toured – the problematic is also central to the interaction of French and English theatre in Canada' (220).[25]

* * *

Apart from the one-act *Encore une fois si vous le permettez* (1998) and the recent *Messe solennelle pour une pleine lune d'été* (1996), which was disastrously received, prompting Robert Lévesque to muse in print about 'la durabilité' of the Tremblay-Brassard alliance ('Le Tandem,' B8), Tremblay's last major theatrical statement came in June 1992 with the premiere of *Marcel poursuivi par les chiens* at the Théâtre du Nouveau Monde, a production mounted as part of city-wide festivities celebrating the 350th anniversary of the 'founding' of Montreal. In this play, Tremblay reacquaints his audience with a familiar protagonist, picking up the threads of this tormented character's story, and filling in the details about the period in between Marcel's adult incarceration in an insane asylum (as documented in 1969's *En pièces détachées*) and his unhappy and violent childhood (outlined in the 1990 novel *La Maison suspendue*). Unable to come to grips with the world around him and, what is worse, fearing that this world is unable to come to grips with him, Marcel takes refuge inside his own head, which is filled with the voices of crying birds.

Yet another allegory of Quebec's collective national consciousness? Perhaps, but surely not so clearly as two of the more recent productions by Tremblay's 'bastard sons,' each timed to coincide with the 1995 referendum. Bouchard's *Voyage du couronnement* opened in Montreal in mid-September of 1995, also at the Théâtre du Nouveau Monde. It tells the story of a group of Québécois travelling aboard an ocean liner to the coronation of Queen Elizabeth II in 1953. The protagonist is a Montreal gangster who has snitched to the police and the government in exchange for money, a new identity and passport, and safe repatriation overseas. However, a high-ranking diplomat on the same 'ship of fools' threatens to renege on the deal unless he is allowed to have sex with the gangster's teenaged son. As Bouchard has commented in a recent interview in the *Globe and Mail*, the gangster's moral dilemma reflects '"the kind of politics which sacrifices tomorrow's generation by obsessing about economics today"' (Conlogue, 'Quebec Theatre's Bright New Hope,' C2).

As for Dubois, the autumn of 1995 was also the occasion for a new production of his award-winning solo piece, *Ne blâmez jamais les Bédouins*. In this twenty-character tour-de-force of artistic creation, Dubois plays all the roles, including that of Michaela, an Italian opera diva tied to a railway track in the desert, with trains speeding towards her on both sides. This would seem to be an apt metaphor for life in Quebec these days. As Pat Donnelly put it in the *Vancouver Sun*, 'even the title sounds like a response to Jacques Parizeau's referendum-night comments about the "ethnic vote"' ('Bad Karma,' C3). And yet, whereas Bouchard remains a committed nationalist, maintaining quixotically that 'the independence of Quebec will come when Canada seizes its own sovereignty' (Conlogue, 'Quebec Artists,' E1), Dubois has recently done an about-face, proclaiming that the PQ is holding Quebec artists hostage, that he will no longer support the sovereigntist movement, and that the supposedly socially democratic province of Quebec is in fact 'a "soft" totalitarian society' (Donnelly, C3).

How these recent theatrical and political developments bode for the future of gay drama in Quebec, which has for so long made issues of national and sexual self-determination almost completely coterminous, remains to be seen. What is certain, however, is that Tremblay's 'sons,' like the various communities (national, sexual, artistic) to which they 'belong,' and from which they write, are divided over the 'problem of identity.' Bouchard appears, for the most part, content to continue 'writing in the father's house,' framing his allegories of national authentification within Tremblay's familiar binary discourse of femininity and masculinity. On the other hand, recognizing that the repeated reading – or, following from de Man and Lacan, the necessary *mis*reading – of homosexuality as symbolic of Quebec's national identity crisis has, paradoxically, contributed to a backlash against queer theatrical images in the province, Dubois is no longer comfortable being at home with Claude. Neither, I have to admit, am I.

I began this chapter on a personal note, and it is on a similar note that I would now like to close. No doubt my conclusions, such as they are, will strike many as far too tentative, others as overly polemical. Nevertheless, as a gay Anglo, and a former resident of Quebec who still has both personal and professional ties to the province, I share some of Schwartzwald's anxieties about the practical implications of Quebec cultural workers' theoretical investments in the discourse of homosexuality. As Quebec's 'identity crisis' grows ever more protracted, and the terms of the debate ever more fractured and polarized, how long can it be, I wonder, before queers, agitating for a different kind of civic recognition, outstrip their symbolic usefulness, and rejoin women and ethnic minorities as part of Aquin's unholy trinity in the nationalist rhetoric of blame? Moreover, should Quebec sovereignty eventually be achieved, what then? For a symbolic role in the Oedipal narrative of a nation-state is, as we shall see in the next chapter, not the same as a political one. The female characters in Nicole Brossard's fiction/theory, for example, are explicitly urban precisely as a means of rupturing the cultural legacy of the *roman de la fidélité*, in which woman, as womb, is abjectly associated with *la terre*. In Brossard's texts, as in Daphne Marlatt's, the construction of an alternative lesbian genealogy becomes a process of self-translation, its (re)production in/as narrative parthenogenic. If, in the end, like Brossard and Dubois, I resist an equivalency of national and sexual identities based on the 'difference of sameness,' it is because I, also like them, am trying to sort out where exactly it is in the overlapping political and erotic spaces of Canada and Quebec that I belong.

5

Towards a Transnational, Translational Feminist Poetics: Lesbian Fiction/Theory in Canada and Quebec

La traduction est un acte de passage par lequel une réalité devient tout à la fois autre et semblable. Qu'il s'agisse de passer de la réalité à la fiction par l'écriture ou de passer de la fiction à la réalité par la lecture ou de faire passer un texte d'une langue à l'autre, ma fascination pour l'acte de passage a toujours été au centre de mon questionnement littéraire et existentiel.[1]

Nicole Brossard, *À tout regard*, 84

... marked, we are
elsewhere,

translated here

Daphne Marlatt, 'Booking passage,' 118

In the concluding chapter of *Imperial Leather*, Ann McClintock claims that nationalism has been 'constituted from the very beginning as a gendered discourse and cannot be understood without a theory of gender power' (355).[2] This historical gendering of nationalism, as she goes on to point out, is 'frequently figured through the iconography of familial and domestic space' (357). Indeed, the term 'nation' itself derives etymologically from the Latin *natio, nasci*, meaning 'to be born.' Similarly, the object of a 'patriot's' (again from the Latin *pater, patros*, meaning 'father') love is usually his 'motherland' (occasionally his 'fatherland'), and he expresses this love in his 'mother tongue.' And yet, while the familiar/familial Oedipal metaphor offers women a symbolic role within the national narrative, it does not yield a concomitant political one, since the hierarchization of citizens within the nation-state is founded 'on the prior naturalizing of the social subordination of women and children within the domestic sphere' (McClintock, 358).

By extension, the standard construction of a national narrative as a genesis story, as an act of birthing,[3] and the allegorical representation of autonomous regions as manifestations of woman's physical and sexual difference, does not allow us to transcend the sex-affective identification of woman solely with the reproductive capacities of her body (a point to which I shall return). This is particularly evident in the New World, where the myth of the landscape as 'virgin' territory to penetrate and populate depends, according to Marianna Torgovnick, on a phallic semiology that says 'if explorers ... are "manly," then what they explore must be female' (61; see also McClintock, 28–30).

The sex-gender paradox at the heart of patriarchal/nationalist discourse (where a narrative of origins is reduced to the level of an active male protagonist and the passive female space through which he moves, and where a male plot can only be refracted through a female setting or landscape) is exposed as a flawed ideological construction in the theoretical fictions (and fictional theories) of lesbian-feminist writers like Nicole Brossard and Daphne Marlatt, who repeatedly return to the body as the site from which to anatomize the tropes and images used to other women, and through which to re-member an alternative genealogy ('a lesbian genealogy' [Meese, 46]) of sexual difference.[4] In Brossard's *L'Amèr; ou, Le chapitre effrité*, this re-inscription can begin only after a ritual killing/sacrifice of the 'symbole apprivoisé' ('domesticated symbol') of women's bodily servitude to men: 'J'ai tué le ventre et je l'écris' (21, 19; 'I have murdered the womb and I am writing it' [*These*, 23, 21]). This primal act of violence – necessary in order to combat the violence of patriarchal discourse – opens up a space for the writing of a new narrative, in which the text's lesbian scriptor is both her own mother and her own daughter: 'Fille-mère lesbienne, j'inscris la dernière contradiction. Minant par l'intérieur l'histoire à laquelle je puis maintenant participer' (34; 'Daughter-mother lesbian, I write down the ultimate contradiction. Undermining from within his-tory in which I can now participate' [*These*, 36]).

Musing on the 'discrepancy between what our patriarchally-loaded language bears (can bear) of our own experience and the difference from it our experience bears out – how it misrepresents, even miscarries, and so leaves unsaid what we actually experience,' Marlatt likewise dismantles her own metaphor of (linguistic) birthing in the essay that concludes

Touch to My Tongue by transforming the (m)other's tongue into the lover's tongue: 'how can the separate nouns mother and child convey the fusion, bleeding woman-infant mouth, she experiences in those first days of feeding? what syntax can carry the turning herself inside out in love when she is both sucking mouth and hot gush on her lover's tongue?' (47, 48). Moreover, in the sequence of poems that precedes this essay, Marlatt uses the cyclical process of separation and return encapsulated in the myth of Demeter and Persephone to parallel the lesbian love story at the 'kore' of her text. In Marlatt's retelling of the myth, however, Demeter and Persephone are no longer figured simply as mother and lost daughter; they are also separated/reunited lovers: '(*amba*, amorous Demeter, / you with the fire in your hand, i am coming to you)' (23). In this regard, the dedication 'for Betsy' (18) links the text, and directs the reader, to another book of poems published the same year, Betsy Warland's *open is broken*, bearing a complementary dedication, 'for Daphne' (5).

But if, as Brossard claims, to write (as) a woman 'est plein de conséquences' (*L'Amèr*, 43; 'is heavy with consequences' [*These*, 45]), then it would seem that '... to write in lesbian' (Marlatt, 'Booking passage,' 118) is fraught with even greater risks. 'One is,' after all, 'not born ... a woman,' as Simone de Beauvoir famously instructed us in *The Second Sex* (267); and, moreover, 'lesbians are not women,' at least in Monique Wittig's estimation ('The Straight Mind,' 32). Waging war against the regulatory structures of language, grammar, and syntax – as per Wittig's *Les Guérillères* – may not ultimately lead to the defeat of patriarchy and its affects/effects, including the nation-state; but a mobilization of this sort will necessarily contribute to their *transformation*, their *translation*.

In her essay, 'Under the Covers: A Synesthesia of Desire (Lesbian Translations),' Alice Parker uses 'the related concepts of *translation* and *passing* ... to de-sign a space of lesbian subjectivity': 'As a woman, a feminist, a lesbian,' writes Parker, 'I translate the materiality of my daily experiences into an alien code, a code that is always already phallic and patriarchal, and which e(xc)ludes me. The only way I can speak/write is by passing as an-other' (322). As my choice of epigraphs to this chapter attests, *translation* and *passing* are also important concepts for Brossard and Marlatt. '[U]ne lesbienne qui ne réinvente pas le monde est une lesbienne en voie de disparition,' is how Brossard puts it in *La Lettre aérienne* (127; 'a lesbian who does not reinvent the world is a lesbian in the process of disappearing' [*The Aerial Letter*, 136]). Consequently, Brossard's writing, like that of Marlatt, is based not so much on a poetics of mimesis, which effaces the materiality of language and erases difference through the transparent splitting of subject and object; rather, I would argue, their texts are framed by a poetics of catachresis, of rupture, of excess, where slippages in/between language, narrative, and syntax are made visible, and where the 'barrier/slash,' as the grammatical site of such 'acts of passage' (cf. the 'j/e' of Wittig's *Le Corps lesbien* [*The Lesbian Body*]),[5] represents, not the limits of subjectivity and difference, but their intersection, their 'interface' (Brossard, *These*, 40; 'entre-deux' [*L'Amèr*, 38]). The translation poetics of Brossard and Marlatt, I want to suggest in this chapter, map a space *between* English-Canadian and Québécoise women in this country, creating a community of feminist writers and readers 'across national and other borders' (Moyes, 'Composing,' 206). This space is, as Brossard claims, 'un espace de fiction' (*L'Amèr*, 38; 'a space for fiction' [*These*, 40]); but it is also a space for theory. A space, in other words, for fiction/theory.

* * *

The term 'fiction/theory,' or 'fiction théorique,'[6] was first coined by Brossard in reference to her 1977 novel, *L'Amèr*. As she puts it,

> Feminist consciousness made me question reality and fiction. For example, when I was writing *L'amèr*, I felt that I had to move reality into fiction because patriarchal reality made no sense and was useless to me. I also had the impression and the certainty that my fictions were reality – they are full of meaning – and that from there I could start a theoretical work. That's why I called the book 'une fiction théorique.' (Quoted as epigraph to Godard, 'Fiction/Theory,' 4)

A definition of sorts is offered by Brossard in the preliminary pages of *L'Amèr*. 'Théorie fictive: les mots n'auront servi que dans la

'Fiction/theory' gained prominence in feminist literary circles in English Canada with the publication, in 1986, of a special issue of *Tessera* devoted to its explication/exploration. As Lianne Moyes notes, this special issue can be read in part 'as the manifestory moment of feminist fiction/theory, the moment in which it stages itself as an event. Such a moment is important, particularly in anglophone Canada where fiction/theory has suffered a certain critical invisibility' ('Into the Fray,' 315). In the opening exchange between the volume's editorial collective, Marlatt defines the term as follows:

> fiction/theory: a corrective lens which helps us see *through* the fiction we've been conditioned to take for the real, fictions which have not

dernière étreinte' (n. pag.; 'Fictive theory: words were used only in the ultimate embrace' [*These*, n. pag.]). Caught in this 'ultimate embrace' of fiction/theory are not just the genres of novel and critical essay, but also the discourses of feminism and postmodernism (or 'modernité,' as Brossard would no doubt term it), the subjective experiences of writer and reader, and the imagined and material spaces of body (*corps*) and text (*texte*), what Brossard refers to elsewhere as 'cortex' (see, for example, her 'Le Cortex exubérant').

And yet, while *L'Amèr* was the first text to which Brossard gave the label 'fiction théorique,' she had for several years prior to its publication been exploring similar issues in shorter pieces – such as 'Vaseline,' 'Le Cortex exubérant,' and '*E* muet mutant' – that appeared regularly in the pages of *La Barre du jour*, an experimental Montreal literary journal that Brossard co-founded (together with Roger Soublière) in 1965.

La Barre du jour, and its successor, *La Nouvelle Barre du jour* (which first appeared in 1977), have since become identified – in large part via their respective editorial associations with Brossard – as important sites of feminist writing in Quebec. Special issues focusing on 'Women and Language,' 'Body, Words,

only constructed woman's 'place' in patriarchal society but have constructed the very 'nature' of woman (always that which has been). fiction *theory* deconstructs these fictions while *fiction* theory, conscious of itself as fiction, offers a new angle on the 'real,' one that looks from inside out rather than outside in (the difference between woman as subject and woman as object). (Quoted in Godard et al., 'Theorizing,' 9)

The experience of being on the outside looking in is a familiar one to Marlatt. Having immigrated to Vancouver from Malaysia at the age of nine, she concedes that, in hindsight, 'most of my writing has been a vehicle for entry into what was for me the new place, the new world' ('Entering In,' 219). This is particularly noticeable in early works like *Vancouver Poems* and *Steveston*, which can be read as attempts to translate the 'immigrant imagination' into a more tangible (i.e., material and locatable) sense of national, or at least regional, self-definition.

In 1963, having 'mastered' being 'Canadian' (see Marlatt, 'Difference,' 191), and fresh from having participated in the Vancouver Poetry Conference, Marlatt once again found herself on the outside looking in, this time as one of the few women members (Gladys Hindmarch was another)

Imaginary,' 'Women and the City,' etc., and showcasing prominently the work of Brossard, Madeleine Gagnon, Louky Bersianik, Suzanne Lamy, Jovette Marchessault, France Théoret, and Louise Cotnoir, among others, have helped solidify this view (see, in this regard, Godard, '*La Barre du jour*'; and Forsyth, 'Les Numéros spéciaux'). But it is worth remembering that *La Barre du jour*, in particular, was established in the midst of the Quiet Revolution and, as such, shared many of the nationalist goals of the avowedly separatist *Parti Pris* magazine, founded only two years earlier. As Brossard and Soublière put it in a special issue of *La Barre du jour* protesting the Canadian government's response to the 1970 October Crisis, an event Brossard would later juxtapose fictively with the 1943 Conscription Crisis in *Sold-out* (1973), 'En 1963, nous avons lu *Parti Pris* et nous avons compris. Il n'y avait pas à discuter: les positions critiques de cette revue ajoutées à notre expérience quotidienne du Québec ... achevèrent de transformer notre impatience en un naturel contestataire' ('De notre écriture,' 3; 'In 1963 we read *Parti Pris* and we understood. There was nothing to discuss: the critical positions of that review, combined with our daily experience of Quebec ... succeeded in transforming our impatience into a natural militancy'). of *Tish*, a Vancouver-based writing collective that included such soon-to-be Canadian literary stalwarts as George Bowering, Frank Davey, and Fred Wah. The *Tish* school, and its eponymous magazine, were very much influenced by the work of the Black Mountain poets (Charles Olson, Robert Creeley, Robert Duncan, Jack Spicer, Allen Ginsberg, among others), and Marlatt quickly set about 'mastering' this 'new writing'as well:

> i trained myself in that poetic, the injunctions to get rid of the lyric ego, not to 'sprawl' in loose description or emotion ungrounded in image, to pay strict attention to the conjoined movement of body (breath) and mind in the movement of the line, though it didn't occur to me then to wonder whether my somewhat battered female ego was anything like a man's or whether my woman's body had different rhythms from his, or whether my female experience might not give me an alternate 'stance' in the world. ('Difference,' 191)

And yet, while 'the implications of Olson's big breaths and giant proprioceptive body remain gender specific' (Williamson, 'It gives me,' 171), Marlatt is the first to acknowledge the 'continuity' (as well as the 'difference') between her early so-called 'phenomenological' writing and her later

For Brossard and the *Barre du jour* collective, this natural militancy itself translated into the creation, quite literally, of a 'new writing,' *la nouvelle écriture* quickly becoming the term of choice to describe the work that the journal regularly published. *La nouvelle écriture*, influenced in its approach to language by French post-structuralism, and materially centred on the body, was closely related to *l'écriture au féminin* (not to be confused with *écriture féminine*),[7] a term that gradually superseded its predecessor in the Brossardian lexicon as *La (Nouvelle) Barre du jour* featured more and more experimental contributions from feminist writers in Quebec. Summarizing the trajectory of Brossard's career to the mid-1970s, Louise Forsyth notes that

> it has been with the *Barre du Jour* group ... that Nicole Brossard has affirmed her solidarities and developed the weapons of her praxis: *la nouvelle écriture* and *l'écriture au féminin*, both aggressively subversive of received ideology and affirmative of dynamic personal freedom. She moved with the original group beyond the political and social nationalism of the sixties and then moved still further beyond its analysis to a new solidarity and complicity as a radical feminist. ('Beyond,' 164)

'lesbian' writing, that just as 'the openness of the "Black Mountain" projective poetics ... allowed for translation from an American to a Canadian *Tish* context,' so did it '[allow] for translation to the explicitly feminist context of [her] writing in the 1980s' (Carr in 'Between,' 99). Emphasizing that 'you can't make a simple transference,' Marlatt nevertheless points out that both kinds of writing are concerned with locating the 'body in the act of composition' ('Between,' 99). Gradually, however, the question became how to write about the differences *between* bodies, and how to make woman's body, in particular, the *subject* of her work, rather than 'the object of someone else's' ('Between,' 99).

Marlatt's involvement with *Tish* led to successful editorial associations with several other West Coast literary journals throughout the 1970s (including *The Capilano Review*, *Island*, and *Periodics*). It was not until the early 1980s, however, that Marlatt started gravitating to a more explicitly feminist community of writers. The immediate occasion for this move (as well as for her first meeting with Brossard) was the 1981 Dialogue Conference at York University, 'which brought together anglophone-Canadian and Quebec feminist writers and critics' (Williamson, 'It gives me,' 172). It was here, as

This movement culminated, to a certain extent, in the creation of yet another monthly periodical. Even before *La Barre du jour* had mutated into *La Nouvelle Barre du jour*, Brossard and five other women (including Michèle Jean, Eliette Roux, and France Théoret) were busy planning and putting together *Les Têtes de Pioche*, a feminist magazine of social and political writing that published its first issue in March 1976. It appeared regularly thereafter until its final issue of June 1979. A community of feminist writers (and readers), brought together in part through journals like *La (Nouvelle) Barre du jour*, *Les Têtes de Pioche*, and *Spirale*, and committed to a radical critique of patriarchal language and culture, was thus already flourishing in Quebec by the time Barbara Godard's 1983 translation of *L'Amèr* (*These Our Mothers*) introduced English Canadians to the pre-eminent form of this critique, 'fiction/theory.'

well as at the 1983 Women and Words / Les Femmes et les mots Conference in Vancouver, that the idea of a bilingual, pan-Canadian feminist periodical was initially conceived.

This periodical, which first appeared in 1984 as a special issue of *Room of One's Own*, was of course *Tessera*. Now in its fourteenth year, the journal's original editorial collective of Marlatt, Barbara Godard, Kathy Mezei, and Gail Scott has long since dispersed and moved on to other projects. Still, as Marlatt notes in her contribution to the introduction of *Collaboration in the Feminine*, several of *Tessera*'s early 'thematic concerns' recur in subsequent issues (13). One such 'abiding concern' is 'fiction/theory.' Another is translation.

* * *

Contemporary post-structuralist theories of meaning production, emphasizing the necessarily reciprocal relationship between writing and reading in the interpretation of texts, 'have made translation a figure of dramatic indeterminacy, invested less with a confident mission of mediation than with the power to reveal the aporia of communication and the irremediable distance between language and the world of reference' (Simon, 'The Language of Cultural Difference,' 160). Just as he deconstructs the binary opposition between speech and writing, so does Jacques Derrida challenge the traditional distinction between writing and translation, between an 'original' text and its reproduction in (an)other's language. For Derrida, whose 'entire philosophic enterprise ... can be seen as an analysis of the translation process at work in every text,' any given piece of writing is perforce its own translation, since language can only signify in terms of *différance*, 'in the space of its own foreignness to itself' (Johnson, 146).[8]

The post-Derridean deconstruction of writing and translation as mimetic modes of representation is a reminder that texts are not composed outside of history, that they are subject to certain enabling and destabilizing constraints, and that the practice of translation, in particular, 'shapes, and takes shape within, the asymmetrical relations of power that operate under colonialism,' frequently perpetuating static and unchanging images of the other (Niranjana, 2). To the extent that it has to do with the transference of 'foreign' into 'native' languages, translation also operates within a decidedly nationalist paradigm, one which carries with it its own 'dissymmetries' and 'relations of dominance' (Simon, 'The Language,' 160). Thus, in the Canadian context, for example, where 'official bilingualism' barely masks the violence of a 'colonial' encounter between two 'founding nations,' translation is weighted with very different historical and cultural meanings in Quebec and English Canada, to say nothing of the First Nations displaced by this encounter. Moreover, as a gender-marked discourse, translation is the site/sign of yet another power struggle.

In much the same way that McClintock discusses the gendering of nationalism in terms of domestic space, Lori Chamberlain has analysed the Oedipal metaphors at work in the historical representation of writing and translation. Whereas the emphasis in writing is on 'paternity,' notes Chamberlain, on the ability of the (masculine) author to *produce* an 'original' work of art, the emphasis in translation tends to be on 'maternity,' on the 'fidelity' or 'infidelity' of the (feminine) translator's *reproduction* of that work. Her 'survey of the metaphors of translation' suggests that the discourse's 'implied narrative concerns the relation between the value of production versus the value of reproduction. What proclaims [itself] to be an aesthetic problem is represented in terms of sex, family, and the state, and what is consistently at issue is power' (66). (Derrida, it turns out, is not outside this representational loop, referring to the 'double bind of translation as a *hymen*, the sign of both virginity and consummation of a marriage' [Chamberlain, 70].) For Chamberlain, a feminist theory of translation must 'rely, not on the family model of oedipal struggle, but on the double-edged razor of translation as collaboration, where author and translator are seen as working together, both in the cooperative and the subversive sense' (70–1).

It is with these material pressures in mind that Brossard began to investigate the theoretical liminalities and fictional possibilities of translation in the mid-1980s. The immediate occasion for this investigation was a series of poetic 'transformations' which yielded, among other texts, *L'Aviva* (1985), 'Polynésie des yeux' (1987) and, with Marlatt, the chapbooks *Mauve* (1985) and *character/jeu de lettres* (1986). I shall be returning to the poetic collaborations/translations between Brossard and Marlatt at the end of this chapter, but first I want to suggest that the interface between lesbian-feminist fiction/theory and translation, its 'entre-deux,' which is also in some senses a 'pas de deux,' is perhaps nowhere more evident than in Brossard's seventh novel, *Le Désert mauve* (1987).

In many respects her most conventionally 'narrative' novel, *Le Désert mauve* is also the first work to which Brossard has been willing to attach the label 'postmodern' (see Parker, 'The Mauve Horizon,' 107).[9] The reader soon discovers, however, that what appears from the cover to be a single coherent text is actually three books in one. The first, by a 'fictional' author named Laure Angstelle, is 'un court récit' entitled *Le Désert mauve*, and published by 'Éditions de l'Arroyo.' It is narrated in the first person by a precocious teenager named Mélanie, who lives with her mother, Kathy Kerouac, and her mother's lover, Lorna Myher, at the Red Arrow Motel, in the middle of the Arizona desert. Angstelle's novella is both a feminist rewriting of the *Bildungsroman* genre, and a lesbian version of the modern American picaresque (in particular, Jack Kerouac's *On the Road*). When Mélanie is not borrowing her mother's Meteor to drive to Albuquerque, New Mexico, seeking wisdom and absolution from her cousin, Grazie, she is haunting the motel's bar in search of answers to puzzling questions of identity and sexuality, hoping to catch a glimpse of the mysterious Angela Parkins, a forty-something geometrist whose voice was 'hystérique, au bord de l'ivresse' (*DM*, 28; 'hysterical, bordering on intoxication' [*MD*, 25]). Mélanie's attraction to the older academic, blooming as it does against such an arid backdrop, has of course a specific transnational lesbian intertext in Jane Rule's *The Desert of the Heart* (1964), which traces the courtship between the young Anne Childs, a change dispenser at one of the local casinos, and Evelyn Hall, an English professor who has come to Reno to obtain a divorce.

Like Anne's questing (and questioning) soul, Mélanie's restless spirit reflects her immediate engagement with the world around her. Although she tells her story for the most part in the past tense, she seems to live her life completely in the present; the future can only be defined in abstract terms: 'Un jour peut-être, je raconterai ma vie. Un jour quand je n'aurai plus quinze ans et le coeur à l'esprit qui s'émerveille. C'est tout dire quand je parle de la nuit et du désert car en cela même je traverse la légende immédiate de ma vie à l'horizon' (*DM*, 25; 'Some day perhaps I will tell my life story. Some day when I am no longer fifteen with a heart whose spirit has a sense of wonder. It's saying it all when I talk about the night and the desert for in so doing I am stepping through the immediate legend of my life on the horizon' [*MD*, 23]). But her horizon of expectations is abruptly foreshortened: while dancing sensuously together in the bar of the Red Arrow Motel, Angela Parkins is gunned downed in Mélanie's arms, most likely murdered by 'l'homme long,' a figure of 'patriarchal violence and nuclear catastrophe' (de Lotbinière-Harwood, 'Geo-graphies,' 59) whose ominous presence shadows the text, and who bears more than a passing resemblance to Robert Oppenheimer. Angstelle's book ends apocalyptically, with a return to 'la réalité, l'aube' ('reality, the dawn'), and an acknowledgment of absence: 'Je ne peux tutoyer personne' (*DM*, 51; 'I cannot get close to any you' [*MD*, 46]).

For Maude Laures, these words are a provocation and a challenge, spoken across a sexual/textual space of desire separating writer and reader. Having read and 's'était laissé séduire, *ravaler*' (*DM*, 59; 'let herself be seduced, *sucked in*' [*MD*, 55]) by Angstelle's book, she has now decided to undertake a translation of it, thereby rescuing it from literary oblivion and, in the process, forging a closer bond with its 'auteure' ('auther') and her characters. The second section of Brossard's novel, 'Un Livre à traduire' ('A Book to Translate'), is thus largely taken up with Laures's working journal, an extended glossalia/marginalia of/on Angstelle's text, recording the reader-turned-translator's annotations and critical commentary over close to two years of near-obsessive engagement with the book, a period that is nevertheless described as 'un *temps de restauration*' [*DM*, 66; 'a *time of restoration*' [*MD*, 62]). Included in Laures's journal are long observations on 'Lieux et Objets' (the motel, its swimming pool and bar, the Meteor, the TV that is always on, Mélanie's butterfly tattoo, revolvers hidden in drawers, glove compartments, briefcases), 'Personnages' (including detailed portraits of author and translator, as well as a blurry photo-montage of 'l'homme long,' someone whom Laures apparently cannot bring herself to evoke in words), various 'Scènes' (in which Laures constructs mock dialogues between herself and the characters, and stages an imaginary and dramatic conversation/confrontation with Angstelle), and, finally, several of the text's thematic and imagistic 'Dimensions' (desert, dawn, light, reality, beauty, fear, and civilization).

The final section of Brossard's novel comprises Laures's eventual translation of Angstelle's book, which she has retitled *Mauve, l'horizon*, and for which she has found a publisher in 'Éditions de l'Angle.' The catch is that it, like the two preceding sections, is also written in French. Whole passages from *Le Désert mauve* are here repeated verbatim, and the story remains largely the same. But this is by no means translation as simulacrum. Subtle differences in phrasing, syntax, sentence structure, and imagery indicate that Laures has made Angstelle's text her own. While several critics (Simon, 'Rites'; Gould) have pointed out that *Le Désert mauve*'s American setting, along with the reappearance of words and phrases in English and Spanish in all three of its sections, 'draw[s] attention to the "problem" of language, to the foreignness of other languages' (Gould, 98), Brossard's novel is less about translation from one language to another than it is about translation from one woman to another. And, as Brossard notes elsewhere, the only language 'foreign' to women is that articulated by patriarchy: 'coincées entre le sens que nous donnons à la réalité et le non-sens que constitue pour nous la réalité patriarcale, nous sommes le plus souvent forcées d'adapter nos vies à la traduction simultanée que nous faisons de la langue étrangère' (*La Lettre aérienne*, 97; 'caught between the sense we give to reality and the non-sense patriarchal reality constitutes for us, we are most often forced to adapt our lives to simultaneous translation of the foreign tongue' [*The Aerial Letter*, 112]). Once again the *inter*textual and *trans*national connections with Jane Rule are striking in this regard. Troping as well on the 'grammar' of gender and woman's enforced cultural immersion in patriarchy, Rule writes, in the opening paragraph of *The Desert of the Heart*, 'For such a woman [as Evelyn] marriage remains a foreign tongue, an alien landscape, and, since she cannot become naturalized, she finally chooses voluntary exile' (7).

Both Angstelle and Laures, like Evelyn Hall, recognize the limits of patriarchal language, as it informs with equal measure 'source' and 'target' texts: 'Le désert est indescriptible' (*DM*, 11, 181; 'The desert is indescribable' [*MD*, 11, 167]) is the phrase that opens and closes both Angstelle's book and Laures's translation. In a world where words can kill, where a man with an accent who reads Sanskrit translates logarithmic formulae and algebraic equations into weapons of mass destruction, virtually the only way to translate, 'de *faire passer*' (*DM*, 61; 'to *carry over*' [*MD*, 57]), women's experience and lesbian desire is by (re)reading and (re)writing – in the words of Brossard's own translator – 'through the body' (de Lotbinière-Harwood, 'Geo-graphies,' 60).[10] Thus, near the end of the second section we read:

> Le temps était venu du corps à corps avec le livre. Un temps qui ferait place à l'étonnement devant les choses que l'on ne voit que très rarement, sises à l'arrière-plan de nos pensées. D'une langue à l'autre, il y aurait du sens, juste distribution, contour et rencontre du moi, cette substance mouvante qui, dit-on, entre dans la composition des langues et qui les rend savoureuses ou détestables. Maude Laures savait que le temps était maintenant venu de se glisser anonyme et entière entre les pages. (*DM*, 177)[11]

Like the image of the hologram in *Picture Theory*,[12] translation in *Le Désert mauve* thus becomes the site/sign of a 'virtual' encounter between women that takes place both inside and outside of language, imagining from a constantly shifting perspective, and a variety of different angles, women's 'corps rayonnants et tridimensionnels, portées vives comme de fluorescentes citées dans la nuit patriarcale' (*La Lettre aérienne*, 75; 'three-dimensional and radiant bodies, carried resplendent through the patriarchal night like fluorescent cities of visionary learned women' [*The Aerial Letter*, 94]). In reading and rewriting *Laure's* text, *Laures* translates herself: 'Perspective répetée de l'aller-retour. Recours à l'original, néanmoins la démarche interposée, la dérive comme un choc culturel, une émotion grave semée de miroirs et de mirages' (*DM*, 61; 'Repeated perspective of the two-way passage. Resorting to the original, nevertheless the intervening process, the drift like a cultural shock, a grave emotion sown with mirrors and mirages' [*MD*, 57]). 'Translation becomes,' to return to my epigraphs, 'an activity of passing, a round-trip journey' (Parker, 'The Mauve Horizon,' 117). It is, to paraphrase Brossard from the first of those epigraphs, a passing from reality to fiction through writing, and a passing from fiction to reality through reading. And the language that emerges from this utopian space of lesbian-feminist translation/collaboration is one of desire.

* * *

In her book, *Body Inc.*, Pamela Banting distinguishes between three different poetics of translation: '*interlingual* translation' refers to the various kinds of pictographic, ideographic, and phonetic transferences that occur between two or more languages; '*intralingual* translation' interrogates the slippages between speech and writing, orality and literacy, theory and rhetoric, within the same language; and '*intersemiotic* translation' takes place at the level of overlapping sign systems, delineating, among other types of translation, that which occurs between 'words and images (paintings, photographs, drawings) or ... between words and bodies, text and flesh' (xvi). As we have just seen, all three operate, to a greater or lesser degree, in Brossard's *Le Désert mauve.* According to Banting, however, Marlatt's feminist writing practices have, at least since the publication of *How Hug a Stone* (1983), been grounded primarily within a poetics of 'intersemiotic translation,' a (re)reading and (re)writing – to return to de Lotbinière-Harwood's phrase – 'through the body.' As Marlatt puts it in her essay 'musing with mothertongue,' language 'relates us to the world in a living body of verbal relations ... putting the living body of language together means putting the world together, the world we live in: an act of composition, an act of birthing, us, uttered and outered there in it' (*Touch*, 49).

Some critics have interpreted the gynecological/maternal rhetoric suffusing this passage, as well as other of her works, as proof of Marlatt's essentialist politics (see Tostevin, 'Daphne Marlatt'; Davey, *Post-National Arguments*, 195–209). But this is in some senses a wilful misreading, a deliberate conflation of patriarchal and nationalistic constructions of the 'mother tongue' with feminist re-inscriptions of what Banting and others have referred to as the '(m)other tongue.' Mapping the spaces between these two different ways of speaking and writing, Marlatt re-*organ*izes women's bodies and texts neither by replacing the metaphorical penis with an equally metaphorical womb (indeed, her metaphorical 'organ' of choice is the tongue, a source of eroticism for both women and men), nor by substituting '"vulvalogocentrism"' for '"phallocentrism,"' as Lola Lemire Tostevin would have us believe ('Daphne Marlatt,' 38); instead, out of this admixture Marlatt creates, in Banting's terminology, a composite language that is at once no one('s) mother tongue and everyone's other tongue,[13] an 'interlanguage' inscribed in the 'spaces between and among' different linguistic and signifying systems, inscribed, in other words, '*only* in the act of translation itself' (*Body Inc.*, 163).

In *Body Inc.* Banting is concerned, for the most part, with the translation poetics articulated by, and elaborated within, Marlatt's long poem sequences – in particular, *How Hug a Stone* and *Touch to My Tongue* – and criticism (most notably 'musing with mothertongue'). However, in another important essay, Banting has also declared that Marlatt's '*Ana Historic* is the novel as translation': 'Marlatt takes on the problem of how to write a book about an historical woman, a contemporary woman, and the relationships among women, when the traces of women's history have been obliterated, and the official version, that is, men's history, is a narrative of subjection, exploitation and domination' ('Translation A to Z,' 125, 123). 'When both speech and writing are coded as masculine,'

Banting goes on to ask, 'how does the woman writer write a novel?' (124). In part, by translating the form(s) of that novel. And, indeed, it is around questions of genre that I would like to frame my discussion of the translational/transnational poetics embodied by/in *Ana Historic.*

The front cover of Marlatt's novel announces itself as just that: *Ana Historic: A Novel.* However, the reader soon discovers that the text that comprises Marlatt's 'novel' does its best to undermine this claim. Within the pages of *Ana Historic,* virtually every novelistic convention is overturned: chapter divisions are dispensed with, as are standard paragraph breaks, complete sentences, orthodox punctuation, and even capital letters. Blank pages and white spaces abound. Parentheses are opened and frequently never closed. Dialogue is indicated variously with dashes, single inverted commas, and italics. And whole passages from other books – Ralph Andrews's *Glory Days of Logging,* Simone de Beauvoir's *The Second Sex,* Leonard Frank's *The History of Shock Treatment,* J.S. Matthews's *Early Vancouver,* and M. Allerdale Grainger's *Woodsmen of the West,* to name just a few – are imported and plunked down in the middle of Marlatt's. The effect is palimpsestic. Whereas Grainger, for example, seems to record unquestioningly 'history the story, Carter's and all the others', of dominance. mastery. the bold line of it' (*Ana Historic,* 25), Marlatt is drawn to 'the lure of absence,' what gets passively effaced and actively erased from history, 'the monstrous lie of it' (24). By repositioning Grainger's text, then, within the space of her own, Marlatt retroactively maps a feminine consciousness onto it, the cedar stumps we are left with at the end of *Woodsmen* becoming in *Ana Historic* not only a symbol of male profligacy and self-castration but also one of sisterly communion, a place 'hollow in the middle where they nestled in a womb, exchanging what if's, digging further with their fingers, sniffing the odour of tree matter become a stain upon their hands like dried blood' (12).

Grainger's literary realism is likewise dispensed with in *Ana Historic.* Indeed, any semblance of a straightforward, linear narrative is thwarted by three overlapping time-frames, or chronologies: the present, which centres on Annie, a Vancouver wife and mother still mourning the death of her own mother, Ina, and gradually coming to awareness of her lesbian identity through her friendship with Zoe; the near past, which focuses on the relationship between Annie and Ina in 1950s Vancouver; and the historical past of one Mrs Richards, a woman whose name Annie comes across while doing research for her history professor husband, Richard, and about whom she starts to invent a life. This third narrative line becomes a kind of *mise en abyme,* and to her novel-within-a-novel Marlatt/

Annie occasionally appends subject headings in bold typeface. In one final subversion of generic conventions, *Ana Historic*, the 'novel,' actually ends with a poem (153).

To be sure, all of this reads pretty much like the standard recipe for postmodern metafiction: certainly the resistance to master narratives (of history, of gender, etc.) is there in Marlatt's text, not to mention the inclusion of a suitably self-reflexive writing subject as protagonist, one prone to statements like 'a book of interruptions is not a novel' and 'this is not a roman / ce, it doesn't deal with heroes' (37, 67). And yet, while *Ana Historic* can conceivably be classified as 'historiographic metafiction,' and has recently been labelled 'documentary-collage' (see Jones, *That Art of Difference*, 140–60), it also defies, or rather exceeds, the representational boundaries – not to mention the *national* economy – circumscribing the two standard generic designations for most contemporary English-Canadian writing.[14]

Ana Historic: A Novel: women written by history, history *re*-written by women, *trans*lated, 'back, backward, reversed / again, anew' (43). *An ahistoric novel*: documents, records, facts – '(f)act. the f stop of act' – quoted out of (con)text, juxtaposed, re-cited/re-si(s)ted 'in the ongoing cinerama' of fiction (31). *A novel (of) histori(c)/ana*: anecdotes, gossip, a collection of memorable sayings, that which is 'suspect at the archives. "inauthentic," fictional possibly, contrived later' (30). In translating History into her story – Mrs Richards's, but also Ina's, as well as her own – Annie is essentially rewriting what remains unwritten, working from only the barest outline of a source text, the sum total of a life encapsulated by two fleeting references in the archival registers of 1873 and 1874: 'that is all that history says ... but i don't want history's voice. i want ... something is wanting in me. and it all goes blank on a word. want. what does it mean, to be lacking? empty. wanton. vanish. vacant, vacuum, evacuate' (48). But, as Annie soon comes to realize, all that history says is not all that history asks: what do women want (Freud)? what do they lack (Lacan)? Ana Historic = Ana Hysteric. History as 'hystery. the excision of women (who do not act but are acted upon)' (88). In this regard, Annie is thinking not only of the disappearance of Ana Richards from history, but also of the more recent silencing of her mother, Ina, her body cut off – and into – by such medically sanctioned procedures as a hysterectomy and electro-shock therapy: 'they erased whole parts of you, shocked them out, overloaded the circuits so you couldn't bear to remember. re-member' (148–9).

Several critics have remarked on Marlatt's self-conscious recuperation of hysteria as a feminist writing practice. For example, Glen Lowry claims that in *Ana Historic* 'Ina, the hysterical mother, is symptomatic of a much larger fear of the grotesque body. In a sense, she is a manifestation of woman driven mad by an inability to cope with a body denied by the dominant discourses of the bourgeois' (89). Manina Jones notes how Annie's re-assembling and re-circulation of 'both official and unofficial discourses of the past' becomes a kind of '"therapeutic" act,' mirroring her imaginary conversations with her dead mother – themselves constitutive of 'a talking cure for that other cure' – and thereby doubly 'regenerating elements of Annie's (absented) heredity' (*That Art,* 146, 144). Similarly, Janice Williamson has interpreted 'Annie as the hysteric Anna O' (*Sounding Differences,* 188), an historical/hysterical connection that Kathleen Scheel has recently expanded upon in 'Freud and Frankenstein: The Monstered Language of *Ana Historic*' (101–3). But once again it is Banting who makes the link with translation, claiming that 'Marlatt's conception of the relation between the body and language is close to the idea of hysterical translation' (*Body Inc.,* 206). Banting defines hysterical translation neither as 'the translation of psychic blockage or pain into bodily symptoms,' nor as 'the expression or imitation of madness, or of femininity,' but rather as an 'intersemiotic translation from one signifying system to another,' the re-presentation of the 'body as pictogram,' a 'literal/littoral' zone from which to 'de-territorialize' phallogocentric language (206, 208, 209). As Annie puts it at one point in *Ana Historic,* 'mouth speaking flesh. she touches it to make it tell her present in this other language so difficult to translate. the difference' (126). Hysterical translation is enacted most explicitly in Marlatt's novel – as in most of her texts – through the etymological investigation of various words, a process of linguistic recovery that attempts to reorganize and re-eroticize woman's body – '*the* body, not even *your* body. split off, schizophrenic, suffering hysteric malfunction' (89) – by excavating its lost meanings. And, in the case of the lesbian body, its hidden meanings: secretly looking up the word 'vagina' in French, the teenaged Annie is 'astonished to discover it was masculine. le vagin. there must be some mistake, i thought, not knowing its history, a word for sheath, the cover of a sword. it wasn't a sword that i was promised' (63).[15]

The history of words translated in/as the hysteria of bodies; and vice-versa. In keeping with the history/hystery *ana*-logy, Marlatt has suggested elsewhere that part of what both she and Annie are doing in *Ana Historic* is performing a kind of self-analysis through fiction, what Marlatt refers to as 'fictionalysis' ('Self-Representation,' 15). Fictionalysis, for Marlatt, is closely linked to autobiography: 'It is exactly in the confluence of fiction (the self or selves we might be) and analysis (of the roles we have found ourselves in, defined in a complex socio-familial weave), it is in the confluence of the two that autobiography occurs, the self writing its way to life, whole life' ('Self-Representation,' 15). Autobiography, and in particular women's autobiography, is employed as a counter-discourse in Marlatt's novel in order to de-centre and dis-place the truth-claims of official history, to point out that a nation's narrative does not tell the stories of all its citizens.[16] For Peggy Kelly, the deconstruction of history is inseparable from life-writing/the writing life in *Ana Historic.* Both constitute 'key element[s] of the [text's] fiction-theory practice': 'At the intersection of life-writing and historiography, Marlatt examines the false oppositions of "factual" history and story-telling, public and private events, truth and fiction' (82–3).

For Annie, then, autobiography – or 'fictionalysis' – becomes a form of self-translation, occasioning her imaginative 'leap' from the domestic sphere of Annie Anderson, wife of Richard, mother of Ange and Mickey, daughter of Ina and Harald, to the lesbian community of Annie Torrent, lover of Zoe. In this regard, Annie's 'maiden' name may constitute Marlatt's intertextual homage to Anne Hébert's classic 1950 novella about sexual repression and Oedipal desire, 'Le Torrent'; or it might be an allusion to Verena Tarrant, the nubile young woman whom Olive Chancellor desires in Henry James's *The Bostonians* (1886). At any rate, there can be no mistaking the 'torrent' of lesbian desire unleashed by Annie's reclamatory act of self-naming.[17]

But, in translating, or rewriting, (her)self, Annie is also translating many other selves. To this end – and 'Not a Bad End' at that, the reader is informed (138) – Annie precedes her own 'monstrous leap of imagination' (135) with Ana's equally 'monstrous' one, attempting to forestall Mrs Richards's translation into Mrs Ben Springer by suggesting an 'other life in a Gastown room' with Birdie Stewart (134). Ana/Ina/Annie; Mrs Ana Richards / Mrs Richard Anderson: 'whose story is this?' (67). All of theirs and none of theirs, it would seem:

> i want to knock: can you hear? i want to answer her who's there? not Ana or Ina, those transparent covers. Ana Richards Richard's Anna. fooling myself on the other side of history as if it were a line dividing the real from the unreal. Annie/Ana – arose by any other name, whole wardrobes of names guarding the limitations – we rise above them. Annie isn't Richard's or even Springer's. (152)

As with Maude Laures's rewriting of Laure Angstelle's text, Annie's rewriting of her life story, as well as the life stories of Ina and Ana, takes place as a collaborative act in/of the feminine, translation as a lesbian-feminist writing practice opening up a space – a passageway – between fiction and theory, bodies and texts, 'the reach of your desire ... reading us into the page ahead' (153).

This is quite literally the case for Marlatt, who has made a point of 'salvaging' various aspects of her novel and reincorporating them into other texts, most notably 'Territory & co.' Which is why the arguments concerning the 'unexpectedly conventional' ending of *Ana Historic* (Tostevin, 'Daphne Marlatt,' 38), and the 'naïve feminis[m]' and 'ingenuous positivism' supposedly inscribed therein (Davey, *Post-National*, 206, 208), are themselves teleologically reductive.[18] They impose a false sense of closure onto the text because the ending of *Ana Historic* – whether 'good' or 'bad' – is, in fact, not an ending at all. It is, rather – to borrow a phrase from Gertrude Stein – 'a beginning again' (and again and again), the writing of a 'continuous present,' which is always (and also) in some ways an occasion for further translations (see Stein, 'Composition as Explanation,' 499).

* * *

The task of the translator, according to Walter Benjamin, 'consists in finding that intended effect [*Intention*] upon the language into which he is translating which produces in it the echo of the original. This is a feature of translation which basically differentiates it from the poet's work ... The intention of the poet is spontaneous, primary, graphic; that of the translator is derivative, ultimate, ideational' ('The Task,' 76–7). It goes without saying that Benjamin's translator, like his poet, is always already male. Each has a stake in naturalizing his patriarchal investments in an original/originary text, and in making these investments transparent in both 'source' and 'target' languages. But what happens when poet and translator are women – women, moreover, committed to making the differences between languages, texts, and subjectivities visible/scriptable/readable? First of all, notes Barbara Godard, 'the traditional boundary set up to separate original works from their translations collapses' ('Theorizing Feminist Discourse/Translation,' 50). Instead, the feminist poet and the feminist translator become co-participants in the creation of meaning. As Susanne de Lotbinière-Harwood puts it, 'feminists translating feminists have placed an emphasis on their co-creator status which represents a refusal of the traditional view of the neutral and invisible servant-translator' (*Re-Belle*, 154). The feminist translator, insisting on visibility, boldly asserts her presence in the text, placing her signature alongside (rather than underneath) the poet/author's (see de Lotbinière-Harwood, *Re-Belle*, 153–5); among her tasks are the 'affirmation' of her 'critical difference,' and the 'flaunting' of the 'signs of her manipulation of the [feminist poet's] text' (Godard, 'Theorizing Feminist,' 50). To this end, de Lotbinière-Harwood has labelled her feminist translation strategies '*re-belles et infidèles*': 'It is a reclaiming of the expression *belles infidèles*, coined in seventeenth-century France to describe translations that deliberately distort or appropriate the source-language work to suit the translator's political or cultural agenda. Literally it means "unfaithful beauties." My addition of the prefix *re-* changes the beauties into rebels and implies repetition with change. Translation as a rewriting in the feminine' (*Re-Belle*, 98–9).

And, I might add, translation as a *rereading of the feminine*. Which, in Lola Lemire Tostevin's opinion, is also an act of re-belle-ion: 'rereading reverses to resist resists to reverse the / movement along the curve of return' ('Re,' 40). *Re*-writing he; *re*-reading she. Consider, in this *re*gard, the following lines of poetry from Marlatt:

> she has no character meaning
> indissoluble boundaries
>
> s/he:
>
> s plural in excess of he (*character/jeu de lettres*)

Line breaks are left deliberately ambiguous in this passage, and so contribute to the multiplicity of readings it produces. Taking the first line as a single unit, we might rewrite it as: 'she' has no character (i.e., no personality), and therefore no meaning. However, if we insert a break after 'character,' and if we interpret 'meaning' as a gerundive phrase rather than a noun, then we might come up with something like the following: 'she' has no character (i.e., no corresponding ideogram), meaning that boundaries remain indissoluble. Either way, Marlatt seems to be saying, 'she' does not signify apart from 'he.' But the colon at the end of the third line propels us on to the fourth, which presents 'she' out of character, and therefore outside of (his) meaning(s) – extra, excessive, supplementary.

The difference a letter makes. But 'what difference does (the) difference make?' (Meese, 15). Apparently a lot, especially if we (re)read this passage from Marlatt through the holo*graphic* prism of Brossard's translation:

> elle est sans caractère signifiant
> insoluble l/imite
> i/lle:
> ℓ plurielles dans l'excès de ce qu'il (*character/jeu de lettres*)

The French equivalent of 'she' is of course 'elle.' But in order to evoke in her translation Marlatt's graphic play on 's/he,' Brossard must invent a new word, compounding 'il' (he) and 'elle.' Far from signifying the 'insoluble l/imite(s)' of her translation, however, I would argue that this neologism becomes the site/sign of its 'critical difference,' in Godard's 'affirmative' use of that phrase. Building upon the spirit of excess signalled by Marlatt's 'original' source text, Brossard here provides an occasion for further linguistic experimentation and polysemic play.

'I/lle' has as a homonym in French, 'île' ('island'), an aural pun visually reinforced by Brossard's marooning of the letter *i* – also the first-person singular pronoun in English (and, in its lower case, Marlatt's preferred self-designation as a writing subject) – on one side of the barrier/slash. By contrast, what is on the other side is always already greater than 'him': after all, 'il,' even when pluralized to 'ils,' only has one *l*. But 'elle/elles' is doubly doubled, redoubled, woman as multiple, she multiplied; and, as Wittig has demonstrated through her strategic experimentation with the latter pronoun in *Les Guérillères*, there is strength in numbers (see also, in the Quebec context, Suzanne Lamy's *d'elles* [1979]). The two *ll*'s at the centre of each pronoun also fuse to become an erotic metonym – as well as a typographic abbreviation – for 'la *l*angue *l*esbienne' ('the lesbian tongue'), in its pleasurable exploration, its sensual translation, of both bodies and texts, a point reinforced later on in the poetic sequence by Brossard's play on 'sibylle, si belle, elfe, ellipse, la lyre' (*character/jeu de lettres*). And, finally, it is worth mentioning that, in its singular form, 'elle' is also a palindrome, that is, a word that reads the same way backwards as well as forwards, suggesting a process of infinite reinvention in/of the feminine (cf. Annie's deliberate 'misspelling' of Ana Richards's first name in *Ana Historic* [43]).[19] Thus, Brossard's 'play of letters' in the final line of her translation substitutes *l* where, given Marlatt's source text, we might have expected the return of the silent *e* from an earlier piece like '*E* muet mutant' (although the fact that the character is handwritten once again makes things ambiguous: as reproduced on the page, ℓ could be either a small *l* or a large *e*). Brossard concludes with another aural pun, *l*, when spoken aloud, being virtually indistinguishable from 'elle' or 'elles,' the latter of which is also nicely incorporated in the final syllable (more double *ll*'s!) of 'plури*elles*.'[20]

This kind of creative manipulation of the text – what Godard has called '*Womanhandling*' ('Theorizing Feminist,' 50) – takes many forms in the poetic collaborations between Brossard and Marlatt. For example, at the end of her translation of Brossard's contribution to *Mauve*, we find Marlatt actually appending an extra stanza, offering a reading of what in effect remains unwritten. Here, first of all, is the passage in question from Brossard's 'source' text:

la peau et preuves à l'appui
penser que parfois
écrire leur ressemble
en des traits indécidables
fiction culture cortex
M A U V E (*Mauve*)

Now here is Marlatt's translation of this passage:

skin and its evidents

to think   to write
sometimes resembles in
undecidable features

fiction culture cortex

M A U V E

M A U V E

cortex fiction culture

stains the other
mew   maiwa   mauve
malva rose core text
fiction rings round
skin immersed in
resemblance takes

the stain, sense
roseblue in tissue re-
membering (*Mauve*)

Marlatt's (re)reading of *Mauve*, her replaying of it, provides us with an example of translation as 'contamination,' in Tostevin's literary critical formulation of that term (see her 'Contamination'). The body ('corps') of Brossard's text, the heart ('core') of it, spills over into Marlatt's, seeping into her coda like fluid from the brain (cerebral 'cortex'), staining (an)other page – a necessary bit of bruising perhaps, obtained in the rough and tumble negotiation of meaning (see Marlatt, 'Translating MAUVE,' 29–30).

How complex, how multitudinous, the vagaries of colour. Mauve: how many ways can you say it? How many ways can you see it? In 'Polynésie des yeux,' one of only a handful of her texts that she herself has translated, Brossard writes: 'Mauve tangible / c'est un long parcours afin que l'oeil' ('tangible mauve finds its atmosphere / in the long course of the eyes' [*À tout regard*, 120]). And this from *L'Amèr*: 'L'ACTE VIOLENT DE L'OEIL AU MAUVE ÉPRIS S'INFILTRE RAVI DÉPLOYANT *LA*' (58; 'The Violent Act of the Eye on Enamoured Purple Infiltrates Enraptured Unfolding *Her*' [*These*, 60]). A different angle of vision: returning the male gaze, deflecting it, to another woman. In this way, mauve becomes the colour of desire, lesbian desire. Laure Angstelle associates this desire with the desert, an endless thirst. But, in her translation of Angstelle's book, Maude Laures prefers to associate it with what lies beyond the desert, the horizon, a place just out of reach, but a place to get to nonetheless, a somewhere that is nowhere (i.e., Brossard's lesbian utopia), lush with expectation, drenched in possibility. So, too, with Marlatt's translation of Brossard. As Marlatt puts it, 'I came to see Nicole's line of letters reading "M A U V E," then, as the horizon line of thought, a horizon line of fluency indicating that point where meaning curves. Taking liberties, i wrote a coda to honour this experience of reading M A U V E, the erotic transgression of borders, both cultural and linguistic' ('Translating MAUVE,' 30).

Skin and its evidence: apprehending meaning in a moment/movement/mauvement. The horizon line in lesbian-feminist translation is, like the barrier/slash in fiction/theory, fluid and diffuse, inviting continuity and encouraging collaboration rather than imposing false limits and reinforcing the myth of solitary authorship; it is a reading which is also a rewriting, and a writing which is also a rereading; it is 'the leap beyond that borderline of words, beyond the edge of the page ... beyond the separateness of two languages, two minds' (Marlatt, 'Translating MAUVE,' 29).

And, in the case of Brossard and Marlatt, it is the leap beyond the separateness of two nations (English Canada and Quebec), a passage booked between the common ground of gender, the shared territory of sexuality: '*women,* another, a double word. *women beside ourselves.* our fierceness our loyalty our loving' (Marlatt, 'Territory & co.,' 91).

According to Sherry Simon, 'translation has ... been important for literary feminism in Canada, this being one of the few areas in which the hermetic cultural barriers between Quebec and English Canada have become somewhat permeable' ('Rites,' 106). But does it necessarily follow that national borders have also become obsolete? In a recent article speculating on 'The (In?)Compatibility of Gender and Nation in Canadian and Québécois Feminist Writing,' Patricia Smart seconds the claims of Ann McClintock sketched at the beginning of this chapter, arguing that 'nations have without exception been the creations of fathers, wild spaces tamed and mapped and bordered by them, in order that they may then be passed on to sons ... Nations without exception have used women as reproducers and educators and nurturers, all the while excluding them from power and from public space' (15). Acknowledging that feminist writers from Canada and Quebec have frequently 'felt that there was no room for them *as women* within the national struggle,' Smart nevertheless worries about the 'more universalist and often utopian feminism' textually employed in response to this exclusion – 'a spiralling out of national reality into mythical, woman-affirming spaces, islands or deserts presented as cut off from national cultures' (17). Included among the writers cited by Smart in this regard we find, not surprisingly, Brossard and Marlatt. For, indeed, the translational, transnational feminist poetics articulated within their work would appear to be in keeping with Virginia Woolf's famous pronouncement, made in *Three Guineas,* that 'as a woman, I have no country. As a woman I want no country. As a woman my country is the whole world' (109).

And yet, prefixes aside, such a poetics need not automatically imply an end point of transcendence. What it does imply is the need for expanding our imaginative horizons to accommodate communities other than the ubiquitous nation-state. In the case of Brossard and Marlatt, this means supplanting or dis-placing the dichotomous geopolitical regions of Canada and/or Quebec with/into alternative physical and psychical spaces, specifically the *civic* space of Montreal and the *(post)colonial* space of Asia Pacific. Throughout the majority of Brossard's writing, and especially in her fiction (from *Un livre* [1970] to *Baroque d'aube* [1995]), the city of Montreal is a vivid presence, signifying both 'surface et totems,' a '[c]osmogonie déarticulée' ('[d]islocated cosmogony'), a place where the women who populate her texts can ride 'ardente sure l'encre délébile' (*French Kiss*, 157; 'eager astride the delible ink' [122]). Or, as Brossard puts it in her most recent novel, using by now familiar imagery, 'Montréal scintille, grand tatouage mauve entre la nuit et les premières lueurs d'aube' (*Baroque d'aube*, 260; 'Montreal scintillates, a great mauve tattoo between the night and the first rays of dawn' [*Baroque at Dawn*, 256]).[21] Similarly, from the Fraser River cannery town documented in *Steveston* (1974) to the childhood haunts of Penang revisited in 'In the Month of Hungry Ghosts' (1979) to the images of Second World War Australia recalled through the prism of the Gulf War in *Taken* (1996), Marlatt has, throughout her oeuvre, devoted herself not just to deconstructing the specific myths of Canadian nationalism but also to unpacking the more general cultural assumptions behind the paternalistic narrative of British imperialism, particularly as that narrative has unfolded along both the Eastern and Western shores of the Pacific Rim. In the process, Marlatt has inscribed, in the feminine, a *counter*-narrative, one in which the voices of the colonial expatriate and her new immigrant daughter, the Memsahib and her Amah, commingle to form part of the 'plausible implausibility of living difference as both other *and* not-other' ('Difference,' 189).

Negotiating the differences that make up this common ground of gender is what mobilizes the feminist concept of the 'politics of location,' which serves as an antidote to the totalizing claims of both patriarchy and nationhood, and about which I will have more to say in the next chapter. Moreover, as my discussion of Dionne Brand's particular politics of *dis*-location in that chapter further suggests, the question is perhaps not so much one of (in)compatibility after all, of which has the greater identitarian claim, gender or nation (or race or sexuality or class, for that matter), but rather the situatedness of each of these affiliative spaces within a given historical moment.

6

'In another place, not here': Dionne Brand's Politics of (Dis)Location

Poetry is here, just *here*. Something wrestling with how we live, something dangerous, something honest.

Dionne Brand, *Bread out of Stone*, 183

I had originally thought that I would begin this chapter on Dionne Brand by locating myself within it, delineating once again the subject positions initially catalogued in chapter 1: white Anglo-Scots gay male literary critic living in Vancouver, British Columbia, Canada ... But, as Adrienne Rich points out in her essay 'Notes toward a Politics of Location,' this kind of Dedalusian game of mapping – a game that Rich admits to playing herself as a child – presumes a fixed centre, 'from which the circles [expand] into the infinite unknown' (212). It is this 'question of feeling at the center that gnaws' at Rich throughout her essay. 'At the center of what?' she asks (212). And if, as Rich implies, my centre 'will not hold,' what does that say about the margins that I have constructed in my overly Cartesian universe, in my work on nationalisms and sexualities in contemporary Canadian literatures, in this chapter? Brand offers a suitably destabilizing and dislocating response when she says: 'I don't consider myself on any "margin," on the margin of Canadian literature. I'm sitting right in the middle of Black literature, because that's who I read, that's who I respond to' ('The Language of Resistance,' 14).[1]

Clearly, then, a more fluid definition of the 'politics of location' is required before beginning any study of Brand's work: something more responsive to the shifting parameters of her identity as a black woman, lesbian, writer, documentary film-maker, academic, scholar, archivist, and cultural activist; something akin to that articulated by Chandra Talpade Mohanty in 'Feminist Encounters: Locating the Politics of Experience.' In this essay, Mohanty sketches the outlines of 'the historical, geographical, cultural, psychic and imaginative boundaries which provide the ground for political definition and self definition for U.S. feminists in 1981' (31). According to Mohanty, these intersecting boundaries open up a 'temporality of struggle,' a site of political 'engagement' that 'suggests an insistent, simultaneous, non-synchronous process characterized by multiple locations,' at the same time as the 'reterritorialization' of said boundaries allows for 'a paradoxical continuity of self,' a 'mapping and transforming [of] political location' that 'suggests a particular notion of political agency, since ... location forces and enables specific modes of reading and knowing the dominant' (41, 42).

In what follows I want to examine the various national and sexual boundaries that both give shape to and delimit, at once legitimate and circumscribe, the production, distribution, and reception of Brand's work in this country, as well as the ways in which Brand 'reterritorializes' these boundaries in her writing, (dis)placing or (dis)locating the national narrative of subjectivity, for example, into the diaspora of cross-cultural, -racial, -gender, -class, and -erotic identifications. In so doing, I hope to illuminate how Brand elaborates both 'a temporality of struggle' and 'a paradoxical continuity of self' that are not only multiply located, but also multi-directional; how, in other words, Brand, as writer, struggles to inscribe her national and sexual experiences in historically defined representational forms, and how I, as reader, accede to those representations through a negotiation of my own historical and experiential contexts. The chapter is divided into two parts: in the first, I present an overview of recent feminist and postcolonial reconsiderations of the 'politics of location,' focusing on how publishing and media technologies in this country frequently contribute to the 'unlocatability' of Brand's work as distinctly 'Canadian'; in the second, I 'perform' a preliminary speech-act reading of her critically acclaimed poetry collection, *No Language Is Neutral*, suggesting that a politics of location must also, in some senses, be accompanied by an ethics of listening.

* * *

As Caren Kaplan summarizes, 'the term "politics of location" emerged in the early 1980s as a particularly North American feminist articulation of difference, and even more specifically as a method of interrogating and deconstructing the position, identity, and privilege of whiteness' (139). Initially used by Adrienne Rich in a series of related essays exploring the effects of racism and homophobia on the women's movement in the United States (most of which have since been published together in *Blood, Bread, and Poetry*), the term, in seeking to account for the production and proliferation of multiple and manifold identities in an era of diaspora and displacement, as well as hegemonic Western interest in those identities, has since '[become] its own academic reification' (Kaplan, 138), at once deconstructing and naturalizing the boundaries between centre and margin.

Central to Rich's conception of a politics of location is her awareness of the impossibility of a 'global' vision of feminist solidarity, which, as she sees it, is merely a creation 'of white Western self-centeredness,' and which, moreover, is frequently founded on a deliberate confusion between what Rich identifies as competing 'claims to the white and Western eye and the woman-seeing eye.' 'Marginalized though we have been as women,' she asserts, 'as white and Western makers of theory, we also marginalize others because our lived experience is thoughtlessly white, because even our "women's cultures" are rooted in some Western tradition' ('Notes,' 219). Yet, as Kaplan points out, such a deconstructive move towards change – what Rich elsewhere refers to as a simultaneous process of 'demasculinizing' and 'de-Westernizing' ('Notes,' 225) – is inherently flawed from the outset because it mistakenly conflates 'Western' and 'white,' thereby 'reinscribing the centrality of white women's position within Western feminism' (141).

If Kaplan politely chastises Rich for failing to consider adequately her own identificatory investments in theorizing and receiving difference, Michele Wallace vehemently denounces Rich's role as a 'gatekeeper' of American feminism, 'somebody who defines the inside, thus keeping me out' (48–9). Describing herself as 'unlocated' and 'schizophrenic' as a black feminist writer and critic in the United States, Wallace advances a theory of location that contrasts sharply with that espoused by Rich. As Wallace puts it, 'when it came to writing, it turned out to be very much a problem of spanning several locations at once, none of which I was able to call home' (50). At the same time, however, she is careful not to discount or elide her sometimes intense feelings of fragmentation and of 'writing in silence' (49). In so doing, she articulates a politics of *un*location that seeks to legitimize 'the multiplicity of positions and allegiances that characterizes the contemporary diasporic or marginal subject'

(Kaplan, 143). For Wallace, then, a politics of location is entirely a matter of 'process,' by which she necessarily means 'more than one process, more than one location, perhaps three or four, none of which connect in any self-evident manner. Or perhaps it is because I haven't found the connections yet. Perhaps this is the level at which my work can be in dialogue with itself without superimposing a premature closure or a false unity' (49).

Brand likewise forestalls 'premature closure' and 'false unity' in her work by embracing 'the dialogue between self and other in herself' (Zackodnik, 206). Unlike Wallace, however, Brand is willing to extend this dialogue to include Rich as well. In *Listening for Something*, her latest documentary feature, and one of the last films to be produced out of the National Film Board of Canada's Studio D, Brand engages the American writer in an extended conversation about the nation-state, citizenship, global capitalism, revolutionary socialism, racism, feminism, sexuality, and the positioning of themselves and their work in relation to each of these subjects. Their ongoing dialogue, shot in grainy black and white, is intercut with lush colour sequences, in which the camera roams across the landscapes of the United States, Canada, and Tobago, visually locating the viewer as Rich and Brand read from their respective poetry.

It is interesting to note that Rich begins her contribution to *Listening for Something* in much the same way that she opens her essay 'Notes toward a Politics of Location': by critiquing Virginia Woolf's declaration, outlined at the end of the previous chapter, that women have no country. As Rich puts it in the film, the challenge of growing up as a middle-class white woman in the racially divided American South was precisely to refuse such transcendent avenues of escape, and to locate herself materially within the historical flux of her country, her city, her home.

And yet, a central paradox within Rich's formulation of a politics of location concerns the fact that her radical rethinking of the U.S. feminist movement, of 'how this *location* affects me, along with the realities of blood and bread within this nation' ('Blood,' 183), was actually occasioned by a trip to Sandinista-governed Nicaragua in the early 1980s. Understanding the meaning of 'being here' meant 'going there,' to reconfigure the title of one of her essays about the visit.[2] Or, as Kaplan succinctly puts it, 'Rich completely rewrites her "home" in terms of "away"' (141).[3] The irony, of course, is that a politics of location – at least as it is initially elaborated here by Rich – does not necessarily travel well as a theory of transnational feminist liberation (just as it must be acknowledged that Brossard and Marlatt's poetics of translation maps only a small and very specific terrain of lesbian-feminist collaboration). Nor does such cultural relativism adequately account for the various historical, material, and situational contingencies attendant upon the diasporic conditions of enslavement, migration, and decolonization, which more often than not contribute to a sense of displacement and exile, of feeling 'away' while 'home' and vice versa, or of feeling 'in between' the two. As I pointed out earlier, in chapter 1, Gloria Anzaldúa has referred to this liminal space, this 'vague and undetermined place created by the emotional residue of an unnatural boundary,' as a 'borderland' (3).[4] Homi Bhabha, in his introduction to *The Location of Culture*, has recently labelled this realm 'the *beyond*,' a term which signals 'neither a new horizon, nor a leaving behind of the past,' but rather 'a sense of disorientation, a disturbance of direction,' a term, moreover, which 'captures something of the estranging sense of the relocation of the home and the world – the unhomeliness – that is the condition of extra-territorial and cross-cultural initiations' (1, 9). '[T]he diaspora has made the world "home,"' according to Claire Harris, but this 'home' is less a tangible locale than a 'space between two worlds,' a 'place of paradox,' a 'limbo' to which poets like Harris and Brand find themselves confined (125). For her part, Brand has enumerated the politics of her particular *dis*locations in *Chronicles of the Hostile Sun* in terms of a further set of spatial paradoxes. Despite having lived *here* – in Canada – for most of her life, what seems to matter most is that Brand was born down *there* – on the Caribbean island of Trinidad. Having one's papers in order, owning a Canadian passport – these things are virtually meaningless in the face of an obdurate national psychology that, official government policies notwithstanding, continues to reinforce in Brand and her fellow immigrants the feeling that they are 'stateless anyway' (*Chronicles*, 70).

What Brand seeks to convey with this statement, and throughout the collection from which it emerges, according to Leslie Sanders, 'is not "home" but rather "other people's experience" and "other places." As a black West Indian and a citizen of that "Third World," her poetic offering legitimately is "other," but it is also conscious of being so, it is consciously oppositional. And it is "here," not "there"' (26). Although Sanders, for the most part, persists in analysing Brand's writing in terms of its imaginative figuring – 'as race, place and heritage' (22) – of the West Indies, she also 'dares' to claim Brand as a 'Canadian' writer. She does so by recuperating Brand's trope of 'statelessness' within and through McLuhan's paradigm of the 'borderline': 'statelessness as an imaginative reality is particularly possible and fruitful in this country of resonances. Claiming

Brand as a Canadian writer is part of daring the identity McLuhan posits is truly Canadian. Similarly, by becoming a Canadian writer, Brand is extending the Canadian identity in a way McLuhan would recognize and applaud' (20).

Sanders's use of the verb 'becoming' is, I believe, telling here, since Brand's race, gender, and sexuality necessarily preclude full participation in national citizenship, and thus prevent her from ever 'being' a Canadian writer. In this sense, then, Brand remains a 'borderline case.' Or, as Carol Morrell suggests, in her introduction to *Grammar of Dissent*, Brand, together with fellow Trinidadian-Canadian poets Harris and Marlene Nourbese Philip, represents 'a particular kind of exiled woman':

> Of African descent, their cultural and linguistic history has been foreshortened: much of Africa was lost when their ancestors were forcibly brought to the New World. Having themselves voluntarily emigrated to Canada, they have become distanced from their childhood experiences of family and community in Trinidad. In Canada, because of what they call subtle but systemic racism, these women do not readily fit in. To many Canadians they 'are' the colour of their skin. Each has had some of her writing rejected by Canadian publishers as not being 'Canadian enough.' (9)

The link between the Canadian publishing industry and nationalist sentiment that Morrell alludes to in passing at the end of this quotation bears further investigation, I believe, especially as it impacts on the 'statelessness' of a writer like Brand, for whom Canada is both home and 'enemy territory' ('At the Lisbon Plate,' 97). For, as Kaplan astutely notes, when it comes to the interpretation of texts, the politics of location cannot be separated from the politics of 'production and reception,' that is, the need to '[historicize] the relations of exchange that govern literacy, the production and marketing of texts, the politics of editing and distribution, and so on' (139).

In constructing itself as *The Canadian Publishers*, McClelland and Stewart helps define and foster, to a certain extent, literary nationalism in this country. As Arun Mukherjee has recently put it, mainstream publishing houses mirror 'the "soul" of the nation, its history and traditions, which are also conceived in terms of a nation's unified "spirit"' (433). But what does this say about the legions of small, independent presses in this country (The Women's Press, Sister Vision, Williams-Wallace, Mercury, Gynergy, Ragweed, Press Gang, Theytus, Fifth House, TSAR, Goose Lane, Polestar, etc.) that have made it their mandate to publish the work of 'racial minority women'[5] writers like Dionne Brand? If large established houses like M&S reflect the 'soul' of Canada (a soul which, needless to say, is overwhelmingly male and white), if such official channels of 'print-capitalism' might be said to help operationalize what Benedict Anderson has called 'imagined nation-ness' (46), then the 'alternative' presses (dare we call them *counter*-presses?) enumerated above would seem to reflect Canada's dark, outered, and exotic 'Other.'[6] As Mukherjee remarks, the dominant discourse here is not one of nationality but of 'ethnicity':

> Many Aboriginal and racial minority women writers have spoken eloquently about how their writing has been turned down time and again because it was not deemed 'Canadian,' but 'ethnic,' that is emerging from and speaking to a minority group. When published by small, usually 'ethnic' presses, the establishment – reviewers and academics – othered it in multiple ways: it was exotic; it was 'Black,' or 'Native,' or 'South Asian'; it was about 'immigrant' experience. The category Canadian has been denied to these writers, their work seldom seen as contributing to 'Canadian' life. (430)

This would perhaps explain why early reviews of Brand's work – which, up until the 1990 release of *No Language Is Neutral*, was published almost exclusively by Williams-Wallace, a small press specializing in writings by Afro-Caribbean women – are so clearly drawn along lines of race and gender. As Mukherjee implies, critical print review media in this country often work hand in hand with the publishing industry to institutionalize dominant views of what it means to write 'as a Canadian.' In the case of two 1983 reviews of Brand's poetry, this process of institutionalization is also one of 'othering.' Douglas Fetherling, for example, opens his *Books in Canada* review of Brand's *Winter Epigrams* by admitting that 'Brand's name is a new one to me, and I know only what the little blurb reveals, that she "is a Toronto Black poet" who's published three earlier titles' (38). By the end of his review, however, Brand is no longer 'a *Toronto* Black poet,' but a 'West Indian' one: 'To this West Indian poet, the winter is not the stuff of the Gilles Vigneault song nor a Calvinist visitation meant to test people; it's a strange and terrible ordeal' (38). Brand's collection thus becomes, in Fetherling's estimation, testimony not to the poet's facility with a satirical and ironic form that dates back to ancient Greece, but to her inability (or unwillingness) to write about that most Canadian of experiences – winter – in a manner representative of the literary traditions of the 'two founding nations' (France and England).[7] For her part, in a *Quill & Quire* mini-review of *Primitive Offensive*, Catherine Russell concludes that much of the book has 'a threatening tone,' Brand's 'African theme' producing a poetic language that likewise becomes 'primitive in its violence and nakedness.' In the end, Russell sighs, 'Brand's persistent reworking of her anguish is ... exhausting. One craves a pair of bongos at least to carry one through the onslaught' (76).

In an interview with Beverly Daurio, also published in *Books in Canada*, Brand responds to the representation of her work in reviews as follows: 'Reviews are equally racist. Work by peoples of colour has to prove universality; a white writer is never asked to prove that. The other things you look for in a review are words like "anger." Reviewers always talk about the anger of Black writers' (14). Thus, in her review of Brand's recent novel, *In Another Place, Not Here*, we find Joan Thomas, in the *Globe and Mail*, praising Brand's 'apparently effortless facility with language' but reacting against the 'bitter tone' which 'seems to be the point of view of the novel': 'there is no hope of a future that transcends the tragedies of the past,' laments Thomas of the book's ending, 'anger is the end of the road' (C10). But in seeking transcendence, and by imposing her own sense of closure onto the text, Thomas ignores the deliberately unfinalizable quality of Brand's novel. Divided into two parts, set in two different locales (Toronto and an unnamed Caribbean island), focalized through two different protagonists (Elizete and Verlia), alternating between first- and third-person narration, using language that combines both a lush participial demotic and a standard English idiom, travelling back and forth in time and space, playing off the themes of home and exile, and complicating dichotomies of race and gender with issues of sexuality and class, *In Another Place, Not Here* repeatedly confounds readerly expectations. Unfortunately, Brand's reframing of intra- and extratextual centre-margin relations in this way tends to get lost on the 'Can lit crit' establishment, which for the most part, still operates under the aegis of an either/or equation of literary nationalism: does she write about Canada or not? And if so, *how* does she write about it?

'Where is here?' Frye's famous query cannot possibly signify to a writer like Brand, because, for her, 'here is not a word with meaning when it can spring legs, vault time, take you ... her away ... here is nothing to hold on to or leave a mark, here you ... hold on to your name until it becomes too heavy and you forget it' (*In Another Place*, 199; first and third ellipses in original). Because Brand's 'here' is necessarily mediated, provisional, evanescent – in a word, 'unlocatable' – her work remains marginal/marginalizable in academic discussions of Canadian literary canons. In this regard, we begin to see how 'national' publishing, reviewing, and teaching priorities further complicate the issue of a politics of location with regard to Brand's work: different notions of location, of what it means to be 'here' and write about 'there,' for example, give rise to contradictory political practices, and agendas.

* * *

I want to conclude this chapter with a brief textual analysis of Brand's 1990 collection of poetry, *No Language Is Neutral.* More specifically, adapting the speech act theory which implicitly informs Judith Butler's *Gender Trouble* and Homi Bhabha's 'DissemiNation,' I want to assess the extent to which Brand's strategic use of 'lesbian' parataxis and 'Caribbean' demotic forms in the text's two long poems, 'hard against the soul' and the title sequence, 'No Language Is Neutral,' 'locates' minority utterance in (performative) opposition to hegemonic patriarchal and nationalist discourses.[8] I only regret that, because of my inability to quote at length from either of these extraordinary pieces, this assessment must necessarily be a foreshortened and partial critical exercise. Readers are therefore strongly encouraged to consult Brand's text directly for further elucidation of what follows.

Although neither explicitly mentions him in their texts, it seems to me that both Butler's and Bhabha's senses of 'the performative' – as applied to the elaboration of gender and cultural differences, respectively – owe something to the definition of the term put forward by J.L. Austin in *How to Do Things with Words* (1962; 1975). In this posthumously published book, Austin distinguishes between two categories of linguistic utterance: 'constatives' and 'performatives.' Whereas the former category is made up of utterances that describe a situation or state a fact that can be assessed as 'true' or 'false,' the latter category comprises utterances that actually perform an action in words, one that is neither true nor false, but rather 'felicitous' or 'infelicitous,' sincere or insincere, well invoked or misinvoked (Austin, 12–18). In other words, performatives are not just utterances that 'say' something; they also 'do' something (133). And, as Austin demonstrates with his analysis of the performative function of the phrase 'I do' in a marriage ceremony (5–11 and *passim*), the *location* in which it is spoken impacts significantly on the production of meaning put into play by a given *locution.*

Despite the fact that he later reverses his own binary opposition between constatives and performatives in favour of a three-tiered iterative/iterable system of 'locutionary,' 'illocutionary,' and 'perlocutionary' acts (see Austin, 94–108), Austin's internal hierarchy of performatives has been the subject of much deconstructive scrutiny. In 'Signature, Event, Context,' for example, Jacques Derrida criticizes, among other things, Austin's refusal to discuss all those performatives labelled 'non-serious' and '*parasitic*,' that is, utterances 'said by an actor on the stage, or ... introduced in a poem, or spoken in soliloquy' (Austin, 22).[9] And, in the final chapter of *Bodies That Matter*, Butler challenges the 'centrality of the marriage ceremony in J.L. Austin's examples of performativity,' once again emphasizing the importance of location: 'from where and when does such a performative draw its force, and what happens to the performative when its purpose is precisely to undo the presumptive force of the heterosexual ceremonial?' (224–5).[10] Moreover, Butler, like Derrida before her, critiques Austin for attributing the 'binding power' of the performative speech act solely to the intentional will or authority of the speaker. As she notes, the issue of power is much more complex here: 'If the power of discourse to produce that which it names is linked with the question of performativity, then the performative is one domain in which power acts *as* discourse' (*Bodies*, 225). Nevertheless, the absent presence of Austin at the end of Butler's earlier book is here invoked (or misinvoked) by name precisely to reassert that 'genders can be neither true nor false, neither real nor apparent, neither original nor derived' (*Gender Trouble*, 141). (Austin is even more of a presence in Butler's *Excitable Speech: A Politics of the Performative* [1997].)

How, then, does gender 'perform'? What exactly does it 'do'? Or, to quote Butler, 'In what senses is gender an act?' 'As in other ritual social dramas [like marriage, for example],' she notes by way of reply to her own question, 'the action of gender requires a performance that is *repeated*. This repetition is at once a reenactment and reexperiencing of a set of meanings already socially established; and it is the mundane and ritualized form of their legitimation' (*Gender*, 140). This '*stylized repetition of acts*' – what Butler (once again following from Derrida) refers to elsewhere as 'citationality' (*Bodies*, 12–16 and *passim*) – 'moves the conception of gender off the ground of a substantial model of identity to one that requires a conception of gender as a constituted *social temporality*' (*Gender*, 140–1). Within the 'social temporality' of Brand's 'hard against the soul,' its 'temporality of struggle,' to reinvoke Mohanty's phrase, the reiteration and re-membering of lesbian desire is thus partly performed through the stylized, paratactical repetition of the homonym 'hear/here.' In the space of a single stanza or even line, one word is called forth and responded to by the other, as in section IV of the poem, for example, where a lover's voice floats up out of sleep and is answered by a warm embrace. It is *here,* in these corporeal 'gestures,' according to the speaker of the poem, that we *hear* the beginnings of time. And time's surcease (see especially 39ff).

Similar tropes of recitation and repetition abound throughout this suite of poems, most notably in the first section, with its successive incantations of 'this is you girl' (6–7), each used to introduce a new stanza, and to catalogue an increasingly vivid progression of concrete images that supplement the opening deictic. The concept of addressivity is of equal importance in this regard. Indeed, the prominent position afforded the pronoun 'you' throughout the collection, and its frequent placement alongside or in conjunction with one or another of the 'hear/here' word pairings (as in 'I hear you / I am here for you'), suggests that Brand's poetry is part of a larger dialogue, that the negotiation and articulation of her identity takes place in a 'dialogic of differences' (Zackodnik, 206).

Of course, gender and sexuality are not the only provisional identities being performed here, as the citational locations/locutions of that word, and its auditory complement, elsewhere in the collection demonstrate. As Brand's text points out, there are no easy equivalencies to be made in terms of the discontinuous 'social temporalities' of gender and race. However, it is interesting to note the degree to which race, in contemporary cultural criticism, is taken as *the* one identity category that defies performative description and theorization. That is, notwithstanding narratives of passing, racial difference is interpreted as 'readily knowable,' and therefore 'readable,' because the signs of difference are always already there, made visible to the naked eye (see Biddy Martin, 110).[11] In other words, races are either 'true' or 'false'; not 'felicitous' or 'infelicitous.' But once again to revert to Austin, this is to conflate performance in its literal or *literary* (i.e., theatrical) sense with linguistic performativity, a discursive equation that Butler, in *Bodies That Matter,* admits to being partly responsible for by earlier 'citing drag [in *Gender Trouble*] as an example of performativity, a move that was taken then, by some, to be *exemplary* of performativity' (230; see also *Gender Trouble,* 137–8). As Butler goes on to clarify, 'if drag is performative, that does not mean that all performativity is to be understood as drag' (*Bodies,* 230–1). Thus it is with Brand's frequent use of Caribbean demotic illocutions in her poetry, the presence of which, in 'No Language Is Neutral' in particular, must not be read reductively as a sign of the text's performance of a kind of racial drag or parodic minstrelism. Indeed, the 'rudiments' of Brand's grammar in this context (which is by no means 'rudimentary'), her 'grammar of dissent' in the words of Carol Morell, are deeply rooted in history, combining a cultural 'morphology' of silent subjection with the whispered 'idioms' of unfettered colloquy, as an early passage in the poem makes clear (23).

In other words, what we are hearing here, in this text, is an act of resistance, performed through the Creolization of a dominant language (English), and resulting in the creation of a 'variable, distinct speech community' (Winer, 12). African peoples, forcibly relocated to the Caribbean by European slave-trading powers in the eighteenth and early nineteenth centuries, were prevented from communicating with each other in their original tribal tongues, and so put together a new, hybrid language, one that deliberately 'contaminated' the official patron discourses of their colonizers (English, French, Dutch, Spanish, etc.) with African idioms and speech patterns. Teresa Zackodnik has recently analysed the interplay between standard English and what she (after Edward Brathwaite) calls Caribbean nation language in Brand's poetry, connecting it with related issues of identity and place: 'Dionne Brand's poetry exhibits this ambivalence [towards place and language], yet also moves toward a notion of the exiled self as place and belonging, and a conception of the language that will voice her experience as a multivoiced discourse in both standard English and Caribbean nation language' (194).[12] Of course, neither language is neutral here; as Brand well knows, each is thoroughly marked by and imbricated in the other: 'Each sentence realized or / dreamed jumps like a pulse with history and takes a / side' (34).

As socio-linguist John Roy has pointed out, in many Caribbean Creole, or nation, languages, 'tense marking is optional'; what is of greater grammatical importance is aspect, that is, whether a given verb phrase describes an event that has already occurred, or whether it describes 'a state that exists at the moment of speech' (146, 147). Within the context of Brand's 'No Language Is Neutral' and within the larger framework of Austin's theory of performative utterances, it is worth pausing over her rather idiosyncratic use of the verb 'to do' throughout the poem. Consider, as but one brief example, the following two lines: 'Silence done curse god and beauty here, / people does hear things in this heliconia peace' (23). In the first instance ('done curse god'), the aspect marked is 'completive,' done, as a 'preverbal marker,' having 'the dominant sense of completion of an activity, event or process' in Lise Winer's schematization of English Creoles in Trinidad and Tobago (27). But as Winer goes on to note, when combined with another auxiliary verb (in Brand's case, the non-stative 'curse'), the meaning of done becomes more ambiguous, either 'emphasizing the end-point of an event,' 'viewing the event as a completed whole,' or assessing 'the situation as having been achieved at some previous point in time, but as still continuing' (28). In the second instance ('does hear things'), the aspect marked is 'habitual' or 'present imperfective,' which 'refers to a repeated activity, a relationship between a dynamic situation and a bounded period of time during which this activity occurs' (Winer, 26). In both instances, however, the aspect is clearly not marked as 'perfective'; that is, we are meant to hear that the racial history Brand is performing for us here is not something in the past, that the Caliban-like cursing informing these lines, and the poem and text from which they emerge, necessarily continues in the present, relocated to metropolitan centres like Toronto and Vancouver, teeming with 'race conscious landlords and their jim crow flats, oh yes! / here!' (31).

Eliding the degree to which racial identities, like gender and erotic identities, are also performative (at least in terms of linguistic speech acts) is to presume that whites are not also racialized in accounts of cultural difference, that whiteness is the free-floating signifier, the undifferentiated, performative ground against which all other (i.e., non-white) hues of the rainbow must figure themselves in fixed and static opposition:[13] 'White. She had thought that it was a style, a way of living well that perhaps anyone could acquire,' writes Brand of Verlia in *In Another Place* (136). One consequence of this stylization of whiteness as normative, according to Brand and Linda Carty in '"Visible Minority" Women: A Creation of the Canadian State,' is that all other non-whites become 'quantitatively aberrant and qualitatively homogeneous' (169). Moreover, as Brand points out in a paper she delivered at the 1994 'Writing thru Race' conference in Vancouver, the construction of 'whiteness' as synonymous with 'Canadianness' carries with it further powers of social legitimation and exclusion: 'The European nation-state of Canada built itself around "whiteness," differentiating itself through "whiteness" and creating outsiders to the state, no matter their claims of birthright or other entitlement. Inclusion in or access to Canadian identity, nationality and citizenship (de facto) depended and depends on one's relationship to "whiteness"' (*Bread out of Stone*, 173–4).

The performative slippage between racial and national identities (not to mention class and sexual ones), between whiteness and Canadianness, that Brand highlights here is also articulated by Bhabha – albeit in a much different context – in his highly influential essay 'DissemiNation.' Like Butler's theories of gender performativity, Bhabha's conception of 'national ambivalence' would also seem to be predicated on the iterative/

iterable premises of speech act theory. In posing the question 'How do we conceive of the "splitting" of the national subject?' Bhabha distinguishes between the 'accumulated temporality' of the pedagogical (or constative, to put it in Austinian terms), which 'founds its narrative authority in a tradition of the people,' and the 'repetitious, recursive strategy,' the '"in-between"' temporality, of the performative, which 'interrupts the self-generating time of national production' through 'its enunciatory "present"' (298–9). In so doing, Bhabha is 'attempting to discover the uncanny moment of cultural difference that emerges in the process of enunciation' (312), a process 'that arises from the ambivalent splitting of the pedagogical and the performative' and from which, as we have seen in connection with Findley in chapter 2, 'there emerges a more instantaneous and subaltern voice of the people, a minority discourse that speaks betwixt and between times and places' (309).

However, in speaking betwixt and between times and places, something inevitably gets lost. '[B]etween my stories / and the time I have to remember,' writes Brand in 'No Language Is Neutral,' 'between me and history,' a verse can still go missing, a chapter may yet disintegrate and turn to dust (26). In the overlapping 'social temporalities' of race and gender, some narratives emerge more clearly than others, and some stories never get told at all. Hence Butler's claim that the repetition of a performative 'act' of gender is always, in some senses, 'a provisional failure of memory' (*Bodies*, 244n); and hence Bhabha's reworking of Ernest Renan's notion, also previously outlined in chapter 2, that the act of national identification also requires a 'syntax of forgetting,' or 'forgetting to remember': 'To be obliged to forget – in the construction of the national present – is not a question of historical memory; it is a construction of a discourse on society that *performs* the problematic totalization of the national will' ('DissemiNation,' 310, 311). In the construction of the 'national [and sexual] present' of Brand's 'No Language Is Neutral,' the here and now of 'race conscious landlords and their jim crow flats,' 'this place where you are a woman and your breasts need / armour to walk. Here' (33), there is an acknowledgment that 'truth' is unimportant, that 'nostalgia' feeds a lie, and that memory is but a 'fiction.'

But if Brand's 'syntax of forgetting' seems to suggest here, in 'No Language Is Neutral,' a process of fragmentation, a violent rending of national identity ('language seemed to split in two,' she writes, 'one branch fell silent, the other / argued hotly for going home ...' [31]), a continuation of the 'statelessness' elaborated in *Chronicles of the Hostile Sun*, in the final section of 'hard against the soul' her language of remembering, her navigation of the various roots/routes of identity, her tracing of their 'map to coming home, the tough geography' (40), implies a provisional alignment of racial, gender, and erotic identities within a single, coherent location, the lesbian body. It is only here, the final lines of the poem suggest, that the speaker finds a true vision of herself ('my eyes followed me to myself' [51]), or more properly, the multiplicity of her *selves.* What others deny exists, or label *terra incognita,* is instantly recognizable to Brand. This is a place she has been before, she tells us in the very last line of the poem. And to which she will no doubt return.

Dis-location from without thus becomes a *re*-location from within. Brand's effecting of sexual/textual closure at the end of this collection as a refusal to be marginalized challenges certain orthodoxies of Canadian literary nationalism, with its emphasis on a presumptive pluralism and notions of multicultural inclusion. And yet, to return to the credo quoted at the outset of this chapter, Brand's self-conscious positioning of herself and her writing 'in the middle' of an/other, trans- or supra-national literary tradition – namely 'Black literature' – would seem merely to reinscribe an aesthetics of 'difference as sameness' similar to the one interrogated in my analysis of Quebec nationalist writing in chapter 4. Indeed, the creation of a seemingly unmediated, self-reflective identity based on race and same-sexuality ('A woman who looks / at a woman ... / I am blackening in my way' [51]) in 'hard against the soul' appears to deny the very situatedness of the discontinuous national and sexual histories informing the poem which dislocates it textually, 'No Language Is Neutral.'

Addressing in part this paradox, Morrell notes that Afro-Caribbean-Canadian writers like Brand, Harris, and Nourbese Philip frequently adopt an essentialist subject position in their work as a tool 'for political intervention': 'This strategy allows them both a community and a coherent sense of self – however fictive or imaginative – from which to act and write' (10). Brand's invention here, at the end of *No Language Is Neutral,* of a 'mythic' space from and through which to speak, her 'reterritorialization' of the shifting boundaries of her identity (as a black woman, as a lesbian, as a black lesbian) in order to map out 'a paradoxical continuity of self,' thus brings us back once again to Mohanty and her characterization of the politics of location as non-synchronous and multivalent. That the locational must also in some senses encompass the locutional, for example, is something taken up by Elspeth Probyn in her essay 'Travels in the Postmodern: Making Sense of the Local.' Here Probyn 'explore[s] a central problematic within feminist cultural theory' – first articulated by Gayatri Spivak – that is, 'whether the subaltern can speak' (177). She does so by organizing her thoughts 'around three current metaphors: locale, location, and local' (177). 'Locale' in Probyn's schema refers to both a discursive and non-discursive place that is the setting for a particular (gendered) event, 'home being the most obvious example.' 'Local' would appear to be the more spatialized locale's temporal equivalent, that which 'directly issu[es] from or [is] related to a particular time.' Finally, 'location' is more methodological in meaning, corresponding to the 'sites of research' through which knowledge is ordered and sequenced (178). Roughly, then, we may classify the three terms as follows: locale = experiential; local = contextual or historical; and location = institutional. The feminist cultural critic's task thus becomes, according to Probyn, to 'make sense' of the local (i.e., the historical and contextual) '[with]in and against' the opposite extremes and conflicting pulls of locale and location. 'Interwoven through these concerns,' Probyn concludes, 'is the very immediate question of whether the subaltern can speak. This question requires that we be continually vigilant to the necessity of bringing to the light the submerged conditions that silence others and the other in ourselves' (186).

But it's always 'in another place, not here,' that such silences will be given their proper hearing. As Brand's textual play on the homonym 'here/hear' demonstrates, and as my analysis of the work of Tomson Highway in the next chapter will further attest, any radical rearrangement of hegemonic figure/ground indices of identity first of all requires us to replace the standard feminist and postcolonial equation of the politics and poetics of location with who can and cannot speak with one that looks more closely at who is listening; it also requires us to examine more closely the nature and intent of this listening, to determine how privileged (white) groups 'can know the difference between occasions for responsive listening and listening as an excuse for silent collusion with the status quo of racial and neocolonial inequalities' (Roman, 79). This is where the concept of the performative, as applied 'theoretically' in this chapter, links up with my somewhat more traditional, 'theatrical' deployment of it in the next. To be sure, the very different uses of this term in both chapters must not be conflated (a point I have already emphasized, and about which I will have more to say in the Coda to this book); nevertheless, what Brand's call-and-response poetry and Highway's Trickster drama *do* demonstrate is that the successful performance of each depends upon the presence of an attentive audience, one fully participant in the production of meaning and its multiple acts of identity and identification.

'[Q]uite here, *I* hear from *you*' is the anaphoric phrase used by Brand throughout 'Phyllis,' another poem included in *No Language Is Neutral* (11–13; my emphasis). Echoing her here, within the 'locale' of my body, and the 'location' of the academic institution, I am striving to hear, to make some sense of the 'local' languages of race, gender, class, and sexuality, and the role each plays in the construction of Canada and its national literatures.

7

Learning New Tricks: Re-Imag(in)ing Community in the Two-Spirited Writing of Tomson Highway

I catch my dark self swimming gracefully
in the mirror frame. Tropical fish.
I see a hook.
New trick.
It's simpler to stay put and wait.
Haul the fisherman in.

Ian Iqbal Rashid, *Black Markets, White Boyfriends, and Other Acts of Elision*, 25–6

Among the many satirical pieces included by the American humorist Fran Lebowitz in her 1978 collection, *Metropolitan Life*, is the witty essay 'Notes on "Trick."' At once a parody of and homage to Susan Sontag's 'Notes on Camp,' the numbered text attempts to define a particular 'trick' aesthetic, to account for the presence (among male homosexuals most explicitly) of a 'trick' sensibility. In note 21, for example, Lebowitz outlines what she sees as 'a distinct Trick taste in literature,' listing works by Carlos Casteneda, Herman Hesse, Djuna Barnes, and Anaïs Nin, among others, as essential reading in this rather esoteric sub-genre (72).

But if any one text can be said to encapsulate a particular 'Trick taste in literature,' then surely it must be Renaud Camus's celebrated attempt to 'utter' homosexuality by recounting his experience – that is to say, the 'history' and 'geography' – of twenty-five random sexual encounters with other men, to 'present' 'each trick ... itself from the start as a *narrative*' (*Tricks*, xi-xiii). In his preface to Camus's text, Roland Barthes comments on the '*passage* from sex to discourse' signalled by *Tricks*, and concludes by offering his own idiosyncratic archaeology of the term: 'a glance, a gaze, an idea, an image, ephemeral and forceful association, which consents to dissolve so lightly, a faithless benevolence: a way of not getting stuck in desire, though without evading it; all in all, a kind of wisdom' (x). Of Barthes's own 'ephemeral and forceful association[s]' in this regard, Robert K. Martin has recently remarked that, excluding the posthumously published *Incidents*, this short, obscure piece of writing gives 'rise to Barthes's most sustained exploration of the possibility of an *écriture gaie*' ('Roland Barthes,' 282).

Within the contemporary Canadian literary scene, explorations of and experiments with an *écriture gaie* have received a number of diverse, not to mention tricky, treatments. For example, in the genre of creative non-fiction, Stan Persky's *Buddy's* is self-consciously styled as an '*homage à Roland Barthes.*' Ruminating on his precursor, Renaud Camus, at one point in the text, Persky notes that while '*Tricks* proposes itself as purely a theatre of surface,' the various epilogues, digressions, and asides which interrupt the episodic narrative of one-night stands 'invoke, however casually, depths of being': 'The "tricks," by definition, argue a kind of anonymity of person ..; the epilogues insist on humanizing them by conceding their endurance beyond the recounted episode' (29, 30–1). To put this into Barthesian terms, the narrative stratagems performed by Camus and Persky ensure that their sexual escapades remain indispensable to the pleasurable productivity – both readerly and writerly – of *jouissance* within their respective texts, at the same time as the former 'trick' allows the latter to continue to exist beyond the bounds of pronominal and parenthetical enclosure, as in the repeated refrain '(*Never saw him again.*)' (see Camus, *passim*; and Persky, 31, 35). This is, I would argue, no mean feat, especially for Persky, since his 'meditations on desire,' unlike Camus's, 'arrive in a time of plague' and are therefore 'shadowed by elegy' (*Buddy's*, 9).

By contrast, in his 1991 collection *Black Markets, White Boyfriends, and Other Acts of Elision*, Tanzanian-Canadian poet Ian Iqbal Rashid includes a series of three linked poems structured around the phrase 'there is this trick ...' Rashid's running/punning play on the signifier 'trick' reveals a Barthesian penchant for repeated transcription without inscription, a fragmentary and momentary textual encounter encapsulated in 'a glance, a gaze, an idea, an image.' It is, to paraphrase Martin on Barthes, the performance of Rashid's sexualized and racialized self 'seen and experienced as cruising' ('Roland Barthes,' 282). Thus, the 'trick' in the first poem is sexual, a casual pick-up, a one-night stand 'met only on rain / -filled nights' (17). The second 'trick' is a magic one, an optical illusion, something 'clever and quick,' performed by a 'handsome conjurer revealing both hands free' (21). The third and final 'trick' is more complicated, although no less ephemeral; it involves a skilful feat of language, a dexterity with identity:

> I begin to wonder what it means when we are told,
> those of us who will never be allowed to claim
> this language as one of our own,
> told by some that have discovered new worlds
> where people have always lived that there is this trick,
> something that *you* must do/read/say
> to restart your heart.
> That *you* have carried an alien burden
> across an alien landscape. (23)[1]

Learning new tricks, although quite conceivably a 'burden,' would certainly not appear to be 'alien' to Indigenous writers in this country, for whom the Trickster figure functions both as a sign of self-definition and cultural alterity, and as 'a comic *holotrope*, an interior landscape "behind what discourse says,"' a 'liberator of the mind,' in the words of Gerald Vizenor, one who mediates the 'language game[s]' that occur between 'the implied author, narrators, the readers, listeners, and the characters' in 'communal discourse' (*The Trickster of Liberty*, xi, x). Unlike the modernist impulses which govern the 'social science monologues' of Paul Radin, wherein the Trickster is invariably homogenized as a thematic figure, an 'aesthetic presence,' or, worse yet, a real person – in other words, a metaphor of individualism that would support the notion of vanishing tribes, and against which could be measured certain theories of 'tabooed' behaviour (see Radin, *The Trickster*) – Vizenor's postmodernist sensibilities maintain that the Trickster, when situated *discursively* as a 'comic holotrope,' part of a communal sign system of representation, 'a consonance of sentences in various voices, ironies, variations in cultural myths and social metaphors,' provides a much-needed corrective critical vocabulary/methodology for the cross-cultural discussion and dissemination of Native American 'oral narratives, translations and modern imaginative literature' ('Trickster Discourse,' 190). This new 'trickster discourse,' according to Vizenor, combines elements of Indigenous theories of 'orality' with aspects of post-structuralist theories of 'textuality,'[2] and, in a 'transvaluation of roles' that signals a 'cultural revolution' of sorts, binds together (that is, both 'liberates' and 'heals') speaker/teller/writer/narrator and interlocutor/listener/reader/audience in what Vizenor calls 'agonistic imagination': 'The trickster summons agonistic imagination in a comic holotrope to a discourse on the revolution in semiotic signs' (193).

Thus, as a figure through which to reimagine both narrative and political/cultural communities, and, moreover, as a 'chance' operation in language aimed at subverting outmoded mythic structures and destabilizing the ontological fixity of 'authentic' or 'essential' representations of the Indigene (be they in the social sciences or the humanities), the Trickster – whether metamorphosized as Coyote, Nanabush, Raven, or Weesageechak – inhabits a discursive site of profound gender ambiguity. And, in the case of two-spirited writers like Beth Brant, profound sexual ambiguity.

In 'Coyote Learns a New Trick,' for example, Brant has a 'female' Coyote transvest as a 'very dapper man of style,' replete with french cuffs, silk tie, fedora and 'a long silver chain ... looped ... from her belt to her pocket, where it swayed so fine' (*Mohawk Trail*, 32). She does this in order to play a trick on the red-haired beauty, Fox, 'that la-di-da female who was forever grooming her pelt and telling stories about how clever and sly she was' (32): 'Now, Coyote's trick was to make a fool out of Fox. To get her all worked up, thinking Coyote was a male, then reveal her true female Coyote self. It would make a good story ... Why, Coyote could tell this story for years to come!' (34).

Unbeknownst to Coyote, however, it is precisely her 'butch' role-playing, her cross-dressed attempt to 'pass,' that sexually arouses the very woman-identified Fox. '"[T]here are no men around here,"' Fox tells Coyote wickedly. '"Just me and sometimes a few girlfriends that stay over"' (33). In the end, it is Fox who 'tricks' Coyote into bed, much to the latter's eventual delight: 'Coyote had not fooled Fox. But somehow, playing the trick didn't seem so important anyway ... Mmmmm yeah, this Fox is pretty clever with all the stuff she knows. This is the best trick I ever heard of. Why didn't I think of it?' (34–5).

In this deceptively simple short story, Brant employs the figural/figurative categories of 'butch' and 'femme,' and the gender ambiguity inherent in transvestism, in order to comment parodically and playfully on the performative exchange of desire in the overlapping scenes of erotic and narrative seduction. Analysing lesbian role-playing at the end of *Gender Trouble*, Judith Butler notes that 'in both butch and femme identities, the very notion of an original or natural identity is put into question; indeed, it is precisely that question as it is embodied in these identities that becomes one source of their erotic significance' (123). Brant's Coyote 'knows that truth is only what she makes it' (31), and, as such, part of the new trick that she learns is to 'divest' herself of the idea that – to paraphrase Butler – the 'object' of lesbian desire is perforce a disembodied femininity and a superimposed masculinity (see *Gender Trouble*, 123). Instead, the butch/femme couple of Coyote/Fox perform an erotic exchange that sunders completely this kind of gendered opposition, 'inhabit[ing] the [lesbian] subject position together' (Case, 283).

Of course, just as the lesbian butch/femme are inextricably intertwined in the *erotic* performance of *identity*, so are the writer-speaker/reader-listener in an Indigenous storytelling event bound together in a somewhat tricky negotiation – through the *oral* performance of *narrative* – of the interpretative spaces of the other. In Tomson Highway's two companion plays about the mythical Wasaychigan Hill Reservation on Manitoulin Island this negotiation is presided over by the figure of Nanabush: in *The Rez Sisters*, 'he' is played by a male dancer; in *Dry Lips Oughta Move to Kapuskasing*, 'she' appears as female. In both plays, however, this 'fantastic creature,' 'this Trickster [who] goes by many names and many guises' (*The Rez Sisters*, xii), imbues the proceedings, and the historical and personal dilemmas faced by the various characters, with a 'liberatory' sense of humour and a 'healing' spiritual magic. If Highway's plays are meant to be read as postcolonial allegories of sorts (*The Rez Sisters*, in particular, seems at least in part to rewrite *The Wizard of Oz*; i.e. 'there's no place like home'), then surely Nanabush is both the metaphoric (albeit ambiguously so) and epistemic epicentre of each.

In the preface to *The Rez Sisters*, Highway claims that, contrary to popular belief, the 'rez' is in fact a really 'cool' place (ix). Judging by his theatrical re-creations of it in these two plays, it is also a profoundly homosocial community. Apart from Nanabush, the cast of *The Rez Sisters* is entirely female, whereas the genders are reversed in *Dry Lips.* Moreover, in each play there is at least one two-spirited character: in *The Rez Sisters*, the tough-talking and hard-drinking Emily Dictionary reveals that the great love of her life was Rosabella Baez; and at one point in *Dry Lips*, Creature Nataways confesses his love for Big Joey. Recognizing that Sedgwick's analyses of 'male homosocial desire' and Butler's theories of performative identities – not to mention Foucault's earlier inquiries into the discursive construction of sexuality – were formulated in Anglo-American and Eurocentric contexts, and that the First World/Third World binary inherent in many academic discussions of race and nationality cannot be adapted to the so-called Fourth World entirely unproblematically, it nevertheless seems apparent to me that in his plays Highway is probing far beyond normative constructions of 'identity,' 'marginality,' and, above all, 'community.' In so doing, he is addressing, within the realm of live theatre and the conventions of oral storytelling, the ways in which performative constructions of multiple subject positions (Indigenous, white, male, female, gay, straight, etc.) are offered to the reader/spectator/listener as part of a participatory exchange of cross-cultural identifications and political agencies.

* * *

In *The Spirit and the Flesh*, an anthropological survey of the North American berdache or two-spirit tradition, Walter Williams notes that post-contact and, in particular, post-independence regulation of sexual diversity and gender variance among various Indigenous cultures by white European settlers was accompanied by a decidedly nationalist fervour.[3] Not only were the assimilationist policies adopted by both the U.S. and Canadian governments directed towards securing 'a nation's doom' by purifying the contaminated blood 'of a weird and waning race' (to quote Duncan Campbell Scott's 'The Onondaga Madonna' [102, 101]); they were also aimed at the simultaneous 'absorption' and 'elimination' of perceived sexual nonconformity,[4] 'mirror[ing] the anti-sexual attitudes of missionaries and public opinion' (Williams, 177). (Mirroring as well the critical consensus regarding Scott's famous sonnet, successive readings of which have so far steadfastly refused to acknowledge the fact that the Deputy Superintendent of Indian Affairs's 'dark lady,' like Shakespeare's, is in some senses 'queer,' her 'careless pose' at least doubly transvestic in its 'mingling' of genders and cultures [101].) According to Gary Kinsman, in *The Regulation of Desire: Sexuality in Canada*, similar attitudes relating to gender hierarchies form the basis of the patriarchal division of (re)productive labour necessary to fuel mercantile capitalist enterprises such as the fur trade. Kinsman, like Williams, believes that '[a] crucial part of the subjugation of ... Native peoples was the destruction of their erotic, gender, and social life and the imposition of European social and sexual organization ... This story of extreme cultural, social, and physical violence lies at the roots of the Canadian State' (71, 73).

Against this dominant anthropological image of the 'vanishing berdache,' of a 'traditional' Native role that has been 'assimilated' by/into white, Western culture in a process akin to cultural genocide, Will Roscoe, building upon his pioneering study, *The Zuni Man-Woman*, has recently argued for a more integrative, inter-cultural approach to 'the history of two-spirit survivance,' one that examines how Indigenous concepts of sex and gender have been '*transformed* in the process of being *reproduced*' ('Was We'wha a Homosexual?,' 218; my emphasis), rather than *absorbed* in the process of being *eliminated* by the dominant 'other.'[5] Such an approach, as Roscoe acknowledges, 'entails questions of authenticity, authority, and interpretation': 'What *is* the true two-spirit tradition? Do two-spirits exist today? Are gay and lesbian Indians their descendants? And is the current interest in two-spirits based merely on romantic projections, or are we involved in the recovery of an important, overlooked chapter of human history?' (194).

The answer to the final three questions, to the extent that they can be answered at all, is of course both 'yes' and 'no.' That is, claims by contemporary North American lesbian and gay aboriginal peoples to a two-spirited identity are mitigated by the first question, any answer to which, in my own opinion, must necessarily be that there isn't one. There is no 'true' or 'essential' category of Indigenous two-spiritedness, just as there is no singular or authentic definition of Western homosexuality; after more than five hundred years of inter- and cross-cultural contact, both terms are thoroughly imbricated with each other's meanings. On this point Roscoe concurs, demonstrating, through an exhaustive survey of eighteenth-century North American frontier discourse and nineteenth-century European sexological studies (many of which concluded that homosexuals comprised an 'intermediate sex' or a 'third gender'; see Carpenter, and Ulrichs), that 'natives actively absorbed European signs and symbols into their cultural systems, and Europeans absorbed accounts of third genders into theirs – to enrich and complicate but not replace existing categories. The term "berdache" and the role itself, to the extent that we know it, is always-already a hybrid, a creative product of complex interactions over an extended period of contact' (218).

This notion of 'hybridity' also lies, as Sheila Rabillard has pointed out, at the heart of Cree-Canadian dramatist Tomson Highway's cycle of 'rez' plays, which would appear to reveal both the deep gender divisions that have resulted from Indigenous communities' historical experiences of colonization, and the panoply of diverse sexual identities that have thrived and adapted in spite of this shared history. The associative, almost metonymical, thread linking issues of political disenfranchisement, cross-gender feuding, and same-sexuality throughout both plays is given its fullest dramatic expression in *Dry Lips*, spooling in particular around the character of Big Joey, who refers to the announcement that his wife, Gazelle Nataways, has been crowned captain of the newly formed Wasy

Wailerettes as follows: 'Wounded Knee Three! Women's version!' (63). This analogy between white oppression and women's usurpation/emasculation of men's traditional roles is extended even further in act 2 when Zachary Jeremiah Keechigeesik and Spooky Lacroix confront Big Joey about his failure to prevent his illegitimate son Dickie Bird Halked from raping Patsy Pegahmagahbow, a traumatic episode that gets equated/conflated in Big Joey's mind not only with the political events of 1973, but also with the accidental premature birth of Dickie Bird at the Belvedere Hotel later that same year:

> 'This is the end of the suffering of a great nation!' That was me. Wounded Knee, South Dakota, Spring of '73. The FBI. They beat us to the ground. Again and again and again. Ever since that spring, I've had these dreams where blood is spillin' out from my groin, nothin' there but blood and emptiness. It's like ... I lost myself. So when I saw this baby comin' out of Caroline, Black Lady ... Gazelle dancin' ... all this blood ... and I knew it was gonna come ... I ... tried to stop it ... I freaked out. I don't know what I did ... and I knew it was mine ... (119–20)

Pressed once more by Zachary to account for his more recent (non)actions, Big Joey finally reveals the full extent of his misogyny: 'Because I hate them! I hate them fuckin' bitches. Because they – our own women – took the fuckin' power away from us faster than the FBI ever did' (120). As Rabillard notes, at this particular juncture Highway's 'drama seems to invite the audience to see the opposition between the genders as a hurtful condition analogous to – if not the product of – the sufferings brought about by White colonization' (15).

But Highway complicates issues of gender and colonization here with added questions of sexuality and erotic object-choice. Previous to Big Joey's testimony, Creature Nataways confesses to Spooky his own reasons for not intervening to stop the rape: 'I love [Big Joey] ... I love the way he stands. I love the way he walks. The way he laughs. The way he wears his cowboy boots ... the way his tight blue jeans fall over his ass ... I always wanted to be like him, William. I always wanted to have a dick as big as his' (104). In the absence of women characters on stage, it is left to Creature to eroticize the hyper-masculinity of Big Joey, of whose many physical attributes we have already heard a great deal in *The Rez Sisters.* The irony, of course, is that in both plays Big Joey, perhaps the one character most associated by Highway with normative patriarchal attitudes, becomes an object of desire for two-spirited characters. Emily Dictionary, back on the 'rez' after having witnessed the death of her lover Rosabella Baez, has recently taken up with Big Joey, much to Gazelle Nataways's consternation. At the end of this first play, we learn that Emily has become pregnant by Big Joey, a plot revelation that Rabillard for one associates with Highway's reappropriation and resignification of the tropes of 'absorption' and 'elimination' (see above) previously used by white government officials, social scientists, and cultural anthropologists (she also cites Radin) to delimit Indigenous sexual identities and gender roles. Emily's baby, Rabillard writes, 'shortly to be expelled into the world, will be the triumphant product of past penetration, vulnerability turned to evidence of the transformative strength of the women before us' (12).

Of equal evidence, in this regard, is Philomena Moosetail's final speech, a hymn she sings in praise of her new toilet bowl: '[I]t's elevated, like a sort of ... pedestal, so that it makes you feel like ... the Queen ... sitting on her royal throne, ruling her Queendom with a firm yet gentle hand ... [I]t's so comfortable you could just sit on it right up to the day you die' (117–18). Again, as Rabillard notes, the 'rez' sisters' voiding of waste, of life's shit, throughout the play becomes 'a comic triumph' (12) by the end, linking the women with Nanabush, who, in the guise of the seagull at the beginning of act 1, we are told, shits liberally and copiously all over Marie-Adele Starblanket's white picket fence. Moreover, as Vizenor reminds us, the coprophilic nature of many Trickster narratives is a comic sign that implicates the audience as well: 'The trickster narrative situates the participant audience, the listeners and readers, in agonistic imagination: there, in comic discourse, the trickster is being, nothingness and liberation; a loose seam in consciousness; that wild space over and between sounds, words, sentences and narratives; and, at last, the trickster is comic shit' ('Trickster Discourse,' 196).

Included as part of the excremental community of Highway's Trickster theatre in this way, white audiences, readers, and critics are forced to wallow in the collective shit as well, to confront our historical complicity in the events unfolding before us on the stage/page, as well as our own particular national and sexual identificatory investments in 'receiving aboriginality' (Filewod), 'recognizing difference' (Maufort), inscribing 'marginality' (Nunn), and asking 'some impure questions of gender and culture' (Rabillard) *vis-à-vis* Native Canadian literatures. My reframing of recent academic essay titles in the preceding sentence demonstrates the wealth of critical articles and studies on Highway that have proliferated in the past few years, most of them by white scholars like myself interested in situating his plays (again like myself) in terms of current theoretical debates in postcolonial and gender studies. What I find remarkable is that in virtually all of these analyses the 'crisis of authenticity' that most agree is enacted in Highway's plays is situated solely within the context of ethnicity and gender, leaving sexuality, for instance, as an undifferentiated aspect of the intersection of these two categories rather than, as I would argue, the 'critical' site of their articulation and elaboration. To be sure, both Rabillard and Alan Filewod briefly mention Highway's homosexuality, but neither comments in any depth on how this might impact on the production and reception of his work. Indeed, Filewod, after having noted that 'when speaking of ethnic culture, the notion of authenticity poses different problems than it does in gender studies,' nevertheless does his best to unproblematize the issue by later suggesting that in *The Rez Sisters* and *Dry Lips* 'Highway implies that ... insight [into female experience] derives from aboriginality rather than sexuality' (365, 369).

Such a potentially throw-away statement belies the fact that it is somewhat too easy for a critic like Susan Bennett not only to accuse Highway of misogyny, but also 'native informancy,' without at all addressing issues of sexuality. In a blistering attack on Jennifer Preston's documentary article on Native Earth Performing Arts Inc.,[6] the theatre company that fostered the development of *The Rez Sisters* and *Dry Lips*, and of which Highway was once artistic director, Bennett claims that 'Highway's representations of Native women merely confirm the negative stereotypes perpetuated in more obviously dominant cultural practice,' a process which allows his predominantly white audiences, according to Bennett, to take 'comfort in knowing that they were right all along – Native women are, indeed, "like that"' (10). In support of her charges, Bennett quotes at length from Saulteaux/Anishnabe-Canadian writer Marie Annharte Baker, who recorded her decidedly ambivalent unease with Highway's depiction of Native women in *Dry Lips* in a special 1991 issue of *Canadian Theatre Review* devoted to aboriginal drama (see Baker, 'Angry Enough to Spit'). Curiously, however, Bennett glosses over another article by Baker included in the same special issue, in which Baker comments on the necessarily mediated representation of Trickster theatre:

> When we see a trickster on the stage in an Aboriginal cultural production, we must become aware not only of the special cultural circumstance of that creation, and its circular totality, we must know something of the playwright, actor, director, or the events of the day which give inspiration to a particular rendition. You are forced to be particular to understand. ('An Old Indian Trick,' 48)

Knowing something of the playwright, and the actor who originated the role of Nanabush in *The Rez Sisters*, is to acknowledge, it seems to me, that both Tomson Highway and his brother, René, brought a particular gay/two-spirited sensibility to bear on the production, one that extends the notion of community identification and subcultural affiliation beyond the categories of gender and ethnicity/aboriginality to include (homo)sexuality as well. Consider, in this regard, Highway's repeated declaration of his desire to 'write plays about "the rez," just as Michel Tremblay wrote about "The Main"' (*The Rez Sisters*, viii). While several critics (see Rabillard, 18; Johnston, 262) have pointed out that The Biggest Bingo in the World, to which the 'rez' sisters head off in Toronto, is almost surely a deliberate echo of the 'Ode to Bingo' performed in act 2 of Tremblay's first play, *Les Belles-Soeurs* – the women in both plays are waiting for the number B-14 to be called (see *The Rez Sisters*, 102; and *Les Belles-Soeurs*, 87) – none of them seems prepared to discuss the potential resonances this allusion has for the creation of what one might call a uniquely gay/postcolonial genealogy of Canadian drama, an alternative or oppositional tradition written from outside the English-speaking 'solitude.'

As I have pointed out in chapter 4, Tremblay's 'Belles-Soeurs cycle' of east-end Montreal plays (of which there are twelve in total) alternates between the 'Main' tenderloin of drag queens and prostitutes and the kitchens and back-alley 'balcons' of working-class families, using both 'as sites for exploring the fears, insecurities, and damage wrought to the colonized psyche' of Quebec (Schwartzwald, 'Fear of Federasty,' 180). Similarly, Highway's own cycle of plays (of which there are a projected seven in total)[7] uses the mythical Wasy Hill Reservation to document Native Canadians' very different experiences of the legacy of imperialism. Moreover, as with Tremblay's use of *joual*, Highway frequently uses the Cree and Ojibway languages in his plays to subvert the hegemony of English-Canadian literary discourse. Finally, and perhaps most importantly, both playwrights 'que(e)ry' representative norms of masculinity, linking 'crises' in gender and sexuality to the process of decolonization. There are no 'male' characters in *Les Belles-Soeurs* (and most of his other plays), according to Tremblay, '"because there *are* no men in Quebec"' (quoted in Schwartzwald, 'Fear of Federasty,' 180). One could make a similar observation with respect to Highway's 'rez,' at least as it is presented in his first play. Certainly Pelajia Patchnose would not bemoan the absence of men from positions of power: 'If that useless old chief of ours was a woman, we'd see a few things get done around here. We'd see our women working, we'd see our men working, we'd see our young people sober on Saturday nights, and we'd see Nanabush dancing up and down the hill on shiny black paved roads' (*The Rez Sisters,* 114).

Of course, it is within the character of Nanabush – like Tremblay's transvestite characters, a 'man-woman prototype' – that Highway locates his most pronounced statements about gender ambiguity and mutable sexual identity. Even when transformed into the Bingo Master at the end of *The Rez Sisters,* Nanabush is incarnated, I would argue, as a specific gay male fantasy type: '*the most beautiful man in the world,*' the stage directions read, '*dressed to kill: tails, rhinestones, and all*' (100). Indeed, his 'trick' waltz with Marie-Adele is at least on the level of genre a subversion of heteronormative conventions, in the sense that a dance of death replaces the traditional marriage dance at the end of classical comedy, just as the bingo table itself becomes a tableau of da Vinci's 'The Last Supper' instead of Veronese's 'The Wedding Feast at Cana.' Marie-Adele succumbs to cancer at the end of the waltz and the Bingo Master changes back into the guise of Nanabush. As danced by René Highway in the original production, the Nanabush/Bingo Master character was suitably 'lascivious, an erotic shimmer, a burn that sunder[ed] dioramas and terminal creeds' for both men and women in the audience; 'an androgyny, *she* ... repudiate[d] translations and imposed representations, as *he* [laid] bare the contradictions of the striptease' (Vizenor, *The Trickster of Liberty,* x; my emphasis).

My paraphrase of Vizenor here in connection with the Trickster's 'tribal striptease' is meant to signal the obverse erotic manifestations of Nanabush in *Dry Lips* as the spirit of Gazelle Nataways, Patsy Pegahmagahbow, and Black Lady Halked. Recognizing that the oversized rubberized breasts and bum that the first two characters wear have been vigorously and vociferously denounced by many feminist critics and reviewers of the play, I want nevertheless to suggest that these prosthetic devices, in their obvious signalling of exaggerated femininity, may provide a link with the particular theatrical excesses of gay drag, where female masquerade is perforce performed as a fantasy of the hyper-real. It is important to remember that René Highway, who was by this time fairly ill from several AIDS-related opportunistic infections, also served as choreographer on *Dry Lips.*[8] With the two brothers collaborating one last time, they were able to turn the striptease performed by Nanabush/Gazelle, for example, into a classic instance of homosocial triangulation and subsequent homosexual panic. In this regard, it is important to listen to the stage directions, which, as Clint Burnham notes, 'resemble nothing so much as novelistic description' and thus 'struggle for priority of meaning' within the text (27):

> *The music is now on full volume and Nanabush/Gazelle's strip is in full swing. She dances on top of the jukebox, which is now a riot of sound and flashing lights. Spooky's kitchen is bathed in a gorgeous lavender light ... In the heat of the moment, as Nanabush/Gazelle strips down to silk tassels and G-string, they begin tearing their clothes off.*
>
> ...
>
> *The lavender lights snap off, we are back to 'reality' and Spooky, Pierre and Zachary stand there, embarrassed. In a panic, they begin putting their clothes back on and reclaim the positions they had before the strip.* (87)

It seems that sooner or later all the male characters in this play are caught with their pants down, the fixation on male buttocks signalled from the opening scene when Zachary's 'bare, naked bum' is displayed prominently for all to see (15). Of course, the peck on the cheek (as it were!) that Nanabush/Gazelle gives Zachary in this scene is repeated by his wife, Hera, in the closing one, a double gesture of (dis)closure, a 'lipstick trace,' that 'marks a feminine presence onto the text' (Burnham, 21) and that effectively takes the play out of the realm of gay fantasy and back into the conventions of bourgeois domestic realism.[9] Still, I would argue that the 'anality' of *Dry Lips*, whether prosthetic or otherwise, is sufficient enough to signify an extension of the notion of a 'crisis of authenticity' in Highway's writing to include not only patriarchal constructions of gender and racialist constructions of ethnicity/aboriginality, but also (hetero)normative constructions of masculinity/sexuality.

This complex confluence of community affiliations and (dis)identifications is highlighted perhaps most explicitly by Highway in 'The Lover Snake,' a short dramatic monologue included in *An Anthology of Native Canadian Literature in English*, edited by Daniel David Moses and Terry Goldie. With a deftness and economy of language, Highway here traces the relationship between the Cree-Canadian speaker and his Sikh-Canadian brother/lover. In so doing, he succeeds in concretizing and materializing (in a way much contemporary psychoanalytical- and deconstructionist-inflected queer and postcolonial criticism seems to avoid at all costs) the politically vexed and historically disjunctive issues of identity and naming, focusing in particular on that most imperialist of signifiers, 'Indian': 'And between us, Dahljeet and me, we would agree that the friendship was an unusual friendship. I mean, there he was, very much an

Indian and here I was, very much an Indian. Only, we were such totally different kinds of Indian. Worlds apart. So different, it was laughable ... And yet, we became close, Dahljeet and I. More than friends, more than brothers, more than lovers, even' (275).

Ironically, the excess of signification, the recursive repetition, heralded by Highway's use of the 'more than' locution in this passage, implies a 'less than' referent elsewhere, a zero sum equation of identity, a minus in the order of dominant discourse, which will not accommodate such a superabundance of difference *within* sameness. This is the paradox of the modern 'calculus' of heteronormativity, according to Eve Sedgwick, a system of binaristic categorization which 'owes its sleekly utilitarian feel to the linguistically unappealable classification of anyone who shares one's gender as being "the same" as oneself, and anyone who does not share one's gender as being one's other' (*Epistemology*, 160). For Homi Bhabha, colonial discourse operates through a similar 'narcissistic' interdiction: '*Almost the same but not white*' ('Of Mimicry,' 130). The cobra, as Dahljeet explains to Highway's narrator, remains faithful to its mate – and to her/his memory – for its entire lifespan. But there is another trick (left unstated in the story) that this 'lover snake' knows how to perform: just as Nanabush can change genders at will, so can the cobra shed its skin.

It's a feat Highway is unable to ask of his characters/actors any more than he can ask it of his audience. Nevertheless, as in the poetry and prose of Dionne Brand, the dominant figure/ground frameworks of identity tend to get deliberately skewed in Highway's plays. The performance of (ab)originality on stage requires white, heterosexual audiences, in particular, to reimagine their relationships not only with Indigenous peoples, but with other marginalized communities as well, including women and queers. It requires, in other words, the learning of a few new tricks.

Coda: The Hats Backwards Syndrome and Other 'Crimes' of Literary Fashion at the End of the Millennium

Much of the analysis in the two preceding chapters – indeed, most of this book – has been informed by concepts of performance and performativity. These terms have increasingly come to dominate contemporary academic discussions of gender and sexuality (thanks, in large part, to Butler and, to a lesser degree, Sedgwick), but only very recently have they also begun to be applied in a more widespread manner (that is, building on Bhabha's pioneering work in the field) to representations of nationality, ethnicity, and race.[1] While I have talked, in chapter 6, about the dangers of conflating the theatrical and the theoretical uses of the terms in these contexts, and while Butler herself has taken great pains to explain her precise position on the performativity of drag in the last chapter of *Bodies That Matter*, there is still a sense in which the performative, especially as it gets discussed and elaborated in queer studies, translates into a kind of critical cross-dressing, a process of self-fashioning, or refashioning, to which anyone can subscribe merely by donning the appropriate apparel or, in this case, availing oneself of the requisite discourse. One doesn't have to *be* queer to *do* queer theory, after all. But it helps if one *looks* queer. It's what I call, after the wave of mostly straight, mostly white, mostly upper-middle-class frat boy/Marky Mark types who jumped on the queer and B-boy bandwagons in the early part of this decade by appropriating the fashion signifiers of the sexually, racially, and economically disenfranchised (oversized flares slung low on hips, exposed Calvin Klein underwear, wallet chains, multiple body piercings, tattoos, goatees, ballcaps worn askew, etc.), the hats backwards syndrome of lit crit. Don't get me wrong, I'm just as guilty as the next person in this regard. The piercing in my right ear was obtained not in celebration of my coming out, but rather in anticipation of my first 'queer' academic conference. My velvet pants and marbled green Doc Martens were purchased for a similar panel. And so on.

'Sometimes the clothes do not make the man,' came George Michael's anguished cry from the closet in 'Freedom 90.' And, indeed, there is a sense in which the metaphorical back-to-front ballcap signifies a process of infinite regression and withdrawal, a desperate shying away from social responsibility and crisis, an escape into the cavernous recesses of 'distressed' denim jeans by boys not quite 'man' enough to fill them (unless, of course, you happen to be a 'boy-dyke' or drag king packing a dildo). So, too, with the refashioning of literary theory in the North American academy over the past decade. Whereas once 'experience' was used as an effective means of resisting the disciplinary/disciplining gaze of the institution in emergent 'minority studies' (i.e., 'Women's Studies,' 'Ethnic Studies,' 'Gay and Lesbian Studies') classrooms, 'performance' is now increasingly being valorized as the privileged episteme from, through, and by which to intervene against dominant social/sexual arrangements. But this, as far as I can tell, is merely to replace one compulsory regime with another. Indeed, it strikes me that in the mosh pit of academe the theoretical movement within queer studies, for example, from 'compulsory heterosexuality,' through 'compulsory homosexuality,' to 'compulsory performance' means that one must not only first be *out*, but also always *on*. Hence the increasing pressure faced by the divas of this movement (Sedgwick and Butler, to cite once again the two most obvious examples) to produce ever more provocative books and articles, to, in effect, perform.

And it is here, in the production of queer theory for mass consumption by a notoriously fickle audience, that the performative starts to mesh with the personal. The very disclosure of the details about the holes in my ears and the clothes in my closet reveals the extent to which the two discourses overlap. Thus it is that we get Terry Castle relating her first lesbian sexual experience in one of the chapters of *The Apparitional Lesbian*; or D.A. Miller talking about who wears boxers and who briefs at his gym in *Bringing Out Roland Barthes*; or David Halperin prefacing his comments about *The History of Sexuality* with a long contextual exegesis of an academic dispute he was involved in with a colleague at MIT in *Saint Foucault*; or Wayne Koestenbaum discussing his favourite female icons in *The Queen's Throat* and *Jackie under My Skin*; or Eve Sedgwick talking about her battle with breast cancer, her friendship with the late Michael Lynch, and her 'poetic' identification with female anal eroticism, particularly spanking, in *Tendencies.*

Why this overwhelming autobiographical impulse in contemporary queer criticism?[2] Why would a group of intellectuals at pains to distinguish the gendered discourse of queerness from anatomical sex and genital erotic identification be so eager to share with the world some of the most intimate aspects of their private lives (and the allusion here to Noel Coward is deliberate, the various permutations of the *practice* of queer theory often resembling a bedroom farce)? I think the answer is at least in part historical and, perhaps even more specifically, millennial. That is, just as the new medicalization and psychiatrization of homosexuality at the end of the nineteenth century led to a panicked dismantling of the discursive scaffolding between the rigidly demarcated Victorian spheres of public and private, culminating in the sensational trials of Oscar Wilde (a prime showcase for the performance of the personal, as Moisés Kaufman's recent play, *Gross Indecency: The Three Trials of Oscar Wilde,* makes abundantly clear), so has the initial pathologization of AIDS as the 'gay plague' at the end of this century prompted many queers, including queer academics, to act out, and up, in public, forfeiting our privacy, offering to display our privation, for expressly political purposes. The difference between the two *fin-de-siècles* is of course one of agency. The compulsion to confess at the end of the nineteenth century was in large measure controlled and regulated by a well-maintained system of state surveillance. While the ubiquity of electronic media has ensured that this policing of 'perverse' desires, not to mention the need to confess those desires on the talk-show circuit, continues at the end of this century,[3] ACT Upers, Queer Nationals, and their various interlocutors in the North American academy have been extremely successful at turning the tables, adopting a *proactive* rather than a *reactive* stance. If, as I implied in the Introduction to this book, the social interdiction of 'Don't ask, don't tell' governs more than just dominant anxieties about the 'presence' of 'subversive' sexualities in the armed forces, then it would seem to me that, as critics on/of the margins, we have a responsibility to resist this cultural muzzling not only by telling, but also by showing, performing the personal *as* political at die-ins and kiss-ins in the streets of major urban centres and, just as importantly, at teach-ins on the campuses of those urban centres.

Which brings me to yet another among the many *p*-words that proliferate throughout these final few pages. I am speaking of pedagogy and, more specifically, of pedagogy's relation, within the antiracist and antihomophobic contexts of postcolonial and queer studies, to what Jane Gallop, in her introduction to a recent collection of essays on the subject, calls the 'performative personal,' the process of 'im-personation' that necessarily 'passes' for teaching at the university level (17). In 'Caliban in the Classroom,' one of the essays included in that volume, Indira Karamcheti summarizes the libidinal economy of the postcolonial studies seminar, where compulsory performance (no less for students than for instructor) is at once a strategy for gaining *political* power and a symptom of *institutional* powerlessness, concluding that the performance of ethnicity by a minority teacher, for example, his or her literal personification of otherness, allows for the 'experience of authority' in a space where he or she had hitherto only been *seen* (again literally) as a native informant (146). This is a salutary reminder to teachers and students alike that textual analysis is performed in a space where bodies are signs as well, and that it is in the positioning of the self *in relation to* institutions (in this case, the academy), that we find the potential for a certain disciplinary dissonance, a wilful pedagogical dissidence, a twisting, bending, queering of curricular theory and classroom practice towards resistance, renewal, and change. If the literature classroom, like the nation (or any other social formation, for that matter), is an imagined community, then it is a community that can be imagined as queer.

At least this is what Joseph Litvak thought. Defiantly flaunting the link between pedagogy and pederasty, and arguing that '*all* teaching, even by heterosexual men, is not just theatrical, but what it somehow seems appropriate to call "queer"' (19), in his contribution to the Gallop collection, Litvak initially posits the gay studies classroom as a primal scene of 'transformative truth-telling' (or 'shaming'), a stage on/from which to work against the heterosexism governing standard pedagogical practices:

> If every teacher, even the most avant-garde queer theorist, is a disciplinarian, every teacher, even the most reactionary custodian of the eternal verities, is also a pervert. But if one's fate as a teacher – especially as a teacher of literature – is to be lovingly forgotten both as the person who, for instance, laid down the law of 'political correctness' *and* as the person who, for instance, 'went too far' in the interpretation of texts, teaching gay studies seems to offer a way of intervening in this cultural work of one's compulsory encrypting. (23–4)

However, having made a point of coming out in several classes, Litvak soon discovered that the personalist discourse he frequently invoked in his pedagogical explorations of the erotic spaces of the classroom often produced in his students a concomitant desire to police those spaces ever more vigilantly. Indeed, his deliberately undisciplined 'truth-telling' in an advanced theory seminar, the 'melodramatic' performance of his sexuality in connection with the specifically 'gay' texts under discussion, was met with open hostility and aggression by the majority of students, several of whom themselves self-identified as queer. The students were responding in this instance to Litvak, not as a person, but as a professor – a 'representative of phallic authority' (25). Thus, as Litvak himself admits, the spectacle the teacher was making of himself could potentially be read as 'autoerotic self-indulgence,' or even bordering on sexual harassment (26).

Ironically, this was exactly the situation that Litvak's and Karamcheti's editor, Jane Gallop, found herself in when, in 1993, two female students accused her of sexual harassment. The students were precise in pinpointing the 'origins' of their dispute against Gallop as stemming from the latter's behaviour at the 1991 Gay and Lesbian Studies Graduate Students' Conference held at the University of Wisconsin at Milwaukee. During the course of this conference, Gallop announced publicly (albeit, in her mind, jokingly) that 'graduate students were [her] sexual preference' and later shared a fairly passionate kiss with one of the complainants at a local lesbian bar. Although Gallop was eventually exonerated of all charges of sexual harassment, she was reprimanded for kissing the student, an act that was deemed to be in direct violation of the university's policy prohibiting 'consenting amorous relations' between students and teachers. As Gallop retails the events in her recent book about the case – one with the deliberately tabloid-style title *Feminist Accused of Sexual Harassment* – the kiss was a performance that, according to her at any rate, had both personal and pedagogical ramifications. 'I was making a spectacle of myself,' she admits, but then goes on to state that 'at the same time, I was being a teacher': 'The performance turned me on and was meant to turn my audience on, literally and figuratively. The spectacle was meant to shock and entertain, and to make people think' (100–1). While Gallop's account of the case is not entirely unsympathetic, what I find most extraordinary, within the context of the present discussion, is that she felt her personal performance was somehow more licensed, or would receive a more positive reception, because it took place at a *gay and lesbian studies* conference, where apparently such *outré* behaviour is *de rigeur.* The feminist scholar was, by her own admission, trying to pass as 'queer.'

My own limited experience on the queer conference circuit and at the front of the (Canadian) literature classroom has not as yet led to more than a partial reconciliation of the national and sexual solitudes in writings of the sort examined throughout this book. Nor has my none too successful 'impersonation' of a university instructor resulted in any lurid personal revelations or displays on my part (and it was most definitely a part I was playing), unless you count the gossipy pleasure I took in recounting to one of my classes the details of my on-camera tiff with 'Tiff' that I alluded to briefly in chapter 2. Notwithstanding the rallies leading up to the 1995 Quebec referendum, the patchwork efforts of Sheila Copps's Heritage Ministry, the parliamentary boosterism of the Reform party, or any of the recent Pride parades in Toronto and Vancouver, Canadians have always tended to be more discreet in our flag-waving than have our neighbours south of the border. It should come as no surprise, then, that our national and sexual *pudeur* extends as well to Canadian academe, which, despite the best efforts of the *Maclean's* annual survey of university rankings, remains steadfast in its repudiation of the American star-system. This is not to say that personalist discourse, for example, hasn't infiltrated the Canadian academic consciousness. Indeed, many of the critics cited throughout the preceding chapters (Probyn, Schwartzwald, Godard, Bannerji, Goldie, Dellamora, Mukherjee, Wallace, to name only a few) strategically make use of this discourse at several key points in their work. Consider as well the not unrelated cultural criticism of scholars as diverse as sociologist Becki Ross, literary critic Helen Hoy, and geographer Cole Harris.[4] Consider the present study.

The fashion system, as Barthes famously instructed us, is conducted wholly in the present tense, a 'vengeful' present, moreover, 'which each year sacrifices the signs of the preceding year' (*The Fashion System*, 289). So, too, with the system of literary criticism. It would be altogether disingenuous of me to pretend that the current vogue for personalist writing in queer studies is much more than a fashionable theoretical moment, and that it won't soon be but a vague memory, eclipsed by a newer, sexier vanguard trend. As I write this, for instance, I notice that the latest edited collection from Sedgwick, *Novel Gazing: Queer Readings in Fiction* (1997), is being touted on the back cover as her 'first move into reparative criticism,' whatever that might be. Certainly this book is a product of a specific historical juncture in the disciplines of queer and postcolonial literary studies. And it is precisely for these reasons of historical specificity that I have retained traces of my own personal narrative (which is by no means pervasive) throughout, risking the disapproval – even outright opprobrium – of some members of the scholarly community, not to mention my own individual 'cringe factor' in looking back on this book several years hence. For it seems important to me, for example, that the initial impetus for this study was occasioned at least in part by a local and personal response to a moment of crisis within another community altogether. Let me conclude by trying to explain.

* * *

Late September 1993. It's my first month as a doctoral student in the English Department at the University of British Columbia. A federal election looms on the horizon, and Kim Campbell is busy whizzing in and out of the West End in a desperate bid to court the gay vote in her home riding of Vancouver Centre. On this particular evening, an intimate group of men and women has gathered at the Firehall Theatre on East Cordova Street to launch a book edited by my friend, Dennis Denisoff. Called *Queeries: An Anthology of Gay Male Prose*, it is, believe it or not, the first anthology of its kind to be published in Canada. I feel honoured, therefore, to have had one of my own stories included among its pages.

The launch is meant to double as a benefit for Little Sister's. Vancouver's much-beloved gay and lesbian bookstore is challenging Canada Customs' right to seize and detain shipments of books destined for its shelves. Little Sister's has been waiting for some time to have its case heard before the Supreme Court of British Columbia: the original statement of claim filed by the bookstore is more than three years old; lawyers' briefs have long been prepared; expert witnesses have been lined up and are anxious to testify; court costs are spiralling out of control as each day goes by.*

* A little historical context may be in order here: On 7 June 1990, after more than five years of systemic harassment in the form of regular detentions of books by Canada Customs, Little Sister's, the store's owners, Jim Deva and Bruce Smyth, and the British Columbia Civil Liberties Association filed a Statement of Claim in B.C. Supreme Court. In it they challenged Canada Customs' right, under Tarriff Code 9956 and Memorandum D9-1-1 of the Customs Act, to exercise 'prior restraint' in seizing any book, magazine, film, or video materials believed to be obscene, as defined by section 163(8) of the Criminal Code of Canada. Little Sister's maintained that the 'prior restraint' clause, which forced the importing business to prove that individually seized items were not obscene, violated the right to freedom of expression guaranteed under section 2(b) of the Canadian Charter of Rights and Freedoms. Further, Little Sister's argued that Canada Customs' routine targeting of a lesbian and gay bookstore violated its owners' personal right to equal treatment under the law (section 15 of the Charter).

That night, before the readings from the anthology begin, Jim Deva, co-owner of Little Sister's, is introduced. He announces to the assembled audience that defence lawyers for the Crown had that very day successfully petitioned the court to postpone the trial date for another full year. My buoyant mood, along with most everyone else's in the room, is immediately deflated. Canada Customs' harassment of Little Sister's staff and customers will, I realize, continue unabated. The legislative and judicial branches of my own government have once again colluded to deny Canadian citizens access to the kind of literature that I both write and have aspirations of teaching some day. Sex, nation, literature: this admixture of discourses implants itself in my brain that night, and the broad parameters of this book begin to take shape.

After four years of delays and postponements while a succession of Crown lawyers prepared their defence, the case finally came to trial before Justice Kenneth Smith in Courtroom 65 of Vancouver's Smithe Street law buildings on 11 October 1994. Representing the plaintiffs was Joseph Arvay, assisted by Irene Faulkner. Over the course of the next two months, the court heard from forty witnesses (who together logged almost two hundred hours of testimony), collected over 260 evidentiary exhibits and documents, and compiled more than a thousand pages of transcripts. On 20 December 1994 the trial came to a close, with Justice Smith reserving judgment.

Just over a year later, on 19 January 1996, that judgment was finally delivered, with Smith upholding Canada Customs' right to detain books at the border. However, Smith added that customs officers frequently exercised their powers in an 'arbitrary and improper' manner, in violation of the Charter of Rights and Freedoms. In response to this ruling, Arvay immediately sought an injunction prohibiting Canada Customs from applying its mandate to Little Sister's until such time as the bookstore's appeal could be heard. Smith responded in late March 1996, noting in his refusal of the injunction that Little Sister's was in effect seeking exemption from what he concluded to be a constitutionally valid law, and that the federal government had already taken steps to remedy the flaws in the enforcement of the Customs Act. At the same time, Smith instructed customs officials to take Little Sister's off the 'look-out' list and to stop targeting materials specifically destined for its shelves. Finally, Smith ordered the federal government to pay $170,000 in courts fees to the bookstore, claiming that the 'financial costs of the presentation of the case are onerous for the plaintiffs and can more easily be defrayed by the federal crown.'

Janine Fuller, Little Sister's tireless and irrepressible manager, has declared both rulings to be partial victories for the bookstore, and has repeatedly vowed to press on with the fight against customs censorship. The latest round of that fight was decided on 24 June 1998, when, in a 2–1 decision against Little Sister's, the B.C. Court of Appeal upheld Smith's original ruling. However, heartened by Justice Lance Finch's dissenting opinion, Little Sister's has launched a final appeal to the Supreme Court of Canada.

For a full summary of the ins and outs of this landmark case, see Janine Fuller and Stuart Blackley, *Restricted Entry*.

Jump with me now to January 1998. Surveying the local political landscape as I begin work on my final revisions, I am forced to ask myself what, in the four years and as many months since I began this study, has changed? Little Sister's, still reeling from the aftershocks of its initial court challenge, has launched the next round of appeals against Justice Kenneth Smith's 1996 decision upholding Canada Customs' right to detain books for inspection; the lobby group Gay and Lesbian Educators (GALE) of B.C. has had its pamphlets, posters, and resource lists, aimed at queer youth in high schools across the Lower Mainland, rejected by school boards in Surrey and Coquitlam; the same month Surrey trustees also ban from their district's school libraries and classrooms three children's books featuring same-sex parents, prompting a challenge to the B.C. Supreme Court on the part of two teachers, one concerned parent, a student, and the author of one of the books; and the curricular efforts of a number of individuals at the University of British Columbia to establish an interdisciplinary lesbian and gay studies minor in the Faculty of Arts have temporarily run aground of institutional bureaucracy. Which makes all the more urgent, as we approach the end of the millennium, the call – to which each of these struggles lends its voice and to which I have attempted to lend my own, however meekly, in this book – for full sexual citizenship within the national body politic:[5] queer is here, and here, and even here ...

If, as I stated at the outset, this study of nationalisms and sexualities in contemporary Canadian, Québécois, and First Nations literatures is in part an attempt to make up for lost time, it is also something else: a declaration that it's about time.

Notes

Introduction: Here Is Queer

1 Patricia Merivale, drawing on the work of Kenneth Bruffee rather than that of Eve Sedgwick, has analysed at least two of these 'couples' within the 'quasi-erotic' triangular paradigm of 'elegiac romance.' See her 'The Biographical Compulsion: Elegiac Romances in Canadian Fiction'; see also Bruffee, *Elegiac Romance: Cultural Change and the Loss of the Hero in Modern Fiction.* Patricia Smart, as we shall see at greater length in chapters 1 and 4, has deduced a similar triangular configuration structuring gender relations within Québécois fiction.

1: Of Triangles and Textuality

1 Indeed, it is interesting to note that Cooper's Leatherstocking novels are themselves heavily steeped in male homosocial desire. In *Love and Death in the American Novel,* for example, Leslie Fiedler has commented at length on the 'austere, almost inarticulate, but unquestioned love' (192) figured between the white woodsman, Natty Bumppo, and the Delaware chief, Chingachgook, in Cooper's *The Pathfinder.*

2 According to Sedgwick, colonialism contributed to the transformation of certain gothic conventions in mid-Victorian England. As she puts it in *Between Men,* the 'literary availability of a thematics of Empire ... replaced the consciousness of class difference that had been endemic in the Gothic with a less discriminate, more dichotomous and fantasy prone distinction between the domestic and the exotic' (182). This process is heightened, of course, in the

'savage' spaces of the New World. On how the gothic gets played out in the Canadian literary context, with particular attention to *Wacousta*, see Margot Northey, *The Haunted Wilderness*.

3 I borrow the term 'indigenization' from Terry Goldie; see his *Fear and Temptation*, 13–17, and *passim*.

4 In Daphne Marlatt's *Ana Historic*, a text which substantially rewrites Grainger's *Woodsmen*, the homosocial triangle – regardless of the configuration of characters – is all female in gender: Annie, Zoe, Mrs (Ana) Richards; Annie, Ina, Mrs (Ana) Richards; Annie, Zoe, Ina; Zoe, Ina, Mrs (Ana) Richards. See chapter 5, below. For a bravura reading of the 'female homosocial triangle' as it relates to the 'counterplot' of modern lesbian fiction, a reading that is as much a polemic against Sedgwick as it is an elaboration of a new critical model, see Terry Castle, *The Apparitional Lesbian*, 66–91. In 'plotting against what Eve Sedgwick has called the "plot of male homosociality,"' Castle concludes, the 'archetypal lesbian fiction decanonizes, so to speak, the canonical structure of desire itself' (90).

5 The photographs accompanying the first edition, inexplicably excised from the initial 1964 McClelland and Stewart New Canadian Library reprint of the text, have since been restored in the most recent 1996 edition. A study of how the photographs impact on the text, both in terms of the construction of literary realism and the ironization of masculinity, bears further investigation.

6 Note, in particular, the homoeroticism which suffuses the following passage: 'Brian stopped and stared across at the Young Ben; he never saw the other boy without excitement stirring within him; as ever it was a wordless attraction strengthening with each additional and fleeting glimpse he got of the Young Ben' (206).

7 See Charles Steele, ed., *Taking Stock: The Calgary Conference on the Canadian Novel*. For dissenting opinions on this assessment, see Malcolm Ross, 'The Canonization of *As For Me and My House*: A Case Study'; Lawrence Mathews, 'Calgary, Canonization, and Class: Deciphering List B'; and Lecker, *Making It Real*, 173–87.

8 See, in this regard, Sedgwick's 'Willa Cather and Others.'

9 I cannot help thinking, in this context, of the fate of Earle Birney's David, in his famous narrative poem of the same name, a poem not without its own homosocial overtones.

10 See, for example, Linda Hutcheon, *The Canadian Postmodern*; Eva-Marie Kröller, *George Bowering: Bright Circles of Colour*; Marin Kuester, *Framing Truths: Parodic Structures in Contemporary English-Canadian Historical Novels*; and Glenn Deer, *Postmodern Canadian Fiction and the Rhetoric of Authority*.

11 In this regard, Merivale has, with characteristic astuteness, privately pointed

out to me that the ending of Aquin's novel is doubly ambiguous: we do not, after all, know the skin colour of Rachel/Anne-Lise Jamieson's unborn child.

12 It is true, as the editors of the recent volume of essays *Nationalisms and Sexualities* claim in their introduction, that Anderson's 'book has relatively little to say about gender or sexuality' (Parker et al., 4). It is worth noting, however, that in his concluding chapter, during a discussion of the nineteenth-century 'imaginings of fraternity' in the American fiction of James Fenimore Cooper (see note 1, above), Herman Melville, and Mark Twain, Anderson does concede – albeit in a footnote – that 'rather than a national eroticism, it is, I suspect, an eroticized nationalism that is at work [in these novels]' (*Imagined Communities*, 202–3n).

13 In his 'Conclusion' to *The Location of Culture*, Homi Bhabha critiques both Foucault and Anderson for failing to introduce the question of race into the historical contests of power at the heart of the disciplinary regimes of sexuality and nationalism: 'If Foucault normalizes the time-lagged "retroverse" sign of race, Benedict Anderson places the "modern" dreams of racism "outside history" altogether. For Foucault race and blood interfere with modern sexuality. For Anderson racism has its origins in antique ideologies of class that belong to the aristocratic "pre-history" of the modern nation' (248).

14 It was Stephen Heath, in his 1978 essay 'Difference,' who first proclaimed that 'the risk of essence may have to be taken' (99). Since then, many post-structuralist feminists have grappled with its import for the theory and practice of gender relations. Diana Fuss offers a critical overview of 'the "risk" of essence' in the first chapter of *Essentially Speaking*, 1–21. See also the essays from the feminist journal *differences* collected by Naomi Schor and Elizabeth Weed in *The Essential Difference*. In her provocative and influential essay, 'Imitation and Gender Insubordination,' Butler also has this to say on the topic of 'identity' and 'risk': 'To propose that the invocation of identity is always a risk does not imply that resistance to it is always or only symptomatic of a self-inflicted homophobia' (14). The ambiguous pronoun reference makes 'it' unclear what exactly is being resisted here, identity or risk-taking.

15 Guillermo Verdecchia makes much the same point about borders in his 1993 Governor General's Award–winning play *Fronteras Americanas*.

16 For theoretical applications of 'post' that are also 'pre,' see Jean-François Lyotard, *The Postmodern Condition*; Richard Cavell, 'Bakhtin Reads De Mille'; and Bakhtin's discussion of the 'chronotope' in *The Dialogic Imagination*, 84–257.

17 See my 'A Queer by Any Other Name?' for a brief linguistic genealogy of 'queer.' For Eve Sedgwick, who has likewise conducted her own etymological

investigation of the word, the power of 'queer' resides not so much in what it means as in what it doesn't mean, what she calls its 'open mesh of possibilities,' its 'lapses and excesses of meaning' ('Queer and Now,' 8). Consider as well the 'open mesh of possibilities' signified by the word 'here.' As Lauren Berlant and Elizabeth Freeman point out, for example, 'Queer Nation's slogan ["We're here, we're queer, get used to it!"] stages the shift from silent absence into present speech, from nothingness to collectivity, from a politics of embodiment to one of space, whose power erupts from the ambiguity of "here." Where?' (199).

2: 'Running Wilde'

1 Wilde's play, subtitled 'The Nihilists,' and based on actual events in Russia, recounts the 'revolutionary and amorous passions' of Vera Saboureff, caught between her political determination to assassinate the Czar and her love for the Czar's nihilist son, Alexis. An operatic political satire reflecting Wilde's attempts to reconcile an inherited Irish nationalism (from his mother, Lady 'Speranza' Wilde) with a nascent aristocratic socialism, the play was to have opened at the Adelphi Theatre in London on 17 December 1881. But following an upsurge in pro-royalist sentiment in the wake of the assassinations of Russian Czar Alexander II and U.S. President James Garfield, the show's backers bowed to government pressure and cancelled the production. *Vera* eventually premiered in New York in 1883, where it received abysmal notices and closed after a week. See Ellmann, 120–4, 153, 241–3.

2 In his 'Playwright's Note' to the published text, Bartley acknowledges the influence that O'Brien's book had on his own: 'The book [*Oscar Wilde in Canada*] set my imagination going and launched me on an obsession lasting five years. The result is *Stephen & Mr. Wilde*' (7). Bartley goes on to note that his play 'begins with history – with what happened – and launched into what might have happened, which is fiction' (8).

3 Arriving at his club on 28 February 1895, Wilde was presented with a calling-card left for him by Queensberry, on the back of which were scrawled the words: 'For Oscar Wilde Posing as a Somdomite [*sic*].' As Ed Cohen notes in *Talk on the Wilde Side*, it was the word 'posing,' more so than the misspelled accusation of 'sodomy,' that became the focus of critical controversy in the ensuing legal proceedings initiated by Wilde against Queensberry: 'the plea of justification tried to shift the focus on sodomy away from its traditional status as a criminally punishable sexual *act* so that it became in the defense's construction a defining characteristic of a type of sexual *actor* (the "sodomite")' (127). Needless to say, the defence's strategy was successful, enabling Queens-

berry's acquittal, and paving the way for the subsequent crown prosecutions of Wilde for 'engaging in acts of gross indecency with another male person,' a new category of criminality and sexual deviancy towards which Wilde was judged to 'exhibit' certain 'tendencies.'

4 To this end, one of the ironies central to Eagleton's play is the fact that Edward Carson, fellow Irishman and later a leader of the Unionist opposition to Home Rule, was one of Wilde's prosecutors. For more of Eagleton's critical commentary on Irish nationalism, and its relation to irony in literature, see his contribution to the Field Day pamphlet (co-authored with Fredric Jameson and Edward Said) *Nationalism, Colonialism, and Literature*, 23–39.

5 Anderson uses the term 'meanwhile' in *Imagined Communities* to describe the 'simultaneity' of the process of nationalism, a 'transverse, cross-time, marked not by prefiguring and fulfilment, but by temporal coincidence, and measured by clock and calendar' (24). Anderson in turn is basing his assertions on Walter Benjamin's notion of 'Messianic time,' as outlined in his 'Theses on the Philosophy of History' (*Illuminations*, 253–64). According to Bhabha, however, 'Anderson fails to locate the alienating time of the arbitrary sign in his naturalized, nationalized space of the imagined community. Although he borrows his notion of the homogeneous empty time of the nation's modern narrative from Walter Benjamin, he fails to read that profound ambivalence that Benjamin places deep within the utterance of the narrative of modernity' ('DissemiNation,' 311). Bhabha's supplementary, subaltern, and substitutive – rather than simultaneous, synchronic, and serial – use of 'the meanwhile' as the ambivalent, 'arbitrary sign of the modern nation-space' (309) in 'DissemiNation' approaches more fully (at least in Bhabha's mind) Benjamin's historical-materialist 'conception of the present as the "time of the now"' ('Theses,' 263). I will be returning to this complex and provocative essay by Bhabha in chapter 6.

6 See also M.L. McKenzie, 'Memories of the Great War: Graves, Sassoon, and Findley.'

7 Gregory Woods supplements Fussell's comments in *Articulate Flesh: Male Homoeroticism and Modern Poetry*.

8 For more on the 'martial formations of masculinity' (189) as they relate to *The Wars*, see Christopher Gittings, '"What are soldiers for?"'

9 The connection between horses and adolescent male sexual object-choice had of course already been explored, to great dramatic effect, by Peter Shaffer in *Equus*, a possible intertext with *The Wars* in this regard. In the case of Shaffer's play, however, Alan's failure to consummate his relationship with his female co-worker prompts him to blind the horses who had hitherto aided him in the pursuit of auto-erotic pleasures.

10 On the importance of 'gesture' in Findley's fiction, see his comments in 'Alice Drops Her Cigarette on the Floor,' 20; see also David MacFarlane, 'The Perfect Gesture'; and Brydon, 'A Devotion to Fragility.'

11 Cf. the following exchange in Findley's recent play, *The Trials of Ezra Pound*:
MUNCIE: You seem not to care for Mister Eliot.
EZRA: I love him. Don't you know he's one of my sons?
MUNCIE: I see.
EZRA: The whole of 20th century English literature is mine. You didn't know that, Muncie? Eliot, Joyce and Yeats: all mine. And Mauberley. The whole of 20th century literature – all – to say nothing of the past, which I've reclaimed ...
MUNCIE: I had thought Hugh Selwyn Mauberley was a fiction, Mister Pound.
EZRA: And he is – he is. So, doesn't that tell you about the rest of them! (38)

12 In a letter to Felix E. Schelling dated 9 July 1922, Pound claims that he is 'no more Mauberley than Eliot is Prufrock,' and that his poem is essentially a 'study in form, an attempt to condense the James novel ... The metre in *Mauberley* is Gautier and Bion's "Adonis"; or at least those are the two grafts I was trying to flavour it with' (*Letters*, 180–1). Ironically, in declaring his 'general distaste for the slushiness and swishiness of the post-Swinburnian British line' (181), Pound also betrays his poem's homophilic lines of influence/filiation: to Henry James; to Théophile Gautier, French aesthete, author of *Mademoiselle de Maupin* (1835), favourite of Wilde; and to the ancient Greek poet Bion, who composed the 'homo-elegiac' 'Lament for Adonis' (c. 100 B.C.E.).

13 For a more in-depth analysis of this 'tendency' within post–Second World War Italian film, see Mellen, 'Fascism in the Contemporary Film.' For an analysis of the configuration of discourses of fascism, homosexuality, and masochism within Alberto Moravia's original literary text, *Il conformista*, see Andrew Hewitt, 'Coitus Interruptus: Fascism and the Deaths of History.'

14 See, in this regard, Richard Plant, *The Pink Triangle: The Nazi War against Homosexuals*.

15 In her essay 'Fascinating Fascism,' Susan Sontag ponders how a generation of post-Stonewall homosexuals could have made fascist aesthetics 'no more than a variant of camp,' how 'a regime which persecuted homosexuals [could have] become a gay turn-on,' concluding (none too moralistically) that it is the prevalence of sado-masochistic sexual practices among gay men 'which make[s] playing at Nazism seem erotic' (97, 102).

16 Findley employs a similar narrative technique in *The Wars*, 9–10 and 181–3.

17 Cf. Barbara Gabriel on *The Butterfly Plague*: 'If the eugenics discourses of *The Butterfly Plague* have been either marginalized or elided altogether in readings of the novel, that is partly due to Findley's own straining for allegory in a fiction in which the unrepresentable of the Holocaust confronts the historical

subject who is *already* outside of the frame of representation' ('Performing the *Bent* Text,' 243).

18 Once again Mosse's study is helpful here, especially chapter 8, 153–80.

19 See especially chapter 2, 31–52, for Frye's discussion of how classical myth functions in relation to the Bible. It is interesting to note the extent to which the symbol of Mount Ararat (or a derivation thereof, most often in the form of a tower or ziggurat) figures in modern Canadian poetry. See, for example, F.R. Scott, 'Lakeshore'; P.K. Page, 'Cry Ararat!'; Dennis Lee, *Civil Elegies*; and Phyllis Webb, 'Leaning,' the last three lines of which serve as the epigraph to Findley's *Voyage*.

20 The term, although it nicely recalls Dollimore, is actually Cindy Patton's. In *Inventing AIDS* she uses 'the idea of dissident vernaculars' in order to '[suggest] that meanings created by and in communities are upsetting to the dominant culture precisely because speaking in one's own fashion is a means of resistance, a strengthening of the subculture that has created new meaning' (148n). On how (homo)sexual 'vernaculars' resist the seductive rhetoric of end-time implicit in 'oracular' pronouncements on AIDS, see my '"Go-go Dancing on the Brink of the Apocalypse": Representing AIDS.' On the 'moral' dimensions of counter-discourse in Findley's metafictions, see Pennee, *Moral Metafiction*; and Ingham, 'Bashing the Fascists.'

21 In a recent article on *Not Wanted on the Voyage*, Cecelia Martell has demonstrated how, 'through a radical infusion of "Camp" elements, Findley not only ironizes social practices, but also criticizes the kinds of binary ideologies that function as filters for exclusivity and inclusion on various, coded levels of a social text – and readers unwilling or unable to move beyond the parameters of the "norms" that construct their readings are forcibly excluded from having access to the encoded criticism inherent in Findley's text' (97). While Martell and I are more or less in agreement in this regard, we differ markedly in our critical 'unpacking' of the camped codes at work in *Voyage*, in part I would argue because of Martell's over-reliance on Susan Sontag 'as a guide on [her] voyage' through the text (103). For example, Martell notes in passing how *Voyage* 'pays tribute to the influences of ... Oscar Wilde' (110n), but fails to explicate in any concrete manner where these influences manifest themselves in the text. See my discussion of *Salome*, below. For her part, Linda Lamont-Stewart argues that 'resistance to authoritarianism' is figured in Findley's text, and specifically in the character of Lucy, through the trope of androgyny.

22 See, for example, Jack Babuscio, 'Camp and the Gay Sensibility' (1984); Jeffrey Escoffier, 'Sexual Revolution and the Politics of Gay Identity' (1985); Martin Humphries, 'Gay Machismo' (1985); Andrew Ross, 'Uses of Camp' (1988); Sue-Ellen Case, 'Toward a Butch-Femme Aesthetic' (1989); and Carole-Anne

Tyler, 'Boys Will Be Girls: The Politics of Gay Drag' (1991). See also the recently edited collections *Camp Grounds* (1993) and *The Politics and Poetics of Camp* (1994). Of course, all of these discussions were preceded by two now-classic studies: Esther Newton's *Mother Camp: Female Impersonators in America* (1972); and Susan Sontag's 'Notes on Camp' (1966). While I take issue with Sontag's assertion that 'Camp sensibility is disengaged, depoliticized' (277), and with her remarks on the 'peculiar relation between Camp and homosexuality' (290), I am in general agreement with her definition of camp as 'a certain mode of aestheticism ... *one* way of seeing the world ... not in terms of beauty, but in terms of artifice, of stylization' (277). See below.

23 The link between femininity and masquerade in psychoanalysis was first made by Joan Rivière in her 1929 essay 'Womanliness as a Masquerade.' More recently, lesbian-feminist theorists like Sue-Ellen Case (in 'Toward a Butch-Femme Aesthetic') and Judith Butler (in *Gender Trouble*) have used Rivière's essay to subvert traditional identity categories, so that gender, for instance, is read ironically or parodically, and is thus displaced into a series of performing signifiers. For his part, Bhabha claims that 'colonial mimicry is the desire for a reformed, recognizable Other, *as the subject of a difference that is almost the same, but not quite* ... Mimicry is, thus, the sign of a double articulation; a complex strategy of reform, and discipline, which "appropriates" the Other as it visualizes power' ('Of Mimicry and Man,' 126).

24 In *The Use of Pleasure*, the second volume of *The History of Sexuality*, Foucault posits the classical Greek model of male-male love in counter-discursive relation to the eighteenth- and early nineteenth-century articulations of (hetero/homo)sexuality outlined in volume 1. More specifically, he focuses on sexual activities as they are elaborated and 'problematized' through technologies of the self, 'bringing into play the criteria of an "aesthetics of existence"' (12). Similarly, what Foucault calls 'a history of "ethics" and "ascetics,"' encapsulated in the phrase 'care of the self' (which would become the title of *The History of Sexuality*'s third volume), is 'concerned with the models proposed for setting up and developing relationships with the self, for self-reflection, self-knowledge, self-examination, for the decipherment of the self by oneself' (*The Use of Pleasure*, 29). In his 'emblematic' reading of the English book 'as an insignia of colonial authority and a signifier of colonial desire' (102), Bhabha notes that 'hybridity represents that *ambivalent* "turn" of the discriminated subject into the terrifying, exorbitant object of paranoid classification – a disturbing questioning of the images of authority' ('Signs Taken for Wonders,' 113; my emphasis).

25 'Blue,' as a signifier, has of course further scopophilic and erotic associations: the gaze solicited and undermined by a 'blue movie,' for example, or the

looks exchanged between model and viewer while flipping through the artistically decadent pages of *L'Amour bleu.*

26 For her part, Sontag claims that 'Camp taste turns its back on the good-bad axis of ordinary aesthetic judgment. Camp doesn't reverse things. It doesn't argue that the good is bad, or the bad is good. What it does is to offer for art (and life) a different – a supplementary – set of standards' (286).

27 Gabriel has perceptively pointed out how Octavius Rivii's 'coding as oriental ephebe' in *The Butterfly Plague* 'anticipates the Lucy figure of Findley's *Not Wanted on the Voyage*, who is even more explicitly drawn as the *Onna gata* of the Japanese Kabuki theatre, that ideal stylization of the feminine, which is always performed by a man' ('Performing the *Bent* Text,' 233).

3: Critical Homophobia and Canadian Canon-Formation, 1943–1967

1 In 'Montreal Poets of the Forties,' Wynne Francis notes that Sutherland's introduction to *Other Canadians* 'does not ring true ... because Sutherland was not a socialist ... *It is probably the one critical article that he sincerely regretted having written* and by 1950 he would have recalled all copies from circulation if he could have had his way' (30; my emphasis).

2 In a recent article, David Leahy has ruminated on the link between Sutherland's 'apparent homosexual panic and some of his aesthetic biases,' arguing that Sutherland's demonization of Anderson's poetry in this context stems at least in part from the former's 'heterorealism,' an 'antiqueer naturalization and valorization of heterosexuality as if it were the only "real" of acceptable way of being sexual' (133, 135).

3 Sutherland's retraction, printed on the front cover of volume 1.20 of *First Statement*, reads as follows: 'I wish to retract all statements made in my article, "The Writing of Patrick Anderson," which in any way concern the motivation of Mr. Anderson's poetry and prose. I apologize for misreadings of Mr. Anderson's works, and for my statement that a story entitled, "Dramatic Monologue," was a part of Mr. Anderson's diary.'

4 A much more generous assessment of Finch's life and work, one that contrasts the 'formalist aesthete' and 'lifelong bachelor' with the 'expatriate wild-man' and 'boastfully homosexual' poet (4) Edward Lacey, has recently been offered by David Helwig in 'Robert and Edward: An Uncommon Obituary.'

5 See Ken Norris, *The Little Magazine in Canada, 1925–80*, especially 27–55, for a full account of the ins and outs of *Preview*, *First Statement*, and *Northern Review.*

6 For Anderson's own – albeit 'fictionalized' – accounts of his relationship with Doernbach, see 'At Baie St. Paul,' in *The Character Ball* (109–28), and 'Remembering Baie St. Paul,' in *A Visiting Distance* (147–9) and *Return to Canada*

(42–3). I will be returning to these pieces and, in particular, the differences between them later in this chapter.

7 For a further analysis of Anderson's affiliation with *En Masse*, see Michael Gnarowski, 'New Facts and Old Fictions: Some Notes on Patrick Anderson, 1945 and *En Masse*.' Unlike Whitney, Gnarowski sees *En Masse* as little more than a 'radical interlude' for an essentially 'bourgeois poet' biding his time between the demise of *Preview* and the birth of *Northern Review*, literary magazines 'less *closeted* within an ideology' (68; my emphasis).

8 On the 'engendering' of competing modernist poetics in *Preview* and *First Statement*, and how this 'echoed' a similar pattern in such important American and European little magazines as *transition*, *Exile*, the *Little Review*, and *This Quarter*, see Edwards, 67–8.

9 'Reverting momentarily to Leonard Cohen' in his article 'The Canadian Bestiary,' Symons asserts 'that [Cohen's] book truly set the stage in Canada for a society whose bravest souls were "beautiful losers" (and whose myriad cowards were the national smuglies). And in French Canada, Hubert Aquin seconded the motion' (14).

10 In '"A National Enema": Scott Symons's *Place d'Armes*,' George Piggford has recently suggested why, in formalist terms, this marginalization might be justified.

11 For a more in-depth reading of the 'anatomies' of homosexual desire encoded in Crane's 'Voyages,' see Thomas Yingling, *Hart Crane and the Homosexual Text*, 91–103; and Robert K. Martin, *The Homosexual Tradition in American Poetry*, 130–6. Martin also discusses Crane's influence on Anderson in 'Sex and Politics,' 116–17.

12 The quotations are from the following poems in *The Colour as Naked*: 'Song of Intense Cold' (26); 'Sestina in Time of Winter' (19); 'Soft Blizzard' (41); 'The Strange Bird' (83); and 'A Monkey in Malaya' (68).

13 My own analysis of Anderson's Malayan excursus owes much to Philip Holden's Barthesian reading of another 'orientalist' text by Maugham, *The Painted Veil*. See Holden, 'An Area of Whiteness.'

14 The Toto who so beguiles Anderson ('You don't have to be a Gide to find a certain fascination in the criminal young' [216]) and, more particularly, Anderson's friend, Bridge, may owe something to the beautiful Italian boy who figures so prominently in Frederick Rolfe, the Baron Corvo's, 'Toto Stories,' weaving fanciful accounts of Catholic piety and pagan decadence. Modelled, in part, on Wilde's *Happy Prince* stories, most of Corvo's tales were originally published in the pages of *The Yellow Book* between 1895 and 1896, alongside writings by Max Beerbohm and Richard Le Gallienne and drawings by Aubrey Beardsley; several more subsequently appeared in a limited edition

Bodley Head 'booklet' called *In His Own Image* (1901). Many have since been gathered together and republished in a single volume under the general title *Stories Toto Told Me* (1969).

15 Ironically, Anderson's introduction of Quebec slang into this passage rings something of a false note: '*le gang*,' although technically correct in terms of Parisian French, actually takes the feminine article, 'la,' in Quebec parlance.

16 Martin lists eleven such items ('Cheap Tricks,' 200–1). The pouch in the copy I consulted contained only ten; it was 'missing' the clipping from *La Patrie* extolling Symons as a 'native son.'

17 On Barthes's 'evanescence,' see Porter, *Haunted Journeys*, 301; on Symons's 'synaesthesia,' see Buitenhuis, 'Scott Symons,' 67, 68.

18 Cf., in this regard, Canadian playwright Sky Gilbert's *More Divine*, in which, after having had his Moroccan boys 'perform,' the character of Barthes proclaims: 'Perhaps if you do not understand it is because there are no words in your language; a thing that contains lust and love, that is fleeting and forever, that is contained in the body and yet read with the soul. If I am remote it is because I wish I was a philosopher and as for truth, I prefer parenthesis' (217).

19 I will be returning to Barthes, and Robert Martin's reading of his '*écriture gaie*,' in chapter 7.

20 There are thirty-three numbered letters, plus one beginning on page 611 headed 'Letter #?,' and one starting on page 722 entitled 'The Last Letter.'

21 In 'Is the Rectum a Grave?' Leo Bersani equates 'psychic tumescence' with sexual 'self-hyperbole,' a struggle for power, for being on 'top,' which is itself 'a repression of sex as self-abolition,' a psychosexual 'shattering' experienced only through penetration, only by being fucked (218). Terry Goldie has recently used Bersani's article to analyse the aesthetics of 'phallic power' and 'anal negation' in Symons's *Place d'Armes*. See his 'The Man of the Land / The Land of the Man,' 161–2.

4: 'Pour exprimer un problème d'identité'

1 'If I start off with ... the subject of the literary variants of homosexuality in French Canada, it's because I recognize a sociological value. Also, this sexual deviationism seems to me the most likely and shameful explanation for a literature that is universally weak, without brilliance, and truly boring ... This sort of inversion, which seems to me to have seriously contaminated almost all of our literature, is not an inversion that wants to show off or that seeks to scandalize. No, this is a profound inversion: thus, it takes care to obscure itself within diversified themes ... The literary categories of inversion have not been

systematically inventoried at this point, but something tells me that these categories are very numerous and contain a majority proportion of stereotypes that present themselves precisely as cases of non-inversion. If there is a human condition generative of dissimulation, it's homosexuality.' All translations from the French are my own unless otherwise indicated.

2 'I don't know that I've talked a lot about homosexuality in the theatre! ... The first times I used homosexual characters, it was to express a problem of identity. *La Duchesse* ... [and] *Hosanna* are not plays about homosexuality. Not that I didn't want to talk about it, but I was making use of them for other reasons, for their willingness to be someone else, a reflection of our society.'

3 On nation-states and linguistic nationalism, Hubert Aquin had this to say in 1962: '... the concept of the nation-state is clearly outdated, corresponding neither to reality nor to the most recent scientific findings ... Ethnic homogeneity no longer exists, or at least is very rare ... [T]he French-Canadian people has been replaced by a cultural-linguistic group whose common denominator is language' ('The Cultural Fatigue of French Canada,' 29). Now consider the following about-face, recorded by Aquin some twelve years later: 'Immigrants are potentially the most insidious aspect of our anglicization. It is no longer the English who want to assimilate us; it is the immigrants who not only want to be assimilated to the English, but who dispute our right to assimilate anyone at all to our culture and our language' ('*Joual*: Haven or Hell?' 104). So much for non-ethnic nationalism, cultural homogeneity, and linguistic harmony in Quebec in 1974, on the eve of a PQ election victory. In fact, I would argue that the xenophobic vitriol expressed by Aquin in this passage is not that far removed from the sentiments behind Parizeau's 1995 referendum-night remarks.

4 For a satirical indictment of anti-Semitism in Quebec, see Richler, *Oh Canada! Oh Quebec!* Many of Richler's harshest observations were based on the research contained within a then undefended Ph.D. dissertation by Delisle, a political science student at Laval University. Delisle's thesis has since been published as *The Traitor and the Jew: Anti-Semitism and Extremist Right-Wing Nationalism in Québec from 1929–1939* (1993). Among other important figures and institutions to come under scrutiny in its pages are Abbé Lionel Groulx, Quebec's iconic nationalist historian, and *Le Devoir*, the province's most popular daily newspaper. On how the Northern Cree of Quebec have adopted a language of national self-determination in order to confront the Quebec government over economic developments like the James Bay hydroelectric project, see Ignatieff, 123–6. An early response by Caroline Bayard to the stand-off at Oka places the crisis within an historical context of mounting tensions between Quebec's francophone and Indigenous communities since the 1960s. See her 'From

Nègres blancs d'Amérique (1968) to Kanesatake (1990).' For further discussion of the non-equivalencies between nationalism and ethnicity in Quebec, particularly as they relate to the province's immigrant Haitian population, see the pioneering postcolonial work of Max Dorsinville, including *Caliban without Prospero* (1974), *Le Pays natal* (1983), *Solidarités* (1988), and his translation of Paul Dejean's *The Haitians in Quebec* (1980). Of course, the very title of Pierre Vallières's *Nègres blancs d'Amérique* highlights some of these non-equivalencies.

5 On how this ideology operates in Quebec literature, see Patricia Smart, *Writing in the Father's House*; and Paula Gilbert Lewis's introduction to *Traditionalism, Nationalism, and Feminism: Women Writers of Quebec*. See also The Clio Collective, eds, *Québec Women: A History*.

6 See also Tremblay's comments in Adrien Gruslin, 'Michel Tremblay achève un premier cycle.' In his essay 'From Alienation to Transcendence: The Quest for Selfhood in Michel Tremblay's Plays,' John Ripley maintains that Tremblay's first cycle is comprised of eleven, and not twelve, plays in total. He lists them as follows: *Les Belles-Soeurs* (1968); *En pièces détachées* (1969); *La Duchesse de Langeais* (1969); *Trois Petits Tours* (1969); *Demain Matin, Montréal m'attend* (1970); *À toi, pour toujours, ta Marie-Lou* (1971); *Hosanna* (1973); *Bonjour, là, bonjour* (1974); *Surprise! Surprise!* (1975); *Sainte Carmen de la Main* (1976); and *Damnée Manon, sacrée Sandra* (1977). However, Ripley is leaving out of this list both 1971's *Les Paons*, a one-act fantasy, and 1976's *Les Héros de mon enfance*, a musical comedy. Since *Les Paons* is the only title among this list that has not been published in Quebec, it is *Les Héros* that I take to be the 'twelfth' play in Tremblay's cycle.

7 As recently as 1993, Yves Jubinville, drama critic at *Spirale* magazine, has continued to endorse this view, noting that Tremblay's use of transvestism in his plays 'est aussi révélateur. Non pas parce qu'il est forcément lié au thème de l'homosexualité, mais parce qu'il développe un autre aspect de la crise du sujet québécois, à savoir son rapport malaisé avec l'identité réelle "habitant" un espace étranger' ('Claude inc.,' 110; 'is also revealing. Not because it is necessarily tied to the theme of homosexuality, but because it develops another aspect of the crisis of the Québécois subject, that is, his/her uneasy relationship with a real identity while "living" in a foreign space'). Robert Wallace, however, questions the sincerity behind some of Tremblay's comments about the 'gayness' of his plays. Quoting from interviews with the author in the Montreal gay press, Wallace implies that Tremblay may in fact be 'hiding' behind the 'political' readings of his plays because of his own unconscious anxieties about his homosexuality and its effect on his relationship with his parents; see Wallace, 'Homo Creation,' 233n. In fact, in later works, most notably the play *Les Anciennes Odeurs* (1981), and the novels *Le Coeur découvert*

(1986) and *Le Coeur éclaté* (1993), Tremblay would explore his alternate 'family' of friends and lovers in much more 'gay-positive' terms.

8 All references to the play-texts under discussion in this chapter are to the original French editions put out by Montreal's Leméac press. The English quotations in parentheses are taken from the published translations of each play, by John Van Burek and Bill Glassco in the case of Tremblay's *Hosanna*, and by Linda Gaboriau in the case of Dubois's *Being at home with Claude* and Bouchard's *Lilies.*

9 See also Koustas, '*Hosanna* in Toronto: "Tour de force" or "détour de traduction?"'

10 In this article, Martin draws important parallels between the staging of Tremblay's *Hosanna* and that of David Henry Hwang's *M. Butterfly*, making use of Hwang's play much in the same way that I did in chapter 2, above.

11 In a recent article, Ruth Antosh has analysed Tremblay's use of what she calls the 'hermaphrodite' (as opposed to 'transvestite') character in *La Duchesse de Langeais, Hosanna*, and *Damnée Manon, sacrée Sandra.*

12 To be sure, Tremblay's original script already makes explicit the manifold ways in which Cuirette is as self-deluded in his identity as Hosanna. For starters, the feminine ending of his nickname (which translates loosely as 'leatherboy,' but which also dovetails as a homonym with the English word 'queer') contrasts with his tough-guy, motorcycle-riding persona. And as Hosanna comments near the end of act 1, with a reference to this persona, 'Tu te promènes en bicycle à gaséline, mais c'est toé qui fait cuire le bacon en dedans! Moé, chus coiffeur dans le jour, pis femme du monde le soir ... Pis j'trouve ça bien mieux que d'être une femme de ménage le jour pis un gars de bicycle le soir!' (47; 'Out there, you cruise around town on your bike, but when you're home, you scrub the pans, and you take out the garbage. Me, I'm a hairdresser by day, and a woman of the world by night ... But what are you? Hein? A cleaning lady who rides a motorcycle when she gets off work!' [67]). In a 1982 interview with Roch Turbide, Tremblay outlined his view of Cuirette as follows: 'Cuirette n'est pas un personnage manqué, mais un demi-personnage ... Il est là au premier acte parce que je voulais vider encore une fois l'histoire des rôles imposés par la société à l'homme et à la femme ... C'est un personnage-accessoire mais il n'est pas manqué' ('Michel Tremblay,' 217; 'Cuirette is not an overlooked character, but a half-character ... He is there in the first act because I wanted once again to empty the history of roles imposed by society on men and women ... He's an accessory-character but he is not overlooked').

13 'The first [production], of modernist inspiration, rallies homosexual and national emancipation around the idea of an identity rediscovered at the end of a hard combat. A liturgy of liberation (in vogue at the time) triumphed

then, a liturgy that was not without a certain lyricism and utopic highlights. In 1990 [*sic*], almost twenty years later, the play gives rise to a reflection on the fragility of identity in the hour of the "end of utopias." No *happy end* here: self-affirmation in the hour of postmodernity is never more than an unachieved project. Which is the better reading? Ultimately, we must without doubt choose both (which is to say that they are both partial!), because the play itself works on these two levels.'

14 Several recent articles have discussed Chaurette's plays in conjunction with those of Dubois and Bouchard: see Jean-Cléo Godin, 'Deux Dramaturges de l'avenir?'; Jane Moss, 'Sexual Games: Hypertheatricality and Homosexuality in Recent Quebec Plays' and '"Still Crazy after All These Years": The Uses of Madness in Recent Quebec Drama'; and Robert Wallace, 'Homo Creation.' On the 'somatic' representation of the gay male body as masochistic, fallible, and dissembling in Lepage and Brassard's play, see Michael Sidnell's 'Polygraph: Somatic Truth and the Art of Presence.'

15 '[F]or the first time, it wasn't the dream his friends stood for that won out, it was the dream I stood for. Instead of changing scenes, while he was on the phone, he stayed there with me. I don't mean there in the kitchen, that's obvious. That's where the phone is. I mean he stayed there with me in his head. So he didn't have to shift back to me, like usual, like a stranger who had to get used to me all over again. It was just the opposite. He talked to them like he was talkin' to me. He told them he had somethin' real urgent to do, and he was looking right at me. I felt hot. I was shivering. Didn't know what to do. He told them he'd call them back the next morning' (429).

16 For an application of this question to Bouchard's text, see Isabelle Raynauld, '"Les Feluettes": Aimer/tuer,' especially 171.

17 On 'absent fathers' and the effect this has on their 'lost sons' in Québécois culture, see Guy Corneau, who postulates yet another triangular model of masculine identity formation: 'Pour évoluer, un homme doit être capable de s'identifier à sa mère et à son père. Le triangle "père-mère-fils" doit pouvoir se former et venir remplacer la dyade "mère-fils." Or, si le père est absent, il n'y a pas de transfert d'identification de la mère au père; le fils demeure alors prisonnier de l'identification à la mère' (22; 'In order to develop, a man must be capable of identifying with both his mother and his father. The "father-mother-son" triangle must be allowed to take shape and replace the "mother-son" dyad. Thus, if the father is absent, there is no transfer of identification from the mother to the father; the son remains a prisoner of his identification with the mother').

18 Compare this statement with one made by Bouchard himself: '[L]a mère est le plus grand personnage mythologique au Québec. La comtesse [dans *Les*

Feluettes] prend une certaine dimension mythique, devient un demi-dieu parce qu'elle est la mère' ('Tout plein d'émotions,' 12; 'The mother is the greatest mythological character in Quebec. The Countess [in *Lilies*] takes on a certain mythic dimension, becomes a demi-god because she is the mother').

19 What has come to be labelled 'l'affaire des enfants de Duplessis' refers to another dark chapter in Quebec's history, when thousands of orphans and illegitimate children placed in provincial institutions and religious homes between 1935 and 1964 were routinely beaten, sexually and psychologically abused, used as cheap labour, and incorrectly classified as mentally challenged. On 11 March 1993 lawyers representing several of the now adult victims launched a $1.4 billion class action suit (the largest in Quebec history) against the provincial government and seven institutions and religious orders. For a comprehensive overview of the social and historical background to this affair, see Micheline Dumont, 'Des religieuses, des murs et des enfants.'

20 'In the whole history of Québécois theatre since the renewal of the 1960s, *Being at home with Claude*, by René-Daniel Dubois, joins those perfectly felt plays ... that give theatre from here its specific appeal, its intrinsic value ... Dubois proves, with *Being at home with Claude*, that he is at once the most aesthetic of our playwrights and, what makes his genius the equal of Tremblay's, the most visceral of dramatic poets.'

21 'One of the particular thematics of Québécois theatre, aside from national affirmation, family realism, feminist poetics, is homosexuality. Already one of the driving forces of Tremblay's theatre, homosexual love and conflicts have given major works to Québécois theatre for the past ten years. Whether we speak of Normand Chaurette, with *Provincetown Playhouse* ..., or Serge Sirois's *Pommiers en fleurs*, or René-Daniel Dubois's *Being at home with Claude*, homosexual plays or plays about homosexuality (there is a difference) have become one of the fields of introspection for Québécois theatre ... Michel-Marc Bouchard ... inscribes himself at the centre of this ring of homosexual reality.'

22 See Tremblay's comments on Dubois in this regard in 'Il y a 20 ans,' 74.

23 It should be pointed out, however, that this symbolic link is made, for the most part, only in the case of male homosexuality. Lesbianism, as portrayed on stage in the plays of Jovette Marchessault, for example, 'ouvre la voie à un nouveau mythe des origines' ('opens the way to a new myth of origins'), but one in which 'les femmes s'identifient aux femmes' ('women identify with women'), and not with the political ideal of national independence (Lynda Burgoyne, 'Théâtre et homosexualité féminine,' 114).

24 See, in particular, Stephen Godfrey, 'Dramatizing the Intensity of Love,' in the *Globe and Mail*; and Geoff Chapman, 'Love's Labor's Almost Lost in Lilies,' in the *Toronto Star*.

25 For similar thoughts on the 'inter-cultural' production of Québécois theatre in English Canada, and, in particular, Toronto, see Annie Brisset, 'Language and Collective Identity: When Translators of Theater Address the Quebec Nation'; and Jane Koustas, 'From "Homespun" to "Awesome": Translated Quebec Theater in Toronto.'

5: Towards a Transnational, Translational Feminist Poetics

1 'Translation is an act of passage whereby one reality becomes all at once different and the same. Whether it's a matter of passing from reality to fiction through writing or of passing from fiction to reality through reading or of making a text pass from one language to another, my fascination for the act of passage has always been at the centre of my literary and existential questioning.'

2 The acuity of McClintock's remarks is underscored by Benedict Anderson's rather blithe statement, in *Imagined Communities*, that 'in the modern world everyone can, should, will "have" a nationality, as he or she "has" a gender' (5).

3 Benedict Anderson would no doubt disagree with this contention. According to him, 'nations ... have no clearly identifiable births,' and their genealogies are not made up of 'a long chain of begettings' (205).

4 For a preliminary list of those writers included in Brossard's 'preface' to an as yet unpublished book of lesbian genealogy, see her 'Tender Skin My Mind.' A revised version of this essay appears in *La Lettre aérienne* as 'Lesbiennes d'écriture.' Brossard's *Picture Theory* (1982) can also be read as an attempt to recuperate two members of this lesbian genealogy from the traditional patriarchal begetting that characterizes the modernist canon: Djuna Barnes and Gertrude Stein. See, in this regard, Lianne Moyes, 'Composing in the Scent of Wood and Roses: Nicole Brossard's Intertextual Encounters with Djuna Barnes and Gertrude Stein.'

5 In 'The Mark of Gender,' Wittig claims that 'the bar in the *j/e* of *The Lesbian Body* is a sign of excess. A sign that helps to imagine an excess of "I," an "I" exalted' (87).

6 Gail Scott notes an important distinction between the two terms: 'in French, the emphasis is on fiction, not theory. That is, the noun in French is *fiction*, the adjective *théorique* is what qualifies it' (Godard et al., 'Theorizing,' 8). As a bilingual English-language writer living in Montreal, and as a member of both the original *Tessera* editorial collective and the 'Sunday/la dimanche' theory group (that also included Brossard, Louky Bersianik, Louise Cotnoir, Louise Dupré, and France Théoret), Scott is, in a sense, uniquely positioned to com-

ment on how 'fiction/theory' and 'writing in the feminine,' for example, have played out differently in the feminist communities of English Canada and Quebec. See, in this regard, her *Spaces Like Stairs.* For insightful analyses of Scott's 1987 novel, *Heroine,* particularly as it relates to the genre of fiction/theory, see Bina Toledo Freiwald, '"Towards the Uncanny Edge of Language": Gail Scott's Liminal Trajectories'; and Peggy Kelly, 'Fiction Theory as Feminist Practice in Marlatt's *Ana Historic* and Scott's *Heroine.*'

7 '*Écriture féminine,*' or 'feminine writing,' is of course the name given by Hélène Cixous in her 1975 essay 'Le Rire de la Méduse' ('The Laugh of the Medusa'), to 'a new *insurgent* writing' that will liberate woman's body and occasion 'her shattering entry into history' (250). While it remains 'impossible to *define* a feminine practice of writing,' according to Cixous, we can nevertheless be sure that such a practice 'will always surpass the discourse that regulates the phallocentric system' (253). Above all, *écriture féminine* is a writing 'through' the body, one that '[sweeps] away syntax,' an 'impregnable language that will wreck partitions, classes, and rhetorics, regulations and codes' (256). Cixous gave several important lectures in Montreal between 1972 and 1973, and while the Québécoise concept of '*écriture au féminin*' owes much to her thinking, it differs from *écriture féminine* in at least one important respect: as Karen Gould points out, writers like Brossard, Bersianik, and Théoret 'have – unlike Cixous – consistently understood their own approach to writing in the feminine as a gender-marked discourse in which women alone are engaged, rather than as an anti-logocentric or anti-phallocentric approach to writing that male and female writers alike might pursue' (38). For Peggy Kelly, the addition of the preposition 'au/in' is significant, emphasizing the woman writer as agent, 'a conscious assertion of feminine subjectivity through the movement of the male or female writer into the realm of the (feminine) imaginary' (95n). While Kelly seems to conflate the two terms somewhat in her assessment (especially where the participation of male writers is concerned), I am in general agreement with her remarks about agency.

8 Although, as Barbara Johnson points out, 'Derrida's work ... has always already been (about) translation' (144), the problematics associated with the discourse are foregrounded most explicitly in texts such as 'Living On / Border Lines' (1979), 'Des Tours de Babel' (1985), and *The Ear of the Other: Otobiography, Transference, Translation* (1985).

9 What in English Canada would be considered prototypically 'postmodern' (Brossard's entire oeuvre, for example) was until the mid-1980s in Quebec usually classified under the literary-critical rubric of 'modernité.' And this despite the fact that the original 1979 French edition of Jean-François Lyotard's *The Postmodern Condition* was commissioned expressly by the Quebec

government. The back cover of Brossard's *Le Désert mauve* actually claims that it is 'le premier roman postmoderne écrit au Québec!' For a response to this claim, see Janet Paterson, *Postmodernism and the Quebec Novel*, 114–30. On Brossard's and Marlatt's rewriting of postmodern metanarratives 'in the feminine,' see Susan Knutson. See also Brossard's conversation with Marlatt in 'Blue Period – That's a Story.'

10 Kristine J. Anderson has recently drawn on the work of Brossard and de Lotbinière-Harwood in formulating an 'em*bodied*' theory of feminist translation; see her 'Revealing the Body Bilingual.' See also Marlene Wildeman's comments on translating *La Lettre aérienne* in 'Daring Deeds: Translation as Lesbian Feminist Language Act.'

11 'The time had come for taking on the book body to body. A time that would give way to astonishment regarding things only very seldom seen, sited in the background of our thoughts. From one tongue to the other there would be meaning, fair distribution, contour and self-encounter, that moving substance which, it is said, enters into the composition of languages and makes them tasteful or hateful. Maude Laures knew that now was the time to slip anonymous and whole between the pages' (*MD*, 161).

12 For a discussion of translation as it relates to *Picture Theory*, see Sherry Simon, *Gender in Translation*, 22–8.

13 I am paraphrasing Banting quoting Jane Gallop here; see Gallop, 'Reading the Mother Tongue,' 328–9.

14 As Manina Jones notes, 'it has become a critical commonplace to say that documentary is the quintessential Canadian form of representation' (*That Art*, 3). 'Historiographic metafiction' is, according to Linda Hutcheon, the hallmark of the English-Canadian postmodern novel. See her *The Canadian Postmodern*.

15 According to Dennis Cooley, Marlatt's 'fascination with etymology ... brings together her interest in origins *and* in reflexive writing within a system. They announce further an engagement in a textual world, and not in any way direct or raw experience, the dictionary presiding over them' (72). As Annie confesses early on in the novel, the dictionary, Ina's 'immigrant weapon,' also 'saves me when the words stop, when the names stick' (17).

16 George Bowering has called *Ana Historic*, 'an autobiographical novel of the imagination,' a label that Marlatt has partially endorsed. See 'On *Ana Historic*: An Interview with Daphne Marlatt,' 96.

17 On 'lesbian self-naming' in *Ana Historic*, see Céline Chan.

18 For Marlatt's emotionally charged response to critics who have 'suggested that the ending of [her] novel is prescriptive,' see the interview 'Changing the Focus' (128ff). Interestingly, Davey has recently invoked Marlatt's 'Not a Bad

End' in foreclosing on his own ongoing debate with Robert Lecker: 'not a bad canon' is how he ends one of the essays in *Canadian Literary Power* (77).

19 Brossard makes an intimate connection between palindromes and translation in her suite of poems *L'Aviva.*

20 For a somewhat different, although no less pleasurable, reading of the 'gap between S and L' in Marlatt and Brossard's suite of poems, and of how this gap 'points to the dimension of cultural specificity in feminist [translation] strategy' (238), see Susan Holbrook, 'Mauve Arrows and the Erotics of Translation.'

21 On the importance of the city – or urban polis – in Brossard's writing, particularly the city of Montreal, see Louise Forsyth, 'Nicole Brossard and the Emergence of Feminist Literary Theory in Quebec since 1970'; M. Jean Anderson, '"We'll All End Up Leavin": Regionalism, Nationalism, and Individual Identity in Some Recent Canadian Novels by Women'; and Kimberley Verwaayen, 'Region/Body: In? Of? And? Or? (Alter/Native) Separatism in the Politics of Nicole Brossard.'

6: 'In another place, not here'

1 Brand says much the same thing in an interview with Dagmar Novak included in the anthology *Other Solitudes*: 'I've heard other writers talk about being on the margins of Canadian writing. I find myself in the middle of black writing. I'm in the centre of black writing, and those are the sensibilities that I check to figure out something that's truthful. I write out of a literature, a genre, a tradition, and that tradition is the tradition of black writing' (273).

2 See her '"Going There" and Being Here,' in *Blood, Bread, and Poetry*, 156–9. Other essays in this volume dealing with Rich's experiences in Nicaragua, particularly as they impacted on her subsequent formulation of a 'politics of location' *vis-à-vis* U.S. feminism, include 'North American Tunnel Vision' and 'Blood, Bread, and Poetry: The Location of the Poet.' It is interesting to note that at the end of the latter essay, 'poems by Dionne Brand' are listed among those writings that Rich turns to 'for signs of [the] fusion I have glimpsed in the women's movement, and most recently in Nicaragua' ('Blood, Bread, and Poetry,' 187). Rich may be referring here to a series of epigrams that Brand wrote to Ernesto Cardenal, Nicaraguan priest, poet, and former Sandinistan politician; see Brand's *Winter Epigrams and Epigrams to Ernesto Cardenal in Defense of Claudia.*

3 For a sustained critique of the concept of 'home' as it figures in feminist cultural criticism, see Biddy Martin and Chandra Talpade Mohanty, 'Feminist Politics: What's Home Got to Do with It?'

4 On how 'Anzaldúa's location in the boderland leads her to deny that there is any place that can be called home' (250), and on how her text 'can be read as oppositional to binaries such as home and exile, center and margin, power and passivity, dominant and dominated, personal and political, public and private histories' (236), see Inderpal Grewal, 'Autobiographic Subjects, Diasporic Locations.' Having said this, however, and, moreover, having acknowledged that Anzaldúa writes from multiple locations precisely in order to 'enable' cross-cultural feminist coalitions, Grewal nevertheless stresses that the 'term "borderlands" has become specific to Chicano culture, thus designating the specific locations of Mexican-Americans' (248).

5 I borrow the locution 'racial minority women' from Arun Mukherjee; see her 'Canadian Nationalism, Canadian Literature, and Racial Minority Women.'

6 Consider, in this regard, an exchange between Brand and Makeda Silvera about the shortlisting of Brand's *No Language Is Neutral* for the 1990 Governor General's Award for poetry. In response to Silvera's query about whether or not Brand thought that *No Language Is Neutral* 'would have been on the shortlist' had it been published by a press 'like Williams-Wallace or Sister Vision' rather than Coach House, Brand says: 'I don't know. I've been on a jury, so I know you just get a whole bunch of books, and you read them. Now me, I might look at a book put out by McClelland & Stewart a little more curiously and say, well, why am I picking this book? Because it's published by an establishment printer or because it's good? ... But I can't consider myself the norm in who's looking at books. I don't know what a white man does when he's looking at books' ('In the Company of My Work,' 370–1). Accepting Brand's comments, it is perhaps no accident, then, that the long overdue *material* recognition of Brand's work coincided with her own recent accession to two of the more 'establishment' publishing houses in this country. *In Another Place, Not Here*, published by Knopf Canada, was shortlisted for the 1996 Chapters / Books in Canada First Novel Award; and Brand's latest collection of poetry, *Land to Light On*, published by McClelland and Stewart no less, won the 1997 Governor General's Award for English-language poetry.

7 For a much different reading of *Winter Epigrams*, one that traces 'the line of ... tradition' in which Brand is writing to the Caribbean (18), see Edward Brathwaite, 'Dionne Brand's Winter Epigrams.'

8 Since she already figures so prominently in this chapter, and since Brand would be the first to acknowledge her influence, it is worth noting that Rich's poetry has recently been examined in terms of a critical methodology fusing 'lesbian theory and speech-act theory' (189); see Colette Peters, '"Whatever Happens, This Is": Lesbian Speech-Act Theory and Adrienne Rich's "Twenty-One Love Poems."' And yet, while Peters correctly acknowledges that Austin-

ian speech act theory, 'with its emphasis on societal conventions already in place, inevitably excludes lesbians and reinforces their invisibility' (196), she curiously makes no mention of Butler's simultaneous adaptation and critique of Austin in formulating her own theory of gender performativity. See below.

9 Critics like Mary Louise Pratt and Shoshana Felman, however, have since made use of Austin's theories to examine the operation of just such a class of performatives in literature. See Pratt, *Toward a Speech Act Theory of Literary Discourse*; and Felman, *The Literary Speech Act: Don Juan with J.L. Austin, or Seduction in Two Languages.*

10 Eve Kosofsky Sedgwick also invokes Austin and 'the weird centrality of the marriage example for performativity in general' to make much the same point regarding 'sexual orthodoxy' in her essay 'Queer Performativity'; see especially 2–4.

11 On the intersections between race and gender in narratives of passing, see Valerie Smith. Butler introduces sexuality into the admixture of competing identities with her readings of Jennie Livingston's film *Paris Is Burning* and Nella Larsen's novella *Passing*, in *Bodies That Matter*, 122–40 and 167–85, respectively.

12 See also Brathwaite, *History of the Voice: The Development of Nation Language in Anglophone Caribbean Poetry.*

13 I am borrowing the figure/ground metaphor from Biddy Martin here; see her 'Sexualities without Genders,' 110 and *passim.* She is in turn borrowing it from Butler; see *Gender Trouble*, 123 and *passim.* Toni Morrison has recently provided a much needed corrective to this prevailing view *vis-à-vis* American fiction in *Playing in the Dark: Whiteness and the Literary Imagination.* See also Ruth Frankenberg, *White Women, Race Matters: The Social Construction of Whiteness.*

7: Learning New Tricks

1 I cannot help thinking that another 'trick' up Rashid's sleeve in these poems, one of the many 'acts of elision' which his text performs, is the subtle intertext with Michael Ondaatje's *There's a Trick with a Knife I'm Learning to Do.* In this sense, Rashid's recoding of Ondaatje's poetic tricks from a gay male point of view mirrors Shayam Selvadurai's recent 'rewriting' of *Running in the Family* in the highly acclaimed *Funny Boy*, which tells the story of a young boy's (homo)sexual awakening in riot-ravaged Sri Lanka. Ondaatje's own writing is frequently suffused with elements of male homoeroticism. See, in this regard, Dennis Denisoff's 'Homosocial Desire and the Artificial Man in Michael Ondaatje's *Collected Works of Billy the Kid.*'

2 See also, in this regard, Arnold Krupat, 'Post-Structuralism and Oral Literature'; and Julia Emberley's analysis of Jeannette Armstrong's *Slash* in *Thresholds of Difference,* 129–50.

3 Although 'berdache' and 'two-spirit' are frequently used interchangeably in much anthropological discourse, the latter term has recently emerged as the preferred designation for alternative male and female gender roles among Indigenous gay and lesbian community leaders. As Roscoe points out ('Was We'wha,' 219n), in 1991 the Toronto-based Gays and Lesbians of the First Nations officially changed its name to 2-spirited People of the 1st Nations. Recognizing that his sexual identity has been informed as much (if not more) by a post-Stonewall, urban gay sensibility as by any unmediated genealogy of aboriginal culture, I nevertheless apply the term 'two-spirit' in this chapter to Tomson Highway. This has less to do with Highway's explicit self-identification with such a label as it does with 'two-spirit's' etymology as a transliteration from Ojibway (Roscoe, 219n), a language with which the playwright is familiar. For further historical/sociological perspectives of the berdache tradition and its influence on modern North American gay and lesbian liberation, see Jonathan Ned Katz, *Gay American History.*

4 I have borrowed – and adapted slightly – the terms 'absorption' and 'elimination' from Sheila Rabillard, whose excellent essay on Highway will remain an important touchstone throughout this chapter. See below.

5 Roscoe borrows the term 'survivance,' defined as 'the capacity for passing on ideas, symbols, identities, and cultural forms from generation to generation' ('Was We'wha,' 193), from Vizenor. See Vizenor, *The Heirs of Columbus.*

6 See Preston, 'Weesageechak Begins to Dance,' *Drama Review* 36.1 (1992). Bennett's response, 'Subject to the Tourist Gaze,' appeared in the same journal a year later.

7 The third instalment, *Rose,* a 'rez motown musical' which focuses on Emily Dictionary and two of the women bikers with whom she used to ride, and which brings both the men and the women of the Wasy Hill Reserve together on stage, is apparently complete. Some of the songs have been workshopped cabaret-style in Toronto, but at present the play awaits a full-scale production. In the meantime, Highway is set to publish his first novel, *Kiss of the Fur Queen,* a semi-autobiographical account of his relationship with René. See Rabillard, 24n; and Winkler.

8 *Dry Lips* premiered at Toronto's Theatre Passe Muraille on 21 April 1989, and René Highway died just over a year later, of AIDS-related meningitis, on 19 October 1990. Gerald Hannon traces the close relationship between the two brothers, as well as their separate – and intertwined – artistic careers in a 1991 *Toronto Life* article, 'Tomson and the Trickster.'

9 Gitta Honegger interprets this visual pun in *Dry Lips* as Highway's postcolonial homage to Shakespeare's *A Midsummer Night's Dream*, Zachary's dream in the former recalling Oberon's mischievous magic in the latter, in which Titania falls in love with Bottom, who has been transformed into an ass. On the oral/anal dialectic that Highway's play performs, see Burnham.

Coda: The Hats Backwards Syndrome

1 See, for example, the essay collections Case et al., eds, *Cruising the Performative*, and Parker and Sedgwick, eds, *Performativity and Performance*; see also Ann Pellegrini, *Performance Anxieties: Staging Psychoanalysis, Staging Race.*
2 To be fair, it seems to be an impulse infusing scholarly work in general of late, especially where the recovery of lost narratives of ethnicity are concerned. See, for example, Marianna De Marco Torgovnick's *Crossing Ocean Parkway* (1994) and Susan Rubin Suleiman's *Budapest Diary* (1996). See also the October 1996 *PMLA* forum on personalist writing in the academy.
3 See, in this regard, Simon Watney, *Policing Desire.*
4 See Ross, *The House That Jill Built: A Lesbian Nation in Formation*; Hoy, '"And Use the Words That Were Hers": Construction of Subjectivity in Beverly Hungry Wolf's *The Ways of My Grandmothers*'; and Harris, *The Resettlement of British Columbia.*
5 The veiled allusion to Canada's pioneering gay liberation monthly is only partly coincidental here. While it is beyond the scope of the present study, a thorough reassessment of *The Body Politic* collective's impact on contemporary Canadian politics, not to mention its important contributions to literary and cultural criticism in this country (many of its columnists – including Jane Rule, Stan Persky, Robert K. Martin, and Michael Lynch – were eminent Canadian writers and literary critics), is long overdue. In the meantime, see Ed Jackson and Stan Persky, eds, *Flaunting It! A Decade of Gay Journalism from 'The Body Politic'*; Gary Kinsman, *The Regulation of Desire: Sexuality in Canada*; and Steven Maynard, 'In Search of "Sodom North": The Writing of Lesbian and Gay History in English Canada, 1970–1990.'

Works Cited

Abelove, Henry. 'From Thoreau to Queer Politics.' *Yale Journal of Criticism* 6.2 (1993): 17–27.

Adorno, Theodor. *Aesthetic Theory*. Ed. Gretel Adorno and Rolf Tiedemann. Trans. C. Lenhardt. London: Routledge, 1986.

Ahmad, Aijaz. 'Jameson's Rhetoric of Otherness and the "National Allegory."' *Social Text* 17 (1987): 3–25.

Anderson, Benedict. *Imagined Communities: Reflections on the Origins and Spread of Nationalism.* 2nd ed. London: Verso, 1991.

Anderson, Kristine J. 'Revealing the Body Bilingual: Quebec Feminists and Recent Translation Theory.' *Studies in the Humanities* 22.1–2 (1995): 65–75.

Anderson, M. Jean. '"We'll All End Up Leavin": Regionalism, Nationalism, and Individual Identity in Some Recent Canadian Novels by Women.' *Regionalism and National Identity: Multi-Disciplinary Essays on Canada, Australia, and New Zealand.* Ed. Reginald Berry and James Acheson. Christchurch: Association for Canadian Studies in Australia and New Zealand, 1985. 71–8.

Anderson, Patrick. *The Character Ball: Chapters of Autobiography*. London: Chatto & Windus, 1963.

– *The Colour as Naked.* Toronto: McClelland and Stewart, 1953.

– 'A Conversation with Patrick Anderson.' With Seymour Mayne. *Inscape* 11.3 (1974): 46–79.

– *Dolphin Days: A Writer's Notebook of Mediterranean Pleasures.* London: Gollancz, 1963.

– *First Steps in Greece.* London: Chatto & Windus, 1958.

– 'Further Notes from Baie St. Paul.' *Preview* 14 (1943): 7–10.

– 'Montreal.' *Preview* (June 1942). N. pag.

– 'Notes from My Journal: Baie St. Paul.' *Preview* 10 (1943): 9–11.
– *Over the Alps: Reflections on Travel and Travel Writing, with Special Reference to the Grand Tours of Boswell, Beckford and Byron.* London: Hart-Davis, 1969.
– 'A Poet Past and Future.' *Canadian Literature* 56 (1973): 7–21.
– *Return to Canada: Selected Poems.* Toronto: McClelland and Stewart, 1977.
– *Search Me: The Black Country, Canada and Spain.* London: Chatto & Windus, 1957.
– *Snake Wine: A Singapore Episode.* London: Chatto & Windus, 1955.
– *A Tent for April.* Montreal: First Statement, 1945. N. pag.
– *A Visiting Distance.* Ottawa: Borealis, 1976.
– *The White Centre.* Toronto: Ryerson, 1946.
Anderson, Patrick, and Alistair Sutherland, eds. *Eros: An Anthology of Friendship.* London: Blond, 1961.
Antosh, Ruth B. 'The Hermaphrodite as Cultural Hero in Michel Temblay's Theater.' Donohoe and Weiss, 207–21.
Anzaldúa, Gloria. *Borderlands/'La Frontera': The New Mestiza.* San Francisco: Spinster/Aunt Lute, 1987.
Aquin, Hubert. *Blackout.* Trans. Alan Brown. Toronto: Anansi, 1974.
– 'Commentaire I.' *Littérature et société canadiennes-françaises.* Ed. Fernand Dumont and Jean-Charles Falardeau. Laval: PU Laval, 1964. 191–3.
– 'The Cultural Fatigue of French Canada.' 1962. *Writing Québec.* Ed. Anthony Purdy. Trans. Paul Gibson et al. Edmonton: U of Alberta P, 1988. 19–48.
– *Hamlet's Twin.* Trans. Sheila Fischman. Toronto: McClelland and Stewart, 1979.
– '*Joual*: Haven or Hell?' 1974. *Writing Québec,* 100–6.
– *Neige noire.* Montréal: Éditions la Presse, 1974.
– *Prochain Épisode.* Ottawa: Cercle du livre de France, 1965.
– *Trou de mémoire.* Ottawa: Cercle du livre de France, 1968.
Ashcroft, Bill, Gareth Griffiths, and Helen Tiffin. *The Empire Writes Back: Theory and Practice in Post-Colonial Literatures.* London: Routledge, 1989.
Austin, J.L. *How to Do Things with Words.* 1962. Ed. J.O. Urmson and Marina Sbisà. 2nd ed. Oxford: Clarendon, 1975.
Babuscio, Jack. 'Camp and the Gay Sensibility.' *Gays and Film.* Ed. Richard Dyer. New York: Zoetrope, 1984. 40–56.
Bad Object-Choices, eds. *How Do I Look?: Queer Film and Video.* Seattle: Bay Press, 1991.
Baker, Marie Annharte. 'An Old Indian Trick Is to Laugh.' *Canadian Theatre Review* 68 (1991): 48–9.
– 'Angry Enough to Spit but with *Dry Lips* It Hurts More Than You Know.' *Canadian Theatre Review* 68 (1991): 88–9.

Bakhtin, M.M. *The Dialogic Imagination: Four Essays.* 1981. Ed. Michael Holquist. Trans. Caryl Emerson and Michael Holquist. Austin: U of Texas P, 1990.

Bannerji, Himani, ed. *Returning the Gaze: Essays on Racism, Feminism and Politics.* Toronto: Sister Vision, 1993.

Banting, Pamela. *Body Inc.: A Theory of Translation Poetics.* Winnipeg: Turnstone, 1995.

– 'Translation A to Z: Notes on Daphne Marlatt's *Ana Historic.*' Barbour, 123–9.

Barbour, Douglas, ed. *Beyond Tish: New Writing, Interviews, Critical Essays.* Edmonton and Vancouver: NeWest / *West Coast Line,* 1991.

Barnes, Clive. '"Hosanna," Witty Play from Quebec.' *New York Times* 15 Oct. 1974: 46.

Barthes, Roland. *Empire of Signs.* Trans. Richard Howard. New York: Hill & Wang, 1982.

– *The Fashion System.* Trans. Matthew Ward and Richard Howard. New York: Hill & Wang, 1983.

– *Incidents.* Trans. Richard Howard. Berkeley: U of California P, 1992.

– Preface. Camus, vii–x.

Bartley, Jim. *Stephen and Mr. Wilde.* Winnipeg: Blizzard, 1993.

Bayard, Caroline. 'From *Nègres blancs d'Amérique* (1968) to Kanesatake (1990).' *World Literature Written in English* 30.2 (1990): 17–29.

Beattie, Munro. 'Poetry 1935–1950.' *Literary History of Canada: Canadian Literature in English.* Gen. ed. Carl F. Klinck. 2nd ed. Vol. 2. Toronto: U of Toronto P, 1976. 254–96.

Benjamin, Walter. 'The Task of the Translator.' *Illuminations: Essays and Reflections.* Ed. Hannah Arendt. Trans. Harry Zohn. New York: Schocken, 1968. 69–82.

– 'Theses on the Philosophy of History.' *Illuminations,* 253–64.

Bennett, Susan. 'Subject to the Tourist Gaze: A Response to "Weesageechak Begins to Dance."' *Drama Review* 37.1 (1993): 9–17.

Bergman, David, ed. *Camp Grounds: Style and Homosexuality.* Amherst: U of Massachusetts P, 1993.

– 'Strategic Camp: The Art of Gay Rhetoric.' Bergman, 92–109.

Berlant, Lauren, and Elizabeth Freeman. 'Queer Nationality.' Warner, *Fear,* 193–229.

Bersani, Leo. 'Is the Rectum a Grave?' *AIDS: Cultural Analysis/Cultural Activism.* Ed. Douglas Crimp. Cambridge, MA: MIT Press, 1988. 197–222.

Bhabha, Homi K. 'DissemiNation: Time, Narrative, and the Margins of the Modern Nation.' *Nation and Narration.* Ed. Homi Bhabha. New York: Routledge, 1990. 291–322.

– 'Introduction: Narrating the Nation.' *Nation and Narration,* 1–7.

– *The Location of Culture.* New York: Routledge, 1994.

– 'Of Mimicry and Man: The Ambivalence of Colonial Discourse.' *October* 28 (1984): 125–36.

– 'Representation and the Colonial Text: A Critical Exploration of Some Forms of Mimeticism.' *The Theory of Reading*. Ed. Frank Gloversmith. Brighton: Harvester, 1984. 93–122.

– 'Signs Taken for Wonders: Questions of Ambivalence and Authority under a Tree Outside Delhi, May 1817.' *The Location of Culture*, 102–22.

Boone, Joseph A. 'Vacation Cruises; or, The Homoerotics of Orientalism.' *PMLA* 110.1 (1995): 89–107.

Bouchard, Michel Marc. *Les Feluettes; ou, La répétition d'un drame romantique.* Montréal: Leméac, 1987.

– *Lilies; or, The Revival of a Romantic Drama.* Trans. Linda Gaboriau. Toronto: Coach House, 1990.

– 'Tout plein d'émotions.' Interview with André Dionne. *Lettres-Québécoises* 53 (1989): 10–13.

Bowering, George. *Burning Water.* Don Mills, ON: Musson, 1980.

Brand, Dionne. 'At the Lisbon Plate.' *Sans Souci and Other Stories.* Toronto: Williams-Wallace, 1988. 95–114.

– *Bread out of Stone: Recollections Sex, Recognitions Race, Dreaming Politics.* Toronto: Coach House, 1994.

– *Chronicles of the Hostile Sun.* Toronto: Williams-Wallace, 1984.

– *In Another Place, Not Here.* Toronto: Knopf Canada, 1996.

– 'In the Company of My Work.' Interview with Makeda Silvera. Silvera, 356–80.

– Interview. With Dagmar Novak. *Other Solitudes: Canadian Multicultural Fictions.* Ed. Linda Hutcheon and Marion Richmond. Toronto: Oxford UP, 1990. 271–7.

– *Land to Light On.* Toronto: McClelland and Stewart, 1997.

– 'The Language of Resistance.' Interview with Beverly Daurio. *Books in Canada* 19.7 (1990): 13–16.

– dir. *Listening for Something ... Adrienne Rich in Conversation with Dionne Brand.* National Film Board of Canada, Studio D, 1996.

– *No Language Is Neutral.* Toronto: Coach House, 1990.

– *Winter Epigrams and Epigrams to Ernesto Cardenal in Defense of Claudia.* Toronto: Williams-Wallace, 1983.

Brant, Beth. 'Coyote Learns a New Trick.' *Mohawk Trail.* 1985. Toronto: Women's Press, 1990. 31–5.

Brathwaite, Edward Kamau. 'Dionne Brand's Winter Epigrams.' *Canadian Literature* 105 (1985): 18–30.

– *History of the Voice: The Development of Nation Language in Anglophone Caribbean Poetry*. London: New Beacon, 1984.

Brie, Albert. 'Tremblay joue et gagne.' *Le Devoir* 15 mai 1973: 10.

Brisset, Annie. 'Language and Collective Identity: When Translators of Theater Address the Quebec Nation.' Donohoe and Weiss, 61–80.

Brossard, Nicole. *À tout regard.* Montréal: NBJ/BQ, 1989.

– *The Aerial Letter.* Trans. Marlene Wildeman. Toronto: Women's Press, 1988.

– *L'Amèr; ou, Le chapitre effrité.* Montréal: Éditions Quinze, 1977.

– *L'Aviva.* Montréal: NBJ, 1985.

– *Baroque at Dawn.* Trans. Patricia Claxton. Toronto: McClelland and Stewart, 1997.

– *Baroque d'aube.* Montréal: Hexagone, 1995.

– 'Le Cortex exubérant.' *La Barre du jour* 44 (1974): 2–22.

– *Le Désert mauve.* Montréal: Hexagone, 1987.

– '*E* muet mutant.' *La Barre du jour* 50 (1975): 10–27.

– *French Kiss.* 1974. Montréal: Éditions Quinze, 1980.

– *French Kiss; or, A Pang's Progress.* Trans. Patricia Claxton. Toronto: Coach House, 1986.

– *La Lettre aérienne.* Montréal: Remue-Ménage, 1985.

– *Mauve Desert.* Trans. Susanne de Lotbinière-Harwood. Toronto: Coach House, 1990.

– *Picture Theory.* Montréal: Nouvelle Optique, 1982.

– 'Tender Skin My Mind.' Trans. Dympna Borowska. *In the Feminine: Women and Words/Les femmes et les mots.* Ed. Ann Dybikowski et al. Edmonton: Longspoon, 1985. 180–3.

– *These Our Mothers; or, The Disintegrating Chapter.* Trans. Barbara Godard. Toronto: Coach House, 1983.

– 'Vaseline.' *La Barre du jour* 42 (1973): 11–17.

Brossard, Nicole, and Daphne Marlatt. 'Blue Period – That's a Story: A Conversation with Nicole Brossard and Daphne Marlatt.' With Jodey Castricano and Jacqueline Larson. *West Coast Line* 28.3 (1994/95): 29–53.

– *Mauve.* Montréal: NBJ/Writing, 1985. N. pag.

Brossard, Nicole, and Roger Soublière. 'De notre écriture en sa résistance.' *La Barre du jour* 26 (1970): 3–6.

Brown, Russell. *Borderlines and Borderlands in English Canada: The Written Line.* Orono, ME: Borderlands Project, 1990.

Bruffee, Kenneth A. *Elegiac Romance: Cultural Change and Loss of the Hero in Modern Fiction.* Ithaca, NY: Cornell UP, 1983.

Brydon, Diana. 'A Devotion to Fragility: Timothy Findley's *The Wars.*' *World Literature Written in English* 26.1 (1986): 75–84.

– 'The Dream of Tory Origins: Inventing Canadian Beginnings.' *Australian-Canadian Studies* 6.2 (1989): 35–46.

– 'Reading Dionne Brand's "Blues Spiritual for Mammy Prater."' *Inside the Poem.* Ed. W.H. New. Toronto: Oxford UP, 1992. 80–7.

– 'Timothy Findley: A Post-Holocaust, Post-Colonial Vision.' *International Literature in English: Essays on the Major Writers.* Ed. Robert L. Ross. New York: Garland, 1991. 583–92.

Buckler, Ernest. *The Mountain and the Valley.* 1952. Toronto: McClelland and Stewart, 1970.

Buitenhuis, Peter. 'Scott Symons and the Strange Case of *Helmet of Flesh.*' *West-Coast Review* 21.4 (1987): 59–72.

Burgoyne, Lynda. 'Théâtre et homosexualité féminine: un continent invisible.' *Cahiers de théâtre jeu* 54 (1990): 114–18.

Burnham, Clint. 'Lips, Marks, Lapse: Materialism and Dialogism in Thomson [*sic*] Highway's *Dry Lips Oughta Move to Kapuskasing.*' *Open Letter* 8.9 (1990): 19–30.

Butler, Judith. *Bodies That Matter: On the Discursive Limits of 'Sex.'* New York: Routledge, 1993.

– *Gender Trouble: Feminism and the Subversion of Identity.* New York: Routledge, 1990.

– 'Imitation and Gender Insubordination.' Fuss, *Inside/Out,* 13–31.

Butler, Judith, and Biddy Martin, eds. *Critical Crossings.* Special issue of *Diacritics* 24.2–3 (1994).

Byron, Lord George. *The Complete Poetical Works.* Ed. Jerome J. McGann. 3 vols. Oxford: Clarendon, 1980–1.

Camerlain, Lorraine. 'Théâtre et homosexualité.' *Cahiers de théâtre jeu* 54 (1990): 5–7.

Camerlain, Lorraine, et al. 'Séminaire (1re séance).' *Cahiers de théâtre jeu* 54 (1990): 43–81.

Campbell, Patrick. 'Attic Shapes and Empty Attics: Patrick Anderson – a Memoir.' *Canadian Literature* 121 (1989): 86–99.

Camus, Renaud. *Tricks: 25 Encounters.* Trans. Richard Howard. New York: Saint Martin's Press, 1981.

Carpenter, Edward. *The Intermediate Sex: A Study in Some Transitional Types of Men and Women.* London: Allen & Unwin, 1908.

Carty, Linda, and Dionne Brand. '"Visible Minority" Women: A Creation of the Canadian State.' Bannerji, 169–81.

Case, Sue-Ellen. 'Toward a Butch-Femme Aesthetic.' *Making a Spectacle: Feminist Essays on Contemporary Women's Theatre.* Ed. Lynda Hart. Ann Arbor: U of Michigan P, 1989. 282–9.

Case, Sue-Ellen, et al., eds. *Cruising the Performative: Interventions into the Representation of Ethnicity, Nationality, and Sexuality.* Bloomington: Indiana UP, 1995.

Castle, Terry. *The Apparitional Lesbian: Female Homosexuality and Modern Culture.* New York: Columbia UP, 1993.

Cavell, Richard. 'Bakhtin Reads De Mille: Canadian Literature, Postmodernism, and the Theory of Dialogism.' *Future Indicative: Canadian Literature and Literary Theory.* Ed. John Moss. Ottawa: U of Ottawa P, 1987. 205–11.

– '"Comparative Canadian Literature" as Crisis and Critique: Towards Comparative Cultural Studies.' *Textual Studies in Canada* 5 (1994): 7–14.

Chamberlain, Lori. 'Gender and the Metaphorics of Translation.' Venuti, 57–74.

Chan, Céline. 'Lesbian Self-Naming in Daphne Marlatt's *Ana Historic.*' *Canadian Poetry* 31 (1992): 68–74.

Chapman, Geoff. 'Love's Labor's Almost Lost in Lilies.' *Toronto Star* 3 Feb. 1991: H2.

Chatterjee, Partha. *The Nation and Its Fragments: Colonial and Postcolonial Histories.* Princeton, NJ: Princeton UP, 1993.

– *Nationalist Thought and the Colonial World: A Derivative Discourse?* London: Zed, 1986.

Cixous, Hélène. 'The Laugh of the Medusa.' Trans. Keith Cohen and Paula Cohen. *New French Feminisms.* Ed. Elaine Marks and Isabelle de Courtivron. New York: Schocken, 1980. 245–64. Originally published as 'Le Rire de la Méduse.' *L'Arc* 61 (1975): 39–54.

Clio Collective, eds. *Québec Women: A History.* Trans. Roger Gannon and Rosalind Gill. Toronto: Women's Press, 1987.

Cohen, Ed. *Talk on the Wilde Side: Toward a Genealogy of the Discourse on Male Sexuality.* New York: Routledge, 1992.

Cohen, Leonard. *Beautiful Losers.* 1966. Toronto: McClelland and Stewart, 1986.

Coleman, Daniel. 'Immigration, Nation, and the Allegory of Manly Maturation.' *Essays on Canadian Writing* 61 (1997): 84–103.

Conlogue, Ray. 'Quebec Artists Face the Fear.' *Globe and Mail* 14 Oct. 1995: E1–E2.

– 'Quebec Theatre's Bright New Hope.' *Globe and Mail* 7 Oct. 1995: C1–C2.

Cooley, Dennis. 'Recursions Excursions and Incursions: Daphne Marlatt Wrestles with the Angel Language.' *Line* 13 (1989): 66–79.

Corneau, Guy. *Père manquant, fils manqué: Que sont les hommes devenus?* Montréal: Éditions de l'homme, 1989.

Cotnam, Jacques. 'Du sentiment national dans le théâtre québécois.' *Le Théâtre canadien-français.* Ed. Paul Wyczynski et al. Montréal: Fides, 1976. 341–68.

Cotnoir, Louise, Barbara Godard, Susan Knutson, Daphne Marlatt, Kathy Mezei, and Gail Scott. 'Introduction: Women of Letters.' Godard, *Collaboration,* 9–19.

Crane, Hart. *The Collected Poems of Hart Crane.* Ed. Waldo Frank. New York: Liveright, 1933.

Crew, Robert. 'Young Quebec Writer Pens Remarkable Play.' *Toronto Star* 8 April 1987: D3.

Crompton, Louis. *Byron and Greek Love: Homophobia in Nineteenth-Century England.* Berkeley: U of California P, 1985.

Crosby, Marcia. 'Construction of the Imaginary Indian.' *Vancouver Anthology: The Institutional Politics of Art.* Ed. Stan Douglas. Vancouver: Talonbooks, 1991. 267–91.

Davey, Frank. 'Canadian Canons: A Response to Robert Lecker.' *Critical Inquiry* 16 (1990): 672–81.

– *Canadian Literary Power.* Edmonton: NeWest, 1994.

– *Post-National Arguments: The Politics of the Anglophone-Canadian Novel since 1967.* Toronto: U of Toronto P, 1993.

de Beauvoir, Simone. *The Second Sex.* Trans. and ed. H.M. Parshley. New York: Knopf, 1957.

de Lauretis, Teresa. 'Film and the Visible.' Bad Object-Choices, 223–84.

de Lotbinière-Harwood, Susanne. 'Geo-graphies of Why.' *Culture in Transit: Translating the Literature of Québec.* Ed. Sherry Simon. Montreal: Véhicule Press, 1995. 55–68.

– *Re-Belle et Infidèle: La Traduction comme pratique de réécriture au féminin / The Body Bilingual: Translation as a Re-Writing in the Feminine.* Montréal and Toronto: Remue-Ménage/Women's Press, 1991.

Dean, Misao. 'The Construction of Masculinity in Martin Allerdale Grainger's *Woodsmen of the West.*' *Canadian Literature* 149 (1996): 74–87.

Deer, Glenn. *Postmodern Canadian Fiction and the Rhetoric of Authority.* Montreal: McGill-Queen's UP, 1994.

Dejean, Paul. *The Haitians in Quebec: A Sociological Profile.* Trans. Max Dorsinville. Ottawa: Tecumseh, 1980.

Delisle, Esther. *The Traitor and the Jew: Anti-Semitism and Extremist Right-Wing Nationalism in Québec from 1929–1939.* Trans. Madeleine Hébert et al. Montreal: Robert Davies, 1993.

Dellamora, Richard. 'Becoming-Homosexual/Becoming-Canadian: Ironic Voice and the Politics of Location in Timothy Findley's *Famous Last Words.*' *Double Talking: Essays on Verbal and Visual Ironies in Canadian Contemporary Art and Literature.* Ed. Linda Hutcheon. Toronto: ECW, 1992. 173–200.

– ed. *Postmodern Apocalypse: Theory and Cultural Practice at the End.* Philadelphia: U of Pennsylvania P, 1995.

Denisoff, Dennis. 'Homosocial Desire and the Artificial Man in Michael Ondaatje's *Collected Works of Billy the Kid.*' *Essays on Canadian Writing* 53 (1994): 51–70.

– '(Re)Dressing One's Self: Artifice and Identity Construction in John Glassco.'

Theorizing Fashion/Fashioning Theory Panel. ACCUTE Conference, University of Calgary, 6 June 1994.

Derrida, Jacques. 'Des Tours de Babel.' Graham, 165–207.

– *The Ear of the Other: Otobiography, Transference, Translation.* Ed. Christie V. McDonald. Trans. Peggy Kamuf. Lincoln: U of Nebraska P, 1985.

– 'Living On/Border Lines.' Trans. James Hulbert. *Deconstruction and Criticism.* New York: Continuum, 1979. 75–176.

– 'Signature, Event, Context.' 1972. *Margins of Philosophy.* Trans. Alan Bass. Chicago: U of Chicago P, 1982. 307–30.

Dickinson, Peter. '"Go-go Dancing on the Brink of the Apocalypse": Representing AIDS: An Essay in Seven Epigraphs.' Dellamora, *Postmodern*, 219–40.

– 'A Queer by Any Other Name?' *Xtra West* 6 Feb. 1997: 11.

Dollimore, Jonathan. *Sexual Dissidence: Augustine to Wilde, Freud to Foucault.* Oxford: Clarendon, 1991.

Donnelly, Pat. 'Bad Karma Haunts Province, Says Critical Quebec Dramatist.' *Vancouver Sun* 4 Dec. 1995: C3.

Donohoe, Joseph I., Jr., and Jonathan Weiss, eds. *Essays on Modern Quebec Theater.* East Lansing: Michigan State UP, 1995.

Dorsinville, Max. *Caliban without Prospero: Essay on Quebec and Black Literature.* Erin, ON: Press Porcepic, 1974.

– *Le Pays natal: Essais sur les littératures du Tiers-Monde et du Québec.* Dakar, Senegal: Nouvelles Éditions Africaines, 1983.

– *Solidarités: Tiers-Monde et littérature comparée.* Montréal: CIDIHCA, 1988.

Dubé, Yves. Préface. Dubois, *Being*, vii–xvi.

Dubois, René-Daniel. *Being at home with Claude.* Montréal: Leméac, 1986.

– *Being at Home with Claude.* Trans. Linda Gaboriau. *The CTR Anthology: Fifteen Plays from 'Canadian Theatre Review.'* Ed. Alan Filewod. Toronto: U of Toronto P, 1993. 389–433.

– *26bis, impasse du Colonel Foisy.* Montréal: Leméac, 1983.

– 'Vivre de sa plume au Québec: Entrevue avec René-Daniel Dubois.' *Lettres-Québécoises* 43 (1986): 10–13.

Dumont, Micheline. 'Des religieuses, des murs et des enfants.' *L'Action nationale* 84.4 (1994): 483–508.

Eagleton, Terry. *Saint Oscar.* Lawrence Hill, Derry: Field Day, 1989.

Eagleton, Terry, Fredric Jameson, and Edward Said. *Nationalism, Colonialism, and Literature.* Introduction by Seamus Deane. Minneapolis: U of Minnesota P, 1990.

Edelman, Lee. *Homographesis: Essays in Gay Literary and Cultural Theory.* New York: Routledge, 1994.

Edwards, Justin D. 'Engendering Modern Canadian Poetry: *Preview, First Statement,* and the Disclosure of Patrick Anderson's Homosexuality.' *Essays on Canadian Writing* 62 (1997): 65–84.

Ellmann, Richard. *Oscar Wilde.* New York: Vintage, 1988.

Emberley, Julia V. *Thresholds of Difference: Feminist Critique, Native Women's Writings, Postcolonial Theory.* Toronto: U of Toronto P, 1993.

Epstein, Steven. 'Gay Politics, Ethnic Identity: The Limits of Social Constructionism.' *Socialist Review* 93/94 (1987): 6–54.

Escoffier, Jeffrey. 'Sexual Revolution and the Politics of Gay Identity.' *Socialist Review* 14.4–5 (1985): 126–96, 133–42.

Faderman, Lillian. *Surpassing the Love of Men: Romantic Friendship and Love between Women from the Renaissance to the Present.* New York: Morrow, 1981.

Fanon, Frantz. *Black Skin, White Masks.* Trans. Charles Lam Markmann. New York: Grove, 1967.

– *The Wretched of the Earth.* Trans. Constance Farrington. New York: Grove, 1968.

Fee, Margery. 'Romantic-Nationalism and the Image of Native People in English-Canadian Literature.' *The Native in Literature.* Ed. Thomas King, Cheryl Calver, and Helen Hoy. Oakville, ON: ECW, 1987. 15–33.

Felman, Shoshana. *The Literary Speech Act: Don Juan with J.L. Austin, or Seduction in Two Languages.* Trans. Catherine Porter. Ithaca, NY: Cornell UP, 1983.

Fetherling, Doug[las]. 'Resurrecting the Long Poem: From Robin Skelton's Old Cornish Ballads to the Pornography of Winter in Montreal.' Rev. of *Winter Epigrams,* by Dionne Brand. *Books in Canada* 12.8 (1983): 37–8.

Fiedler, Leslie. *Love and Death in the American Novel.* New York: Stein and Day, 1966.

Filewod, Alan. 'Receiving Aboriginality: Tomson Highway and the Crisis of Cultural Authenticity.' *Theatre Journal* 46 (1994): 363–73.

Finch, Robert. *Poems.* Toronto: Oxford, 1946.

Findley, Timothy. 'Alice Drops Her Cigarette on the Floor ... (William Whitehead Looking over Timothy Findley's Shoulder).' *Canadian Literature* 91 (1981): 10–21.

– *Famous Last Words.* Markham, ON: Penguin, 1982.

– *Inside Memory: Pages from a Writer's Notebook.* Toronto: HarperCollins, 1990.

– Interview. With Eugene Benson. *World Literature Written in English* 26.1 (1986): 107–15.

– Interview. With Graeme Gibson. Gibson, 15–49.

– 'The Marvel of Reality: An Interview with Timothy Findley.' With Bruce Meyer and Brian O'Riordan. *Waves* 10.4 (1982): 5–11.

– *Not Wanted on the Voyage.* Markham, ON: Viking, 1984.

– *The Trials of Ezra Pound.* Winnipeg: Blizzard, 1995.

– *The Wars.* Toronto: Clarke, Irwin, 1977.

Fisher, Neil H. *First Statement, 1942–1945: An Assessment and an Index.* Ottawa: Golden Dog, 1974.

Forsyth, Louise. 'Beyond the Myths and Fictions of Traditionalism and Nationalism: The Political in the Work of Nicole Brossard.' Lewis, 157–72.

– 'Nicole Brossard and the Emergence of Feminist Literary Theory in Quebec since 1970.' *Gynocritics: Feminist Approaches to Canadian and Quebec Women's Writing.* Ed. Barbara Godard. Toronto: ECW, 1987. 211–21.

– 'Les Numéros spéciaux de *La (nouvelle) barre du jour.* Lieux communs, lieux en recherche, lieu de rencontre.' Lamy and Pagès, 175–84.

'Forum.' *PMLA* 111.5 (1996): 1146–69.

Foucault, Michel. *The Care of the Self.* Vol. 3 of *The History of Sexuality.* Trans. Robert Hurley. New York: Pantheon, 1986.

– *The History of Sexuality, Volume 1: An Introduction.* 1978. Trans. Robert Hurley. New York: Vintage, 1990.

– *The Use of Pleasure.* Vol. 2 of *The History of Sexuality.* Trans. Robert Hurley. New York: Pantheon, 1985.

Francis, Wynne. 'Montreal Poets of the Forties.' *Canadian Literature* 14 (1962): 21–34.

Frankenberg, Ruth. *White Women, Race Matters: The Social Construction of Whiteness.* Minneapolis: U of Minnesota P, 1993.

Fraser, Keath. *As for Me and My Body: A Memoir of Sinclair Ross.* Toronto: ECW, 1997.

Fréchette, Carole, and Michael Vaïs. 'Questions sur un malaise.' *Cahiers de théâtre jeu* 54 (1990): 9–14.

Freiwald, Bina Toledo. '"Towards the Uncanny Edge of Language": Gail Scott's Liminal Trajectories.' *Essays on Canadian Writing* 54 (1994): 60–79.

Frye, Northrop. *The Bush Garden: Essays on the Canadian Imagination.* Toronto: Anansi, 1971.

– *The Great Code: The Bible and Literature.* New York: Harcourt Brace Jovanovich, 1982.

– *The Modern Century.* 1967. New York: Oxford UP, 1969.

Fuller, Janine, and Stuart Blackley. *Restricted Entry: Censorship on Trial.* 2nd ed. Ed. Nancy Pollak. Vancouver: Press Gang, 1996.

Fuss, Diana. *Essentially Speaking: Feminism, Nature and Difference.* New York: Routledge, 1989.

– 'Inside/Out.' Fuss, *Inside/Out,* 1–10.

– 'Interior Colonies: Frantz Fanon and the Politics of Identification.' Butler and Martin, 20–42.

– ed. *Inside/Out: Lesbian Theories, Gay Theories.* New York: Routledge, 1991.

Fussell, Paul. *The Great War and Modern Memory.* New York: Oxford UP, 1975.

Gabriel, Barbara. 'Performing the *Bent* Text: Fascism and the Regulation of Sexualities in Timothy Findley's *The Butterfly Plague.*' *English Studies in Canada* 21.2 (1995): 227–50.

– 'Staging Monstrosity: Genre, Life-Writing, and Timothy Findley's *The Last of the Crazy People.*' *Essays on Canadian Writing* 54 (1994): 168–97.

Gallop, Jane. *Feminist Accused of Sexual Harassment.* Durham, NC: Duke UP, 1997.

– 'Reading the Mother Tongue: Psychoanalytic Feminist Criticism.' *Critical Inquiry* 13.2 (1987): 314–29.

– ed. *Pedagogy: The Question of Impersonation.* Bloomington: Indiana UP, 1995.

Garber, Marjorie. *Vested Interests: Cross-Dressing and Cultural Anxiety.* New York: Routledge, 1991.

Gates, Henry Louis, Jr. 'Critical Fanonism.' *Critical Inquiry* 17.3 (1991): 457–70.

Germain, Jean-Claude. 'Le Théâtre – ne pas confondre tréteaux et tribunes.' *Magazine Maclean* 13.9 (Sept. 1973): 52.

Gibson, Graeme. *Eleven Canadian Novelists.* Toronto: Anansi, 1973.

Gilbert, Sky. *More Divine: A Performance for Roland Barthes.* In *This Unknown Flesh: A Selection of Plays,* by Sky Gilbert. Toronto: Coach House, 1995. 183–233.

Gittings, Christopher E. '"What are soldiers for?" Re-Making Masculinities in Timothy Findley's *The Wars.*' *Kunapipi* 18.1 (1996): 184–91.

Gnarowski, Michael. 'New Facts and Old Fictions: Some Notes on Patrick Anderson, 1945 and *En Masse.*' *Canadian Poetry* 6 (1980): 61–8.

– 'The Role of "Little Magazines" in the Development of Poetry in English in Montreal.' *The Making of Modern Poetry in Canada: Essential Articles on Contemporary Canadian Poetry in English.* Ed. Louis Dudek and Michael Gnarowski. Toronto: Ryerson, 1967. 212–22.

Godard, Barbara. 'Fiction/Theory: Editorial.' *Tessera* 3, in *Canadian Fiction Magazine* 57 (1986): 4–5.

– '*La Barre du jour*: Vers une poétique féministe.' Lamy and Pagès, 195–205.

– 'Theorizing Feminist Discourse/Translation.' *Tessera* 6 (1989): 42–53.

– ed. *Collaboration in the Feminine: Writings on Women and Culture from Tessera.* Toronto: Second Story Press, 1994.

Godard, Barbara, Daphne Marlatt, Kathy Mezei, and Gail Scott. 'Theorizing Fiction Theory.' *Tessera* 3, in *Canadian Fiction Magazine* 57 (1986): 6–12.

Godfrey, Stephen. 'Dramatizing the Intensity of Love.' *Globe and Mail* 28 Jan. 1991: C4.

Godin, Jean-Cléo. 'Deux Dramaturges de l'avenir?' *Études-Litteraires* 18.3 (1985): 113–22.

Godin, Jean-Cléo, and Laurent Mailhot. *Théâtre québécois II: Nouveaux auteurs, autres spectacles.* Montréal: Hurtubise HMH, 1980.

Goldie, Terry. *Fear and Temptation: The Image of the Indigene in Canadian, Australian, and New Zealand Literatures.* 1989. Montreal: McGill-Queen's UP, 1993.

– 'The Man of the Land/The Land of the Man: Patrick White and Scott Symons.' *SPAN* 36 (1993): 156–63.

– 'W.O. Mitchell and the Pursuit of the Homosocial Ideal.' Queer Disruptions Panel. ACCUTE Conference. University of Calgary, 4 June 1994.

Gould, Karen. *Writing in the Feminine: Feminism and Experimental Writing in Québec.* Carbondale: Southern Illinois UP, 1990.

Graefe, Sara. 'Reviving and Revising the Past: The Search for Present Meaning in Michel Marc Bouchard's *Lilies, or The Revival of a Romantic Drama.*' *Theatre Research in Canada* 14.2 (1993): 165–77.

Graham, Joseph F., ed. *Difference in Translation.* Ithaca, NY: Cornell UP, 1985.

Grainger, M. Allerdale. *Woodsmen of the West.* 1908. Toronto: McClelland and Stewart, 1996.

Grewal, Inderpal. 'Autobiographic Subjects, Diasporic Locations: *Meatless Days* and *Borderlands.*' Grewal and Kaplan, 231–54.

Grewal, Inderpal, and Caren Kaplan, eds. *Scattered Hegemonies: Postmodernity and Transnational Feminist Practices.* Minneapolis: U of Minnesota P, 1994.

Gruslin, Adrien. 'Michel Tremblay achève un premier cycle.' *Le Devoir* 26 fév. 1977: 15.

Hannon, Gerald. 'Tomson and the Trickster: Scenes from the Life of Playwright Tomson Highway.' *Toronto Life* 25.4 (1991): 28–31, 35–44, 81–5.

Harris, Claire. 'Poets in Limbo.' Kamboureli and Neuman, 115–25.

Harris, R. Cole. *The Resettlement of British Columbia: Essays on Colonialism and Geographical Change.* Vancouver: U of British Columbia P, 1997.

Heath, Stephen. 'Difference.' *Screen* 19.3 (1978): 50–112.

Helwig, David. 'Robert and Edward: An Uncommon Obituary.' *Canadian Notes & Queries* 50 (1996): 4–6.

Hewitt, Andrew. 'Coitus Interruptus: Fascism and the Deaths of History.' Dellamora, *Postmodern,* 17–40.

Highway, Tomson. *Dry Lips Oughta Move to Kapuskasing.* Saskatoon: Fifth House, 1989.

– 'The Lover Snake.' *An Anthology of Native Canadian Literature in English.* Ed. Daniel David Moses and Terry Goldie. Toronto: Oxford UP, 1992. 275–7.

– *The Rez Sisters.* Saskatoon: Fifth House, 1988.

Holbrook, Susan. 'Mauve Arrows and the Erotics of Translation.' *Essays on Canadian Writing* 61 (1997): 232–41.

Holden, Philip. 'An Area of Whiteness: The Empty Sign of *The Painted Veil.*' *English Studies in Canada* 20.1 (1994): 61–77.

Honegger, Gitta. 'Native Playwright: Tomson Highway.' *Theater* 23.1 (1992): 88–92.

Hoy, Helen. '"And Use the Words That Were Hers": Construction of Subjectivity in Beverly Hungry Wolf's *The Ways of My Grandmothers.*' *Essays on Canadian Writing* 60 (1996): 32–58.

Humphries, Martin. 'Gay Machismo.' *The Sexuality of Men.* Ed. Andy Metcalf and Martin Humphries. London: Pluto, 1985. 70–85.

Hutcheon, Linda. *The Canadian Postmodern: A Study of Contemporary English-Canadian Fiction.* Toronto: Oxford UP, 1988.

– *Narcissistic Narrative: The Metafictional Paradox.* Waterloo, ON: Wilfrid Laurier UP, 1980.

Ignatieff, Michael. *Blood and Belonging: Journeys into the New Nationalism.* Toronto: Viking, 1993.

Ingham, David. 'Bashing the Fascists: The Moral Dimension of Findley's Fiction.' *Studies in Canadian Literature* 15.2 (1991): 33–54.

Jackson, Ed, and Stan Persky, eds. *Flaunting It! A Decade of Gay Journalism from 'The Body Politic.'* Vancouver: New Star, 1982.

Jameson, Fredric. 'Third-World Literature in the Era of Multinational Capital.' *Social Text* 15 (1986): 65–88.

JanMohamed, Abdul R. 'The Economy of Manichean Allegory: The Function of Racial Difference in Colonialist Literature.' *Critical Inquiry* 12.1 (1985): 59–87.

Johnson, Barbara. 'Taking Fidelity Philosophically.' Graham, 142–8.

Johnston, Denis W. 'Lines and Circles: The "Rez" Plays of Tomson Highway.' *Canadian Literature* 124–5 (1990): 254–64.

Jones, Manina. 'Beyond the Pale: Gender, "Savagery," and the Colonial Project in Richardson's *Wacousta.*' *Essays on Canadian Writing* 54 (1994): 46–59.

– *That Art of Difference: 'Documentary-Collage' and English-Canadian Writing.* Toronto: U of Toronto P, 1993.

Jubinville, Yves. 'Claude inc: Essai socio-économique sur le travestissement.' *Le Monde de Michel Tremblay*. Ed. Gilbert David and Pierre Lavoie. Montréal: Cahiers de théâtre jeu/Lansman, 1993. 109–23.

Kahn, Madeleine. *Narrative Transvestism: Rhetoric and Gender in the Eighteenth-Century English Novel.* Ithaca, NY: Cornell UP, 1991.

Kamboureli, Smaro, and Shirley Neuman, eds. *A Mazing Space: Writing Canadian Women Writing.* Edmonton: Longspoon, 1986.

Kaplan, Caren. 'The Politics of Location as Transnational Feminist Practice.' Grewal and Kaplan, 137–52.

Karamcheti, Indira. 'Caliban in the Classroom.' Gallop, *Pedagogy*, 138–46.

Katz, Jonathan Ned. *Gay American History.* New York: Thomas Crowell, 1976.

Kelly, Peggy. 'Fiction Theory as Feminist Practice in Marlatt's *Ana Historic* and Scott's *Heroine.*' *Open Letter* 9.4 (1995): 69–98.

Kinsman, Gary. *The Regulation of Desire: Sexuality in Canada.* Montreal: Black Rose, 1987.

Knutson, Susan. 'Daphne Marlatt and Nicole Brossard: Writing Metanarrative in the Feminine.' *Signature: A Journal of Theory and Canadian Literature* 3 (1990): 28–43.

Koestenbaum, Wayne. *Double Talk: The Erotics of Male Literary Collaboration.* New York: Routledge, 1989.

Koustas, Jane. 'From "Homespun" to "Awesome": Translated Quebec Theater in Toronto.' Donohoe and Weiss, 81–108.

– '*Hosanna* in Toronto: "Tour de force" or "détour de traduction?"' *Traduction, Terminologie, Redaction* 2.2 (1989): 129–39.

Kristeva, Julia. *Nations without Nationalism.* Trans. Leon S. Roudiez. New York: Columbia UP, 1993.

Kroetsch, Robert. Afterword. Sinclair Ross, 217–21.

– 'The Fear of Women in Prairie Fiction: An Erotics of Space.' *The Lovely Treachery of Words: Essays Selected and New.* Toronto: Oxford UP, 1989. 73–83.

Kröller, Eva-Marie. *George Bowering: Bright Circles of Colour.* Vancouver: Talonbooks, 1992.

Krupat, Arnold. 'Post-Structuralism and Oral Literature.' *Recovering the Word: Essays on Native American Literature.* Ed. Brian Swann and Arnold Krupat. Berkeley: U of California P, 1987. 113–28.

Kuester, Martin. *Framing Truths: Parodic Structures in Contemporary English-Canadian Historical Novels.* Toronto: U of Toronto P, 1992.

Lamont-Stewart, Linda. 'Androgyny as Resistance to Authoritarianism in Two Postmodern Canadian Novels.' *Mosaic* 30.3 (1997): 115–30.

Lamy, Suzanne. *d'elles.* Montréal: Hexagone, 1979.

Lamy, Suzanne, and Irène Pagès, eds. *Féminité, subversion, écriture.* Montréal: Remue-Ménage, 1983.

Lane, Christopher. *The Ruling Passion: British Colonial Allegory and the Paradox of Homosexual Desire.* Durham, NC: Duke UP, 1995.

Lawrence, T.E. *Seven Pillars of Wisdom: A Triumph.* London: Jonathan Cape, 1952.

Leahy, David. 'Patrick Anderson and John Sutherland's Heterorealism: "Some Sexual Experience of a Kind Not Normal."' *Essays on Canadian Writing* 62 (1997): 132–49.

Lebowitz, Fran. 'Notes on "Trick."' *Metropolitan Life.* New York: Dutton, 1978. 66–74.

Lecker, Robert, ed. *Canadian Canons: Essays in Literary Value.* Toronto: U of Toronto P, 1991.

– 'The Canonization of Canadian Literature: An Inquiry into Value.' *Critical Inquiry* 16 (1990): 656–71.

– *Making It Real: The Canonization of English-Canadian Literature.* Toronto: Anansi, 1995.

– 'Response to Frank Davey.' *Critical Inquiry* 16 (1990): 682–9.

Lee, Dennis. *Civil Elegies and Other Poems.* Toronto: Anansi, 1972.

Lévesque, Robert. 'Michel-Marc Bouchard: Roberval, 1912, j'avais 19 ans ...' *Le Devoir* 12 sept. 1987: C1–C2.

– 'René-Daniel Dubois livre une pièce majeure.' *Le Devoir* 19 nov. 1985: 23.

– 'Le Tandem Tremblay-Brassard a-t-il fait son temps?' *Le Devoir* 19 fév. 1996: B8.

Lévesque, Solange. 'À propos des "Feluettes": Questions et hypothèses.' *Cahiers de théâtre jeu* 49 (1988): 174–9.

Lévesque, Solange, and Diane Pavlovic. 'Comédiens et martyrs.' *Cahiers de théâtre jeu* 49 (1988): 152–67.

Lewis, Paula Gilbert. Introduction. Lewis, 3–10.

– ed. *Traditionalism, Nationalism, and Feminism: Women Writers of Quebec.* Westport, CN: Greenwood, 1985.

Litvak, Joseph. 'Discipline, Spectacle, and Melancholia in and around the Gay Studies Classroom.' Gallop, *Pedagogy*, 19–27.

Lowry, Glen. 'Risking Perversion and Reclaiming Our Hysterical Mother: Reading the Material Body in *Ana Historic* and *Double Standards*.' *West Coast Line* 25.2 (1991): 83–96.

Lyotard, Jean-François. *The Postmodern Condition: A Report on Knowledge.* Trans. Geoff Bennington and Brian Massumi. Minneapolis: U of Minnesota P, 1989.

McCarthy, Dermot. 'Early Canadian Literary Histories and the Function of a Canon.' Lecker, *Canadian*, 30–45.

McCaughna, David. 'Tremblay Scores Again.' *Motion* July/August 1974: 48.

McClintock, Ann. *Imperial Leather: Race, Gender and Sexuality in the Colonial Contest.* New York: Routledge, 1995.

Macdonald, Marianne. 'Oscar's Grandson Recalls a Century of Pain.' *Independent on Sunday* 12 February 1995: 6.

MacFarlane, David. 'The Perfect Gesture.' *Books in Canada* 11.3 (1982): 5–8.

McGregor, Gaile. *The Wacousta Syndrome: Explorations in the Canadian Langscape.* Toronto: U of Toronto P, 1985.

McKenzie, M.L. 'Memories of the Great War: Graves, Sassoon, and Findley.' *University of Toronto Quarterly* 55.4 (1986): 395–411.

McLuhan, Marshall. 'Canada: The Borderline Case.' *The Canadian Imagination.* Ed. David Staines. Cambridge, MA: Harvard UP, 1977. 226–48.

– *Culture Is Our Business.* Toronto: McGraw-Hill, 1970.

Marlatt, Daphne. *Ana Historic: A Novel.* Toronto: Coach House, 1988.

– 'Between Continuity and Difference: An Interview with Daphne Marlatt.' With Brenda Carr. Barbour, 99–107.

– 'Booking passage.' *Salvage*, 115–19.

– 'Changing the Focus.' Interview with Betsy Warland. *InVersions: Writing by Dykes, Queers & Lesbians.* Ed. Betsy Warland. Vancouver: Press Gang, 1991. 127–34.

– 'Difference (em)bracing.' *Language in Her Eye: Views on Writing and Gender by Canadian Women Writing in English.* Ed. Libby Scheier et al. Toronto: Coach House, 1990. 188–93.

– 'Entering In: The Immigrant Imagination.' *Canadian Literature* 100 (1984): 219–23.

– 'musing with mothertongue.' *Touch to My Tongue*, 45–9.

– 'On *Ana Historic*: An Interview with Daphne Marlatt.' With George Bowering. *Line* 13 (1989): 96–105.

– *Salvage.* Red Deer: Red Deer College Press, 1991.

– 'Self-Representation and Fictionalysis.' *Tessera* 8 (1990): 13–17.

– 'Territory & co.' *Salvage*, 71–91.

– *Touch to My Tongue.* Edmonton: Longspoon, 1984.

– 'Translating *MAUVE*: Reading Writing.' *Tessera* 6 (1989): 27–30.

Marlatt, Daphne, and Nicole Brossard. *character/jeu de lettres.* Montréal: NBJ/Writing, 1986. N. pag.

Martell, Cecelia. 'Unpacking the Baggage: "Camp" Humour in Timothy Findley's *Not Wanted on the Voyage.*' *Canadian Literature* 148 (1996): 96–111.

Martin, Biddy. 'Sexualities without Genders and Other Queer Utopias.' Butler and Martin, 104–21.

Martin, Biddy, and Chandra Talpade Mohanty. 'Feminist Politics: What's Home Got to Do with It?' *Feminist Studies/Critical Studies.* Ed. Teresa de Lauretis. Bloomington: Indiana UP, 1986. 191–212.

Martin, Robert K. 'Cheap Tricks in Montreal: Scott Symons's *Place d'Armes.*' *Essays on Canadian Writing* 54 (1994): 198–211.

– 'Gender, Race, and the Colonial Body: Carson McCullers's Filipino Boy, and David Henry Hwang's Chinese Woman.' *Canadian Review of American Studies* 23.1 (1992): 95–106.

– *The Homosexual Tradition in American Poetry.* Austin: U of Texas P, 1979.

– Introduction. *Lesbian and Gay Studies, Vol. I.* Ed. Robert K. Martin. Special issue of *English Studies in Canada* 20.2 (1994): 125–8.

– 'Roland Barthes: Toward an "*Écriture Gaie.*"' Bergman, *Camp*, 282–98.

– 'Sex and Politics in Wartime Canada: The Attack on Patrick Anderson.' *Essays on Canadian Writing* 44 (1991): 110–25.

– 'Two Days in Sodom: or, How Anglo-Canadian Writers Invent Their Own Quebecs.' *The Body Politic* 35 (1977): 28–30.

Mathews, Lawrence. 'Calgary, Canonization, and Class: Deciphering List B.' Lecker, *Canadian*, 150–66.

Maufort, Marc. 'Recognizing Difference in Canadian Drama: Tomson Highway's Poetic Realism.' *British Journal of Canadian Studies* 8.2 (1993): 230–40.

Maynard, Steven. 'In Search of "Sodom North": The Writing of Lesbian and Gay History in English Canada, 1970–1990.' *Canadian Review of Comparative Literature* 21.1–2 (1994): 117–32.

Meese, Elizabeth A. *(Sem)erotics: Theorizing Lesbian: Writing.* New York: New York UP, 1992.

Mellen, Joan. 'Fascism in the Contemporary Film.' *Film Qaurterly* 24.4 (1971): 2–19.

Mercer, Kobena. 'Skin Head Sex Thing: Racial Difference and the Homoerotic Imaginary.' Bad Object-Choices, 169–222.

Merivale, Patricia. 'The Biographical Compulsion: Elegiac Romances in Canadian Fiction.' *Journal of Modern Literature* 8.1 (1980): 139–52.

– 'Hubert Aquin and Highbrow Pornography: The Aesthetics of Perversion.' *Essays on Canadian Writing* 26 (1983): 1–12.

Meyer, Moe, ed. *The Politics and Poetics of Camp.* New York: Routledge, 1994.

Mitchell, W.O. *Who Has Seen the Wind.* Toronto: Macmillan, 1947.

Mohanty, Chandra Talpade. 'Feminist Encounters: Locating the Politics of Experience.' *Copyright* 1 (1987): 30–44.

– 'On Race and Voice: Challenges for Liberal Education in the 1990s.' *Cultural Critique* 18 (1989–90): 179–208.

Morrell, Carol. Introduction. *Grammar of Dissent: Poetry and Prose by Claire Harris, M. Nourbese Philip, Dionne Brand.* Ed. Carol Morrell. Fredericton: Goose Lane, 1994. 9–24.

Morrison, Toni. *Playing in the Dark: Whiteness and the Literary Imagination.* Cambridge, MA: Harvard UP, 1992.

Moss, Jane. 'Sexual Games: Hypertheatricality and Homosexuality in Recent Quebec Plays.' *American Review of Canadian Studies* 17.3 (1987): 287–96.

– '"Still Crazy after All These Years": The Uses of Madness in Recent Quebec Drama.' *Canadian Literature* 118 (1988): 35–45.

Mosse, George. *Nationalism and Sexuality: Middle-Class Morality and Sexual Norms in Modern Europe.* Madison: U of Wisconsin P, 1985.

Moyes, Lianne. 'Composing in the Scent of Wood and Roses: Nicole Brossard's Intertextual Encounters with Djuna Barnes and Gertrude Stein.' *English Studies in Canada* 21.2 (1995): 206–25.

– 'Into the Fray: Literary Studies at the Juncture of Feminist Fiction/Theory.' *Canada: Theoretical Discourse/Discours théoriques.* Ed. Terry Goldie et al. Montreal: Association for Canadian Studies, 1994. 307–25.

Mukherjee, Arun P. 'Canadian Nationalism, Canadian Literature, and Racial Minority Women.' Silvera, 421–44.

Newton, Esther. *Mother Camp: Female Impersonators in America.* Chicago: U of Chicago P, 1972.

Niranjana, Tejaswini. *Siting Translation: History, Post-Structuralism, and the Colonial Context.* Berkeley: U of California P, 1992.

Norris, Ken. *The Little Magazine in Canada, 1925–80: Its Role in the Development of Modernism and Post-Modernism in Canadian Poetry.* Toronto: ECW, 1984.

Northey, Margot. *The Haunted Wilderness: The Gothic and Grotesque in Canadian Fiction.* Toronto: U of Toronto P, 1976.

Nunn, Robert. 'Marginality and English-Canadian Theatre.' *Theatre Research International* 17 (1992): 217–25.

O'Brien, Kevin. *Oscar Wilde in Canada: An Apostle for the Arts.* Toronto: Personal Library, 1982.

Page, P.K. 'Cry Ararat!' *Cry Ararat!: Poems New and Selected.* Toronto: McClelland and Stewart, 1967. 102–7.

Parker, Alice. 'The Mauve Horizon of Nicole Brossard.' *Québec Studies* 10 (1990): 107–19.

– 'Under the Covers: A Synesthesia of Desire (Lesbian Translations).' *Sexual Practice/Textual Theory: Lesbian Cultural Criticism.* Ed. Susan J. Wolfe and Julia Penelope. Cambridge, MA: Blackwell, 1993. 322–39.

Parker, Andrew, et al., eds. *Nationalisms and Sexualities.* New York: Routledge, 1992.

Parker, Andrew, and Eve Kosofsky Sedgwick, eds. *Peformativity and Performance.* New York: Routledge, 1995.

Paterson, Janet M. *Postmodernism and the Quebec Novel.* Trans. David Homel and Charles Phillips. Toronto: U of Toronto P, 1994.

Patton, Cindy. *Inventing AIDS.* New York: Routledge, 1990.

Pellegrini, Ann. *Performance Anxieties: Staging Psychoanalysis, Staging Race.* New York: Routledge, 1996.

Pennee, Donna Palmateer. *Moral Metafiction: Counterdiscourse in the Novels of Timothy Findley.* Toronto: ECW, 1991.

Persky, Stan. *Buddy's: Meditations on Desire.* Vancouver: New Star, 1989.

Peters, Colette. '"Whatever Happens, This Is": Lesbian Speech-Act Theory and Adrienne Rich's "Twenty-One Love Poems."' *English Studies in Canada* 21.2 (1995): 189–205.

Piggford, George. '"A National Enema": Scott Symons's *Place d'Armes.*' Canadian Gay Writing in Context Panel. ACCUTE Conference. Brock University, St Catharine's, ON. 23 May 1996.

Plant, Richard. *The Pink Triangle: The Nazi War against Homosexuals.* New York: Henry Holt, 1986.

Porter, Dennis. *Haunted Journeys: Desire and Transgression in European Travel Writing.* Princeton, NJ: Princeton UP, 1991.

Pound, Ezra. 'Hugh Selwyn Mauberley (Life and Contacts).' *Selected Poems.* Ed. T.S. Eliot. London: Faber, 1948. 171–87.

– *The Letters of Ezra Pound: 1907–1941.* Ed. D.D. Paige. New York: Harcourt, Brace & World, 1950.

Pratt, Mary Louise. *Imperial Eyes: Travel Writing and Transculturation.* New York: Routledge, 1992.

– *Toward a Speech Act Theory of Literary Discourse.* Bloomington: Indiana UP, 1977.

Preston, Jennifer. 'Weesageechak Begins to Dance: Native Earth Performing Arts Inc.' *Drama Review* 36.1 (1992): 133–59.

Probyn, Elspeth. *'Love in a Cold Climate': Queer Belongings in Québec.* Montreal: GRECC, 1994.

– 'Travels in the Postmodern: Making Sense of the Local.' *Feminism/Postmodernism.* Ed. Linda J. Nicholson. New York: Routledge, 1990. 176–89.

Rabillard, Sheila. 'Absorption, Elimination, and the Hybrid: Some Impure Questions of Gender and Culture in the Trickster Drama of Tomson Highway.' *Essays in Theatre* 12.1 (1993): 3–27.

Radin, Paul. *The Trickster: A Study in American Indian Mythology.* London: Routledge, 1956.

Rashid, Ian Iqbal. *Black Markets, White Boyfriends, and Other Acts of Elision.* Toronto: TSAR, 1991.

Raynauld, Isabelle. '"Les Feluettes": Aimer/tuer.' *Cahiers de théâtre jeu* 49 (1988): 168–73.

Renan, Ernest. 'Qu'est-ce qu'une nation?' *Oeuvres complètes.* Vol. 1. Paris: Calmann-Levy, 1947–61. 887–906.

Rich, Adrienne. 'Blood, Bread, and Poetry: The Location of the Poet.' *Blood, Bread, and Poetry: Selected Prose, 1979–85.* New York: Norton, 1986. 167–87.

– 'Compulsory Heterosexuality and Lesbian Existence.' *Blood,* 23–75.

– '"Going There" and Being Here.' *Blood,* 156–9.

– 'North American Tunnel Vision.' *Blood,* 160–6.

– 'Notes toward a Politics of Location.' *Blood,* 210–31.

Richard, Hélène. 'Le Théâtre gai québécois: Conjuncture sociale et sentiment de filiation.' *Cahiers de théâtre jeu* 54 (1990): 15–23.

Richardson, Major [John]. *Wacousta: A Tale of the Pontiac Conspiracy.* 1832. Toronto: Musson, 1924.

Richler, Mordecai. *Oh Canada! Oh Quebec! Requiem for a Divided Nation.* New York: Viking, 1992.

Ringrose, Christopher Xerxes. 'Patrick Anderson and the Critics.' *Canadian Literature* 43 (1970): 10–23.

Ripley, John. 'From Alienation to Transcendence: The Quest for Selfhood in Michel Tremblay's Plays.' *Canadian Literature* 85 (1980): 44–59.

Rivière, Joan. 'Womanliness as a Masquerade.' *International Journal of Psycho-Analysis* 10 (1929): 303–13.

Rolfe, Frederick [Baron Corvo]. *Stories Toto Told Me.* London: Collins, 1969.

Roman, Leslie G. 'White Is a Color! White Defensiveness, Postmodernism, and Anti-racist Pedagogy.' *Race, Identity, and Representation in Education.* Ed. Cameron McCarthy and Warren Chrichlow. New York: Routledge, 1993. 71–88.

Roscoe, Will. 'Was We'wha a Homosexual? Native American Survivance and the Two-Spirit Tradition.' *GLQ* 2.3 (1995): 193–235.

Ross, Andrew. 'Uses of Camp.' *Yale Journal of Criticism* 2.1 (1988): 1–24.

Ross, Becki L. *The House That Jill Built: A Lesbian Nation in Formation.* Toronto: U of Toronto P, 1995.

Ross, Malcolm. 'The Canonization of *As for Me and My House*: A Case Study.' *Figures in a Ground: Canadian Essays on Modern Literature Collected in Honor of Sheila Watson.* Saskatoon: Western Producer, 1978. 189–205.

Ross, Sinclair. *As for Me and My House.* 1941. Toronto: McClelland and Stewart, 1989.

Roy, John D. 'The Structure of Tense and Aspect in Barbadian English Creole.' *Focus on the Caribbean: Varieties of English around the World, G8.* Amsterdam: John Benjamins, 1986. 141–56.

Rule, Jane. *The Desert of the Heart.* London: Secker & Warburg, 1964.

Russell, Catherine. Review of *Primitive Offensive*, by Dionne Brand. *Quill & Quire* 49.9 (1983): 76.

Sanders, Leslie. '"I Am Stateless Anyway": The Poetry of Dionne Brand.' *Zora Neale Hurston Forum* 3.2 (1989): 19–29.

Scheel, Kathleen M. 'Freud and Frankenstein: The Monstered Language of *Ana Historic*.' *Essays on Canadian Writing* 58 (1996): 93–114.

Schor, Naomi, and Elizabeth Weed, eds. *The Essential Difference.* Bloomington: U of Indiana P, 1994.

Schwartzwald, Robert. 'Fear of Federasty: Québec's Inverted Fictions.' *Comparative American Identities: Race, Sex, and Nationality in the Modern Text.* Ed. Hortense J. Spillers. New York: Routledge, 1991. 175–95.

– 'From Authenticity to Ambivalence: Michel Tremblay's *Hosanna*.' *American Review of Canadian Studies* 22.4 (1992): 499–510.

– '"Symbolic" Homosexuality, "False Feminine," and the Problematics of Identity in Québec.' Warner, *Fear*, 264–99.

Scobie, Stephen. 'Eye-Deep in Hell: Ezra Pound, Timothy Findley, and Hugh Selwyn Mauberley.' *Essays on Canadian Writing* 30 (1984–5): 206–27.

Scott, Duncan Campbell. 'The Onandaga Madonna.' *Canadian Poetry, Volume One.* Ed. Jack David and Robert Lecker. Toronto: General Publishing/ECW, 1982. 101–2.

Scott, F.R. 'Lakeshore.' *Selected Poems.* Toronto: Oxford UP, 1966. 12–13.
Scott, Gail. *Spaces Like Stairs.* Toronto: Women's Press, 1989.
Sedgwick, Eve Kosofsky. *Between Men: English Literature and Male Homosocial Desire.* New York: Columbia UP, 1985.
– *Epistemology of the Closet.* Berkeley: U of California P, 1990.
– 'Nationalisms and Sexualities in the Age of Wilde.' Andrew Parker et al., 235–5.
– 'Queer and Now.' *Tendencies.* Durham, NC: Duke UP, 1993. 1–20.
– 'Queer Performativity: Henry James's *The Art of the Novel.*' *GLQ* 1.1 (1993): 1–16.
– 'Willa Cather and Others.' *Tendencies,* 167–76.
Sidnell, Michael. 'Polygraph: Somatic Truth and the Art of Presence.' *Canadian Theatre Review* 64 (1990): 45–8.
Silvera, Makeda, ed. *The Other Woman: Women of Colour in Contemporary Canadian Literature.* Toronto: Sister Vision, 1994.
Silverman, Kaja. *Male Subjectivity at the Margins.* New York: Routledge, 1992.
Simon, Sherry. *Gender in Translation: Cultural Identity and the Politics of Transmission.* New York: Routledge, 1996.
– 'The Language of Cultural Difference: Figures of Alterity in Canadian Translation.' Venuti, 159–76.
– 'Rites of Passage: Translation and Its Intents.' *Massachusetts Review* 31.1–2 (1990): 96–109.
Slemon, Stephen. 'Monuments of Empire: Allegory/Counter-Discourse/Post-Colonial Writing.' *Kunapipi* 9.3 (1987): 1–16.
Smart, Patricia. 'The (In?)Compatibility of Gender and Nation in Canadian and Québécois Feminist Writing.' *Essays on Canadian Writing* 54 (1994): 12–22.
– *Writing in the Father's House: The Emergence of the Feminine in the Québec Literary Tradition.* Toronto: U of Toronto P, 1991.
Smith, A.J.M., ed. *The Book of Canadian Poetry: A Critical and Historical Anthology.* Chicago: U of Chicago P, 1943.
–, ed. *The Book of Canadian Poetry.* Rev. ed. Toronto: Gage, 1948.
Smith, Valerie. 'Reading the Intersection of Race and Gender in Narratives of Passing.' Butler and Martin, 43–57.
Smith-Rosenberg, Carroll. 'The Female World of Love and Ritual: Relations between Women in Nineteenth Century America.' *Signs* 1.1 (1975): 1–29.
Söderlind, Sylvia. *Margin/Alias: Language and Colonization in Canadian and Québécois Fiction.* Toronto: U of Toronto P, 1991.
Sontag, Susan. 'Fascinating Fascism.' 1974. *Under the Sign of Saturn.* New York: Farrar, Straus & Giroux/Noonday, 1989. 71–105.
– 'Notes on Camp.' *Against Interpretation.* New York: Farrar, Straus & Giroux, 1966. 275–92.

Spivak, Gayatri Chakravorty. 'Subaltern Studies: Deconstructing Historiography.' *In Other Worlds: Essays in Cultural Politics*. New York: Methuen, 1987. 197–221.

Steele, Charles, ed. *Taking Stock: The Calgary Conference on the Canadian Novel*. Downsview, ON: ECW, 1982.

Stein, Gertrude. 'Composition as Explanation.' 1926. *A Stein Reader*. Ed. Ulla E. Dydo. Evanston, IL: Northwestern UP, 1993. 493–503.

Suleiman, Susan Rubin. *Budapest Diary: In Search of the Motherbook*. Lincoln: U of Nebraska P, 1996.

Suleri, Sara. *The Rhetoric of English India*. Chicago: U of Chicago P, 1992.

Sutherland, John. 'The Poetry of Patrick Anderson.' *Northern Review* 2.5 (1949): 8–34.

– Retraction. *First Statement* 1.20 (1943): n. pag.

– Review of *Poems*, by Robert Finch. *Northern Review* 1.6 (1947): 38–40.

– 'The Writing of Patrick Anderson.' *First Statement* 1.19 (1943): 3–6

– ed. *Other Canadians: An Anthology of New Poetry in Canada, 1940–1946*. Montreal: First Statement, 1947.

Symons, Scott. 'The Canadian Bestiary: Ongoing Literary Depravity.' *West-Coast Review* 11.3 (1977): 3–16.

– *Civic Square*. Toronto: McClelland and Stewart, 1969.

– *Combat Journal for Place d'Armes: A Personal Narrative*. Toronto: McClelland and Stewart, 1967.

– *Helmet of Flesh*. Toronto: McClelland and Stewart, 1986.

– Interview. With Graeme Gibson. Gibson, 301–24.

Taylor, Charles. *Six Journeys: A Canadian Pattern*. Toronto: Anansi, 1977.

Taylor, Charles. 'Why Do Nations Have to Become States?' *Reconciling the Solitudes: Essays on Canadian Federalism and Nationalism*. Ed. Guy Laforest. Montreal: McGill-Queen's UP, 1993. 40–58.

Thomas, Joan. 'Poetry Fires Hot Brand Novel.' Rev. of *In Another Place, Not Here*, by Dionne Brand. *Globe and Mail* 29 June 1996: C10.

Torgovnick, Marianna De Marco. *Crossing Ocean Parkway: Readings by an Italian American Daughter*. Chicago: U of Chicago P, 1994.

– *Gone Primitive: Savage Intellects, Modern Lives*. Chicago: U of Chicago P, 1990.

Tostevin, Lola Lemire. 'Contamination: A Relation of Differences.' *Tessera* 6 (1989): 13–14.

– 'Daphne Marlatt: Writing in the Space That Is Her Mother's Face.' *Line* 13 (1989): 32–9.

– 'Re.' Godard, *Collaboration*, 40–3.

Trehearne, Brian. 'Critical Episodes in Montreal Poetry of the 1940s.' *Canadian Poetry* 41 (1997): 21–52.

Tremblay, Michel. *Les Belles-Soeurs*. Montréal: Leméac, 1972.

– 'Entrevue avec Michel Tremblay.' With Rachel Cloutier, Marie Laberge, and Rodrigue Gignac. *Nord* 1 (1971): 49–81.

– *Hosanna.* Trans. John Van Burek and Bill Glassco. Vancouver: Talonbooks, 1974.

– *'Hosanna' suivi de 'La Duchesse de Langeais.'* Montréal: Leméac, 1973.

– 'Il y a 20 ans, "Les Belles-Soeurs" ... "par la porte d'en avant ...": Entretien avec Michel Tremblay.' With Pierre Lavoie. *Cahiers de théâtre jeu* 47 (1988): 57–74.

– 'Michel Tremblay.' *Stage Voices: Twelve Canadian Playwrights Talk about Their Lives and Work.* Ed. Geraldine Anthony. Toronto: Doubleday, 1978. 279–86.

– 'Michel Tremblay: Du texte à la représentation.' Interview with Roch Turbide. *Voix et Images* 7.2 (1982): 213–24.

Tyler, Carole-Anne. 'Boys Will Be Girls: The Politics of Gay Drag.' Fuss, *Inside/Out,* 32–70.

Ulrichs, Karl H. *Vindex: Social-Juridical Studies in the Sexual Love between Men.* Trans. Michael Lombardi. Los Angeles: Urania Manuscripts, 1979.

Usmiani, Renate. *Michel Tremblay*. Vancouver: Douglas & McIntyre, 1982.

Vallières, Pierre. *Nègres blancs d'Amérique: Autobiographie précoce d'un 'terroriste' québécois.* Montréal: Parti pris, 1968.

Venuti, Lawrence, ed. *Rethinking Translation: Discourse, Subjectivity, Ideology*. New York: Routledge, 1992.

Verdecchia, Guillermo. *Fronteras Americanas.* Toronto: Coach House, 1993.

Verwaayen, Kimberley. 'Region/Body: In? Of? And? Or? (Alter/Native) Separatism in the Politics of Nicole Brossard.' *Essays on Canadian Writing* 61 (1997): 1–16.

Vizenor, Gerald. *The Heirs of Columbus.* Hanover, NH: UP of New England/Wesleyan UP, 1991.

– 'Trickster Discourse: Comic Holotropes and Language Games.' *Narrative Chance: Postmodern Discourse on Native American Literatures.* Ed. Gerald Vizenor. Albuquerque: U of New Mexico P, 1989. 187–211.

– *The Trickster of Liberty: Tribal Heirs to a Wild Baronage.* Minneapolis: U of Minnesota P, 1988.

Waddington, Miriam. Introduction. *Essays, Controversies and Poems.* By John Sutherland. Ed. Miriam Waddington. Toronto: McClelland and Stewart, 1972. 7–15.

Wallace, Michele. 'The Politics of Location: Cinema/Theory/Literature/Ethnicity/Sexuality/ Me.' *Framework* 36 (1989): 42–55.

Wallace, Robert. 'Homo Creation: Towards a Poetics of Gay Male Theatre.' *Essays on Canadian Writing* 54 (1994): 212–36.

– *Producing Marginality: Essays on Theatre and Criticism in Canada.* Saskatoon: Fifth House, 1990.

Warland, Betsy. *open is broken.* Edmonton: Longspoon, 1984.

Warner, Michael. 'Something Queer about the Nation-State.' *After Political Correctness: The Humanities and Society in the 1990s.* Ed. Christopher Newfield and Ronald Strickland. Boulder, CO: Westview, 1995. 361–71.

– ed. *Fear of a Queer Planet: Queer Politics and Social Theory*. Minneapolis: U of Minnesota P, 1993.

Watney, Simon. *Policing Desire: Pornography, AIDS, and the Media.* 2nd ed. Minneapolis: U of Minnesota P, 1989.

Watson, Scott. 'Voice without Words.' *Stories.* Vancouver: Talonbooks, 1974. 8–14.

Webb, Phyllis. 'Leaning.' *The Literary Half-Yearly* 24.2 (1983): 91–2.

Whitman, Walt. *Leaves of Grass: A Textual Variorum of the Printed Poems.* 3 vols. Ed. Sculley Bradley et al. New York: New York UP, 1980.

Whitney, Patricia. '*En Masse*: An Introduction and an Index.' *Canadian Poetry* 19 (1986): 76–91.

– 'From Oxford to Montreal: Patrick Anderson's Political Development.' *Canadian Poetry* 19 (1986): 26–48.

Whittaker, Herbert. 'Hosanna a Heart-Pounding Tour de Force.' *Globe and Mail* 16 May 1974: 15.

Wilde, Oscar. 'The Decay of Lying.' 1889. *The Artist as Critic: Critical Writings of Oscar Wilde.* Ed. Richard Ellmann. Chicago: U of Chicago P, 1969. 290–320.

– *Selected Letters of Oscar Wilde.* Ed. Rupert Hart-Davis. New York: Oxford UP, 1979.

Wildeman, Marlene. 'Daring Deeds: Translation as Lesbian Feminist Language Act.' *Tessera* 6 (1989): 31–40.

Williams, Walter L. *The Spirit and the Flesh: Sexual Diversity in American Indian Culture.* Boston: Beacon, 1986.

Williamson, Janice. 'It gives me a great deal of pleasure to say yes: Writing/Reading Lesbian in Daphne Marlatt's *Touch to My Tongue.*' Barbour, 171–93.

– *Sounding Differences: Conversations with Seventeen Canadian Women Writers.* Toronto: U of Toronto P, 1993.

Winer, Lise. *Trinidad and Tobago: Varieties of English around the World, T6.* Amsterdam: John Benjamins, 1993.

Winkler, Donald, dir. *Tomson Highway: Thank You for the Love You Gave.* Life and Times. CBC. Toronto. 9 April 1997.

Wittig, Monique. 'The Mark of Gender.' 1985. *The Straight Mind and Other Essays.* Boston: Beacon, 1992. 76–89.

– 'The Straight Mind.' 1980. *The Straight Mind,* 21–32.

Woods, Gregory. *Articulate Flesh: Male Homoeroticism and Modern Poetry.* New Haven: Yale UP, 1987.

Woolf, Virginia. *Three Guineas.* New York: Harcourt, 1938.

Yingling, Thomas E. *Hart Crane and the Homosexual Text: New Thresholds, New Anatomies.* Chicago: U of Chicago P, 1990.

York, Lorraine. *Front Lines: The Fiction of Timothy Findley*. Toronto: ECW, 1991.

Zackodnik, Teresa. '"I Am Blackening in My Way": Identity and Place in Dionne Brand's *No Language is Neutral*.' *Essays on Canadian Writing* 57 (1995): 194–211.

Credits and Permissions

The author gratefully acknowledges permission to reproduce material from the following sources:

Les Feluettes; ou, La répétition d'un drame romantique, by Michel Marc Bouchard. Montréal: Leméac, 1987.

'Polynésie des yeux,' by Nicole Brossard, courtesy of the author. From *À tout regard*, by Nicole Brossard. Montréal: NBJ/BQ, 1989.

Mauve, by Nicole Brossard and Daphne Marlatt, courtesy of the authors. Montréal: NBJ/Writing, 1985.

Being at home with Claude, by René-Daniel Dubois. Montréal: Leméac, 1986.

Dry Lips Oughta Move to Kapuskasing, by Tomson Highway, courtesy of the author. Saskatoon: Fifth House, 1989.

The Rez Sisters, by Tomson Highway, courtesy of the author. Saskatoon: Fifth House, 1988.

'Booking passage' and 'Territory & co.,' by Daphne Marlatt, courtesy of the author. From *Salvage*, by Daphne Marlatt. Red Deer: Red Deer College Press, 1991.

Touch to My Tongue, by Daphne Marlatt, courtesy of the author. Edmonton: Longspoon, 1984.

character / jeu de lettres, by Daphne Marlatt and Nicole Brossard, courtesy of the authors. Montréal: NBJ/Writing, 1986.

Black Markets, White Boyfriends, and Other Acts of Elision, by Ian Iqbal Rashid, courtesy of the author. Toronto: TSAR, 1991.

'Hosanna' suivi de 'La Duchesse de Langeais,' by Michel Tremblay. Montréal: Leméac, 1973.

A portion of chapter 2 appeared earlier as '"Running Wilde": National Ambivalence and Sexual Dissidence in *Not Wanted on the Voyage*,' in *Essays on Canadian Writing* 64 (1998), and in Anne Geddes Bailey and Karen Grandy, eds, *Paying Attention: Critical Essays on Timothy Findley* (Toronto: ECW, 1998), 125–46.

Chapter 6 appeared earlier in somewhat different form as '"In another place, not here": Dionne Brand's Politics of (Dis)Location,' in Veronica Strong-Boag et al., eds, *Painting the Maple: Essays on Race, Gender, and the Construction of Canada* (Vancouver: U of British Columbia P, 1998).

Index